Thirty copies
of this book,
numbered I to XXX,
have been produced
on Encore
high gloss paper,
bound in Skivertex,
and boxed
in a case faced
with "ocean" velvet

© 1993 "A L'ENSEIGNE DU RAYON VERT" GPO Box 1626. NOUMEA - NEW CALEDONIA

ISBN 0 646 105 19 1

ABROLHOS PUBLISHING PTY. LTD

QVI Building. 25th level. 250 St George's Terrace. Perth 6000
Western Australia

# the first and last voyage of the
# Batavia

by
## Philippe Godard

With the contribution of
## Phillida Stephens

Abrolhos
Publishing

# Contents

# Foreword

One hundred and fifty years before Captain Cook came to fame, the Dutch East India Company, leading world traders, lost its flagship, *Batavia*, on a coral reef that lies just 45 miles from my home town Geraldton, Western Australia.

The mutiny on the *Bounty* was a small incident compared to this immense tragedy. First told in 1656 by various Dutch authors (theirs was really the first book on Australia), it has been related by many since.

Philippe Godard, who is about my age (very young late fifties), who is both explorer and photographer, and is also one of the few extraordinary men I have met, has now discovered Australia's greatest story.

I was keenly awaiting the story that he had to tell and that he has been chasing since I first met him, several years ago. And now we have before us his marvellous book, exhaustive, detailed and superbly illustrated!

In the time that we have travelled together through Western Australia, Philippe and I have acquired much and we look forward to doing more in the future!

**Max Cramer**
*Diver*
*Discoverer of the Batavia's wreck*

# Introduction

This book claims no more, apart from offering the reader a wealth of illustrations, than to throw some light on many details of the dramatic story of the *Batavia*, the broad lines of which were already well known thanks to the work of the late Henrietta Drake-Brockman and the archaeologists of the Western Australia Maritime Museum (Fremantle). They have done remarkable work on the subject and I would like to take this opportunity to pay them the tribute they deserve.

My thirst for open spaces and for the extraordinary, my love of History and, above all, my passion for Western Australia, led me about eight years ago to discover the Abrolhos archipelago, where one of the great dramas of the history of maritime navigation was played out.

On three occasions, with the enlightened guidance of my friend Max Cramer, I paced up and down the islands and islets of the Wallabi group, the southernmost of the three groups that make up the archipelago, site of the tragedy that occurred towards the middle of the year 1629.

The harsh beauty of the almost bare landscape, the exhilarating feeling of having travelled back with the "time machine" and finally, but particularly, the solitude — except for a short season each year during which the lobster fishermen occupy their second homes — all worked on me like a spell. I immediately became imbued with a passionate love for this strange world and in all the time I attentively observed and photographed it, I never found it really inhospitable despite the fact that intrinsically it is.

This book unfolds in text and pictures the décor of each act of the tragedy. When you close it, you will feel that there is nothing you do not know of this cruel story and its setting — the mysterious archipelago of the "Houtman Abrolhos" — and you will have a clear idea of what must have been the physical and moral suffering of the men, women and children who, nearly four hundred years ago, set foot, aghast, on these fragments of bare land, where there was nothing familiar, surrounded on all sides by the threatening ocean, tormented by hunger, thirst, the despair that undermines the spirit and, a little later, the bloody madness of some of their companions in misfortune.

This is without doubt the most disturbing page of the history of Australia.

**Philippe GODARD**

*The author*
*in "Cornelisz' prison"*
*on Beacon Island*

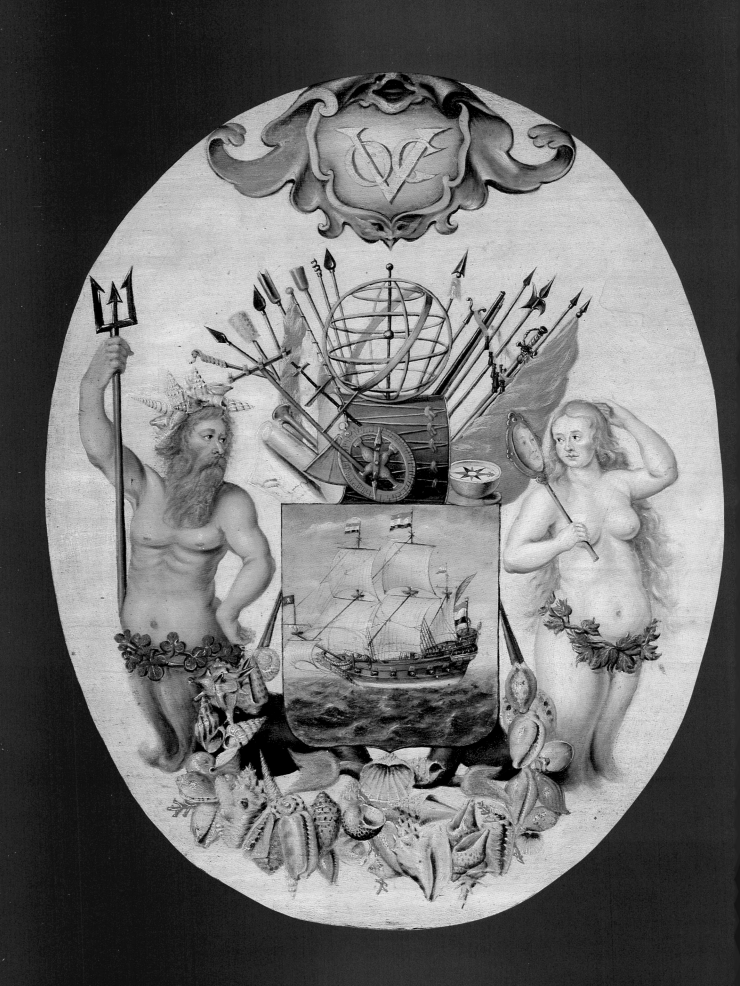

# act I

# The all-powerful "V.O.C."

Fifteen hundred and ninety-eight : Philip II of Spain has just "shuffled off this mortal coil" and the Vervins peace treaty recently signed by France and Spain has tolled the knell of Catholic Spain's hopes, nurtured since the reign of Charles V, the Holy Roman Emperor, of hegemony over the provinces of the northern part of the Netherlands, very largely won over to the reforming ideas of Calvin.

1598... This was also the year in which these "United Provinces", whose religious affinity had for seventeen years now been matched by political ties[1], realized finally what their trading future could be. It was Cornelis de Houtman, a native of Gouda, who had opened their eyes to this potential. He had been employed by the Portuguese as a maritime pilot in the East Indies, as they were known at that time, but having fallen foul of the courts of the Inquisition whose aim was to make him abnegate the heresies of the reformed religion, he had no choice but to seek a new employer; it was thus quite natural that he should go and propose to his compatriots that they profit from his valuable experience. A group of nine Amsterdam merchants took a favourable view of his proposal that they try to break the Lusitanian monopoly of the spice trade, and accordingly a company known as the "Far Lands Company" was set up with a capital stock of 300,000 guilders (as florins were then called), which was ample to build and commission three vessels of large tonnage and a yacht to accompany them — and also to purchase a cargo of merchandise for trading, and to engage the crews they needed.

This small fleet had set out on 2nd April 1595 and returned safely, save for one ship, a little more than two years later with quite a fine cargo of spices and, better still, a contract for exclusive supply concluded with the

*It was on 28th February 1603 that the Heeren XVII chose a monogram for their company that was to become famed throughout the world for nearly two centuries.*

*Left :
The coat of arms of the East Indies Company.*

---

1 Since its formation in 1548, the "Cercle impérial de Bourgogne" (Imperial Circle of Burgundy) had amalgamated seventeen provinces, which included present-day Netherlands, Belgium and Luxemburg, and also part of Flanders and French Artois. With the Union of Utrecht in 1579 the Circle's Protestant component unilaterally laid the foundations of a new political entity called the "Republic of the Six United Provinces". These were the provinces of Guelders, Holland, Zealand, Utrecht, Friesland and Overijsel. Their number became seven when the province of Groningen was added in 1594.

*The date is 1596. Cornelis de Houtman's and Gerrit van Beuningen's four ships are riding at anchor at Bantam, surrounded by small native boats. The very first, modest settlement of the Dutch has been established outside the township. The English were in turn to establish themselves at Bantam in 1603 only to be chased away definitively some eighty years later by their Dutch rivals. The Dutch could not run the risk of allowing such competition to develop in the immediate neighbourhood of Batavia.*

Sultan of Bantam in the western part of the island of Java. Loss of human life had, it must be admitted, been considerable and the financial results of the undertaking were not such as to arouse great enthusiasm, but a breach had been made and on that account alone the expedition was considered a success. From that time on the Dutch, traders and sailors to the marrow, found themselves all the more inclined to believe that the

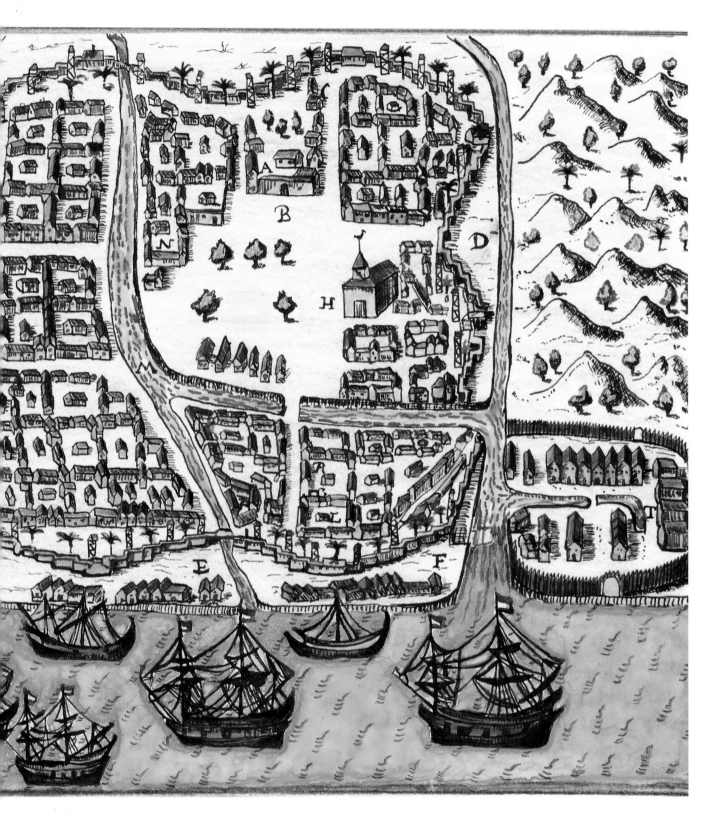

source of their future prosperity lay in the East Indies ; furthermore, in 1596, Jan Huyghen van Linschoten of Amsterdam, who had been appointed at the age of 20 to the post of junior clerk to the Portuguese archdiocese at Goa, had caused a sensation by publishing his *Itinerario*. This voluminous work revealed to his compatriots the mystery of the fruitful trade that the Portuguese, who had been present for nearly a century in

*The signature is authentic but this portrait of Cornelis de Houtman, which hangs in the museum of his birth-place, Gouda, is nevertheless a work of pure imagination. Houtman was instructed, together with Gerrit van Beuningen, to open the "spice route" for his compatriots and he set sail for this purpose in April 1595. The voyage began with three vessels, the Mauritius, the Hollandia and the Amsterdam, accompanied by a small yacht, the Druyfken ("Little pigeon"). The convoy returned home, two years later, but without the Amsterdam which they had been obliged to leave at Java there being no longer enough sailors to work her, nearly two-thirds of the crews having died of scurvy and other illnesses.*

*Right :*
*Etching done in 1597 by Pieter Bast. His birds' eye view of Amsterdam shows the city's expansion (one can see the new and the old ramparts, the latter not yet completely demolished). On the left, within the palisade, the artist has shown the very first Dutch ships to have returned from the East indies, that year. This is also the earliest picture of the lee-boards incorporated in the new generation of barges designed to carry the ever-increasing traffic along the shallow waterways serving the hinterlands.*

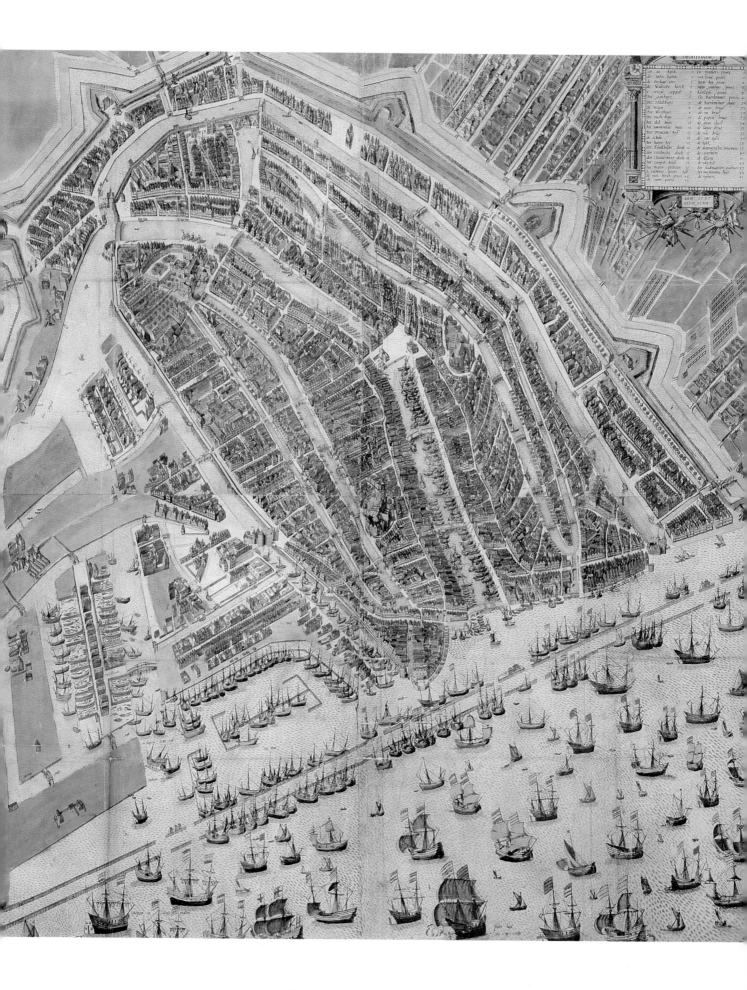

# ITINERARIO,

## Voyage ofte Schipvaert/ van Jan Huygen van Linschoten naer Oost ofte Portugaels In-

dien inhoudende een corte beschrijvinghe der selver Landen ende Zee-custen/ met aen-
wijsinge van alle de voornaemde principale Havens, Revieren/ hoecken ende plaetsen/ tot noch
toe vande Portugesen ontdeckt ende bekent: Waer by ghevoecht zijn/ niet alleen die Conter-
feytsels vande habijten/ drachten ende wesen/ so vande Portugesen aldaer residerende/ als van
de ingeboornen Indianen/ ende huere Tempels, Afgoden, Huysinge/ met die voornaemste
Boomen, Vruchten, kruyden/ Specerijen/ ende diergelijcke materialen/ als ooc die
manieren des selfden Volckes/ so in hunnen Godts-diensten/ als in Politie
en Huys-houdinghe: maer ooc een corte verhalinge van de Coophan-
delingen, hoe en waer die ghedreven en ghevonden worden/
met die ghedenckweerdichste gheschiedenissen/
voorghevallen den tijt zijnder
residentie aldaer.

Alles beschreven ende by een vergadert, door den selfden, seer nut, oorbaer,
ende oock vermakelijcken voor alle curieuse ende Lief-
hebbers van vreemdigheden.

## 't AMSTELREDAM.

By Cornelis Claesz. op 't Water, in 't Schrijf-boeck, by de oude Brugghe.
Anno CIƆ. IƆ. XCVI.

the Indies, maintained with the sultans and other notables of this area so little known to the rest of the world, and at the same time it supplied much information that until then had been a state secret, concerning navigation along the maritime routes that Portugal and Spain regarded as their preserve.

The Dutch merchants, who were motivated by the prospect of quickly winning total political autonomy [2] as much as they were intoxicated by the fragrance emanating from the first bags of spices stocked in the warehouses of Amsterdam's port, threw themselves into the adventure of trading with the Far East. In the short space of time between then and 1601 no fewer than eighteen expeditions, representing in all some hundred vessels, were set up by groups of owners belonging to different cities of the United Provinces. Nowadays one would talk of a "rush".

*The Itinerario : a mine of information purloined from the Spanish and the Portuguese and published in 1596 by Jan Huyghen van Linschoten. In it he describes, accompanied by much detail, the maritime routes leading to the Indies, the wealth of the countries recently discovered, the ways and customs of their peoples, and their botanical and zoological life. For a century, the Itinerario was considered indispensable and served as a guide for every ship making for the Orient. Van Linschoten's work proved to be a revelation to his compatriots and was the origin of their intrusion in full force into the archipelagos of Asia that the two Iberian nations considered their preserve.*

But the simultaneous arrival on the scene of so many competing companies carried with it the risk that the United Provinces would not weigh very heavily in the balance with the Portuguese who were already firmly implanted in the Indies, as mentioned above, or with the English who had just set up the "Company of London Merchants trading with the East Indies" (*sic*) which nourished similar ambitions regarding the spice islands. Very soon it became evident that petty local quarrels must be set aside and a commercial structure built up that would offer a united front to foreign competition. Thus there came into being on 20th March 1602 the "Vereenigde Oost-Indische Compagnie" (abbreviated to

*Next spread :*
*This map, drawn by Cornelis Claesz in 1597, shows the outward and homeward routes followed by the first Dutch expedition to the East Indies.*

---

2 The Netherlands Peace, signed in 1601 by the Republic of the Seven United Provinces and Spain, under pressure from both France and England, was to introduce a twelve years' truce. The final emancipation of the United Provinces — on the initiative of William I of Nassau, Prince of Orange, who was the pioneer in the revolt against the Crown of Spain — was achieved in 1648 with the Treaty of Munster and put an end to the "Eighty Years' War".

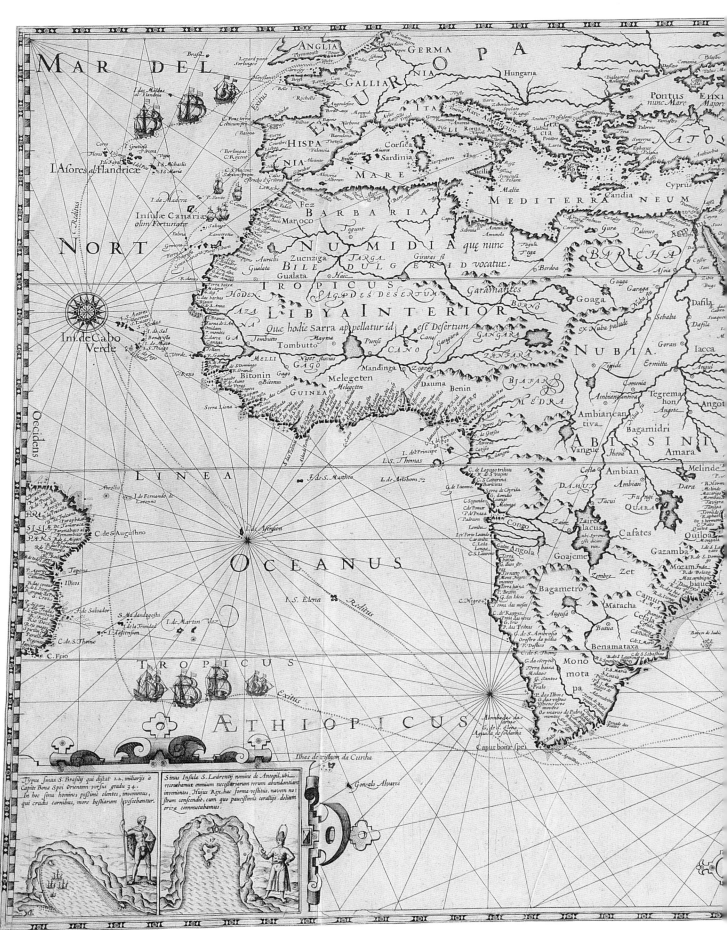

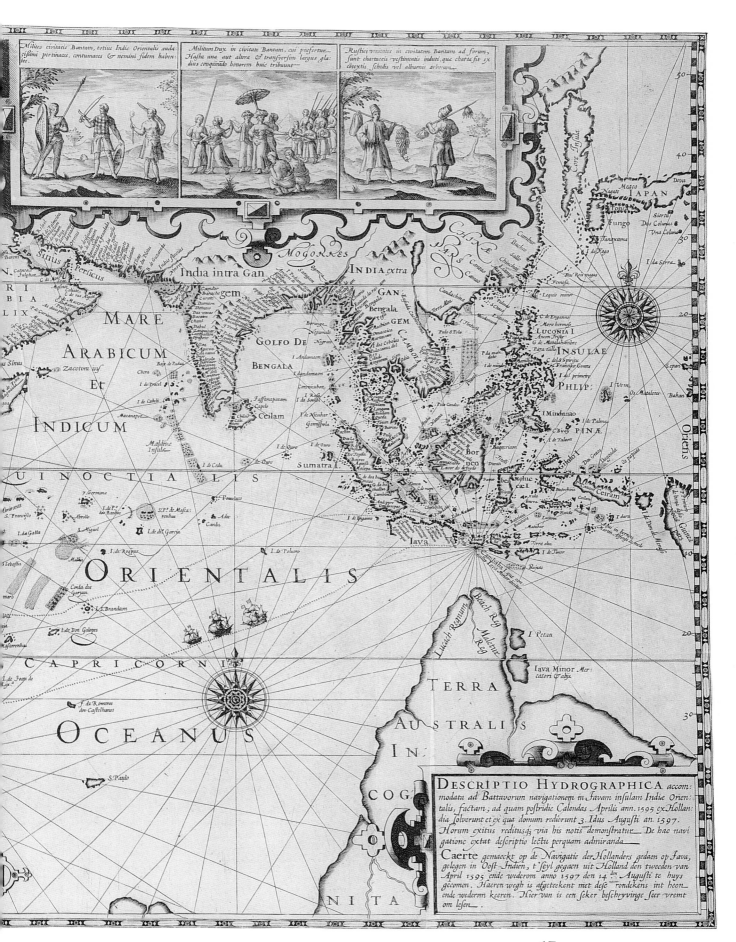

# Middelburg
### Prov. Zeeland

# Amsterdam
### Prov. Noord-Holland

# Enkhuizen
### Prov. Noord-Holland

*Johan van Oldenbarnevelt bore the title of "Grand Pensionnaire", which made him the most important person of the State machinery in the Republic of the Seven United Provinces. He was able to win the support of Stathouder Maurice de Nassau regarding the formation of an amalgamated maritime company and may thus be considered the spiritual father of the V.O.C. Protesting against the excessive rigidity of calvinism, he was politically defeated by his religious adversaries, removed from office, arrested and sentenced to death. His execution (beheading by axe) at The Hague in 1618 is one of the most tragic episodes of Netherlands history.*

"V.O.C."), the United East India Company. The new-born company was given the monopoly of navigation and trade to the east of the Cape of Good Hope. To this end, the former companies gave way to six Chambers of Commerce representing six towns that lived on overseas trade : Amsterdam, Middelburg, Hoorn, Delft, Rotterdam and Enkhuizen.

Each of these Chambers was presided over by a *bewindhebber*, who was himself chosen by a small college of electors composed of the burgomaster and aldermen of the city in question. The managing body of the new company, the equivalent of the Board of Directors of a modern company, comprised seventeen members, the *Heeren XVII*, who were appointed by the Chambers in proportion to each Chamber's commercial importance. Thus Amsterdam had the lion's share, with eight representatives, followed by Middelburg with four, while the others were entitled to only one seat each. In addition to these sixteen delegated directors, there was a seventeenth member, usually a *bewindhebber* whose choice had to meet the approval of the four Chambers carrying the least weight.

Persons of considerable distinction, the *Heeren XVII* met two or three times a year, in order to define or amend the Company's commercial strategy and to settle the more serious of its internal squabbles. The States General, or government, of the United Provinces remained in the background but gave its fullest support while delegating exceptional powers to an enterprise which, by its very structure, constituted the Batavian economic spearhead.

Thus it was that the V.O.C. was authorized to legislate, to hand down justice, to establish colonies and even to engage hostilities against foreign powers if there was any risk that such powers might

# Hoorn
## Prov. Noord-Holland

# Delft
## Prov. Zuid-Holland

# Rotterdam
## Prov. Zeeland

Compagnie Souveraine des Indes Orientales.

*Above :*
*The coats of arms of the six towns whose Chambers of Commerce joined together to form the V.O.C.*

*The ushers are guarding the doors. In a few moments, the seventeen "High and Mighty" lords of the V.O.C. are going to begin one of their annual meetings. According to the Company's rules of procedure, such meetings were to be held six years consecutively at Amsterdam and for the following two years at Middelburg. Each meeting might last as long as two weeks.*

thwart its legitimate interests[3]. In a word, it was a state within a state with an initial capital of 6,500,000 florins collected by national subscription, each share being worth 3,000 florins. However — and this was the novel feature — shareholders were warned that they were making a long-term investment and that the time when an investor received fat dividends on the return of a single voyage was now long

---

3 This explains the regular presence on board its ships of large contingents of soldiers, recruited by the V.O.C. itself and whose task was to put down any whisper of rebellion against the colonial yoke by the indigenous peoples of the East Indies.

past. Nevertheless the investors, though often critical of both the voting methods and the decisions taken by the Supreme Council, were never to regret their investment, for the V.O.C., which thus had at its disposal a substantial fund of ready money, was from the very first years of its existence to make colossal profits thanks to which, until the first third of the 18th century, it was the world's foremost commercial enterprise. It is true that its leaders' motto was no less than "Jesus Christ is good but trade is better"!

In addition to the remarkable spirit of initiative that inspired all its directors and senior officers, the V.O.C. had another overwhelming asset. It was the flagship of a country of outstanding sailors who were rapidly to design and construct a whole range of vessels demonstrating undeniable technical supremacy, as regards their construction and fitting out, compared with the other maritime powers of the time.

Amongst these ships, the "retourships" were by far the most important. As their name indicates, they were designed to ply between the mother country and the Indies. They were exceptionally sturdy vessels and were thus able to carry a maximum of passengers and cargo and repeatedly brave the most violent weather.

After them came the "flûtes" or storeships, which were actually conceived before the "retourships". They were smaller in size though still fairly big, and were designed specifically for interisland traffic in the Indies. Lastly there were the "yachts", support vessels that were the smallest of the range and were intended for what might be termed domestic requirements.

It was of course the spice trade that earned the V.O.C. the greater part of its profits. Amongst the spices, pepper, nutmeg, clove, cinnamon, mace and saffron were the most sought after in the markets of the old world. In addition, but to a lesser degree, the ships brought back products for pharmaceutical use including benzoin, opium and camphor, colouring substances such as indigo and sappan-wood, and lastly various materials appreciated throughout Europe such as silk, cotton, sugar, tortoise-shell, mother-of-pearl, wax and ambergris, the latter well-known as a fixative in making

*A venerable gabled house, well situated beside a canal : it was here, on the ground floor, behind these brick walls that are several hundred years old, that the Hoorn Chamber had its warehouses.*

perfume. It soon became clear that it was essential to have a home port in the Indies and the Company, following in the path of Cornelis de Houtman, fixed its sights on the port of Bantam at the western extremity of the great island of Java. So it was there that the immense warehouse was erected in 1604 in which the precious cargoes that the "retourships" would carry back to the distant homeland were assembled.

On the outward journey, in addition to their quota of passengers, the ships carried the tools and materials needed for the vessel's maintenance, and basic foodstuffs — cheese, wine, beer, spirits, biscuits — mainly intended for the Company's expatriate employees. The cargo also included various metals such as lead, silver and gold in ingots or coins, mirrors and glass, red colouring stuffs such as cochineal and vermilion (much valued in this part of the world), mercury for medicinal purposes (to treat syphilis) or manufacturing (silvering of mirrors) and merchandise for barter such as fabrics, utilitarian objects of china-ware or metal, a variety of baubles and *objets d'art* etc. All this wealth and

*A stirring sight : the polychrome escutcheon that still exists on the façade of the building.*

21

The Dutch were not the only Europeans to dote on spices. At a time when most dishes lacked flavour and when meat, even copiously salted, could not be entirely preserved and tended to go off, spices were used to mask some of the disagreeable after-taste. In Holland they were also used to prepare soused herrings and in spiced wine and "saffron milk" which was made by gently boiling milk to which had been added sugar and a mixture of spices including saffron, cloves, cinnamon and mace. Spices were used too for various medicinal purposes, which explains how it was that they were sold by both grocers and apothecaries.

Giroflier aromatique.

The clove tree (Eugenia caryophyllata) belongs to the Myrtaceae family, and has long, glossy leaves. It can reach a height of ten metres and the inflorescence occurs at the tip of its branches. The spice is the dried bud of the flower, its scent and flavour coming from the essential oil contained in the bud. The clove is used not only for its gustatory pro-perties, but also in medicine on account of its stimulative, anti-spasmodic and carmina-tive properties, and in dentistry it is used to cauterize the dental pulp inside decayed teeth.

Cinnamomum Zeylanicum Breyn.

The cinnamon tree (Cin-namomum zeylanicum) is a small tree of the Laura-ceae family found mainly in Ceylon and in some parts of South India and in Malaysia. Cinnamon powder, obtained by crushing the bark taken from young branches, was known and appreciated from earliest antiquity. The Portuguese had been the sole importers of this spice to Europe ; then the Dutch stole the monopoly from them in 1645 and kept it until 1796, when the island of Ceylon came under the control of the United Kingdom.

Myristica fragrans Houttuin

The nutmeg tree (Myristica flagrans) is fairly similar to the clove tree in size, and belongs to the Myristicaceae family. Like the clove tree it originally grew in only a small part of the Moluccas archipelago. Its fruit is like an apricot in colour and size. When it ripens, it bursts open revealing the nut (inside which is the coveted "seed") which itself is partially covered by a fleshy seed coat, a beautiful orange-red colour ; this too, after drying and crushing, becomes a well-liked spice, mace. In medicine, nutmeg is sought for its stimulative, carminative, astringent, aphrodisiac and tonic qualities.

The pepper plant (Piper nigrum), a vine of the Piperaceae family, is much more widespread than the clove and the nutmeg ; it grows in various Asian countries and has in fact been cultivated since the 6th century. It is the fruit, which grows in elongated bunches, that is used after drying. Until the 14th century it was so rare and so appreciated that it was called "seed of paradise" and apothecaries sold it by the ounce. In the 17th century the V.O.C. merchants obtained it mainly from Sumatra and Bantam as well as from the coast of Malabar in India. Towards the middle of the same century, some six million pounds (in weight) of pepper was being sent to Europe and accounted for more than half the spice cargo of the "retourships". The V.O.C. also sold a further three million pounds of pepper to China and India. In addition to its universally appreciated gustatory qualities, pepper is of use in medicine to stimulate the digestion and on account of its tonic, aphrodisiac, carminative and febrifugal qualities. It is also liked by hens, and causes them to lay more quickly but, unlike humans, does not make them sneeze !

23

these trinkets would serve as currency to obtain the favours of the princes or sultans with whom the Company wished to establish an agreement for the purpose of ensuring exclusive access for itself to the best possible sources of supply.

The task of collecting the spices was left to the "upper merchants", "under merchants" and "assistant merchants", titles which, as regards the first two at least, scarcely reflect the qualities and skills of those to whom they were applied and who were in fact high level commercial officers. Were they not required to exercise the finesse of diplomats — and if need be the cunning of spies — to contract alliances, to hamper the activities of competitors (the Portuguese being of course their primary target), to verify the quality of the produce, negotiate prices and arrange for its collection and transport to Bantam? The under merchant, and all the more so the upper merchant himself, thus formed one of the Company's essential links, and only men with proven qualities ever gained such posts.

The pragmatism of the *Heeren XVII* soon led them to realize that their officers could not be in two places at once and the very wide range of tasks with which their agents overseas were charged was in effect restricting their efficacy. Considering the expansion, no less exceptional than it was unexpected, of the Company's activities, the Council therefore decided at an extraordinary meeting held in Amsterdam on 1st September 1602 to appoint a resident Governor General in the East Indies.

His task would be to look after all major questions of a political nature and, if need be, military matters also, while at the same time putting into practice locally the broad directives decreed by the *Heeren XVII*.

*Previous spread :
An expatriate "upper merchant" and his wife, in the first quarter of the 17th century. In the background one can see the citadel of Batavia.*

*A mid-17th century engraving, depicting the collection, weighing and negotiation of nutmeg by V.O.C. merchants residing in the Moluccas.*

Sagou Boom
Ziet

Peper

Sagou

Peper

Peper

Pieter Both, the first to hold the post, was a man of great competence and strong personality, but he wore himself out visiting his various agencies. Thus he spent far too much time on incessant travelling and was able in actual fact to do only very little to promote the imperialistic aims of the Company. Neither of his two successors had more luck in their task.

Everything changed when Jan Pieterszoon Coen, a native of Hoorn, arrived on the scene in 1618. Aged thirty-one when he took up his duties, he was "different" from the others in that he had begun his career with the Company, ten years earlier, as an under merchant. Physically, he was tall and slim, with fine features. Fierce determination could be read in his eyes, and he had already shown that his devotion to the V.O.C. was boundless.

*1619 : the embryo of what was to become, much later, the megalopolis of Djakarta, has taken shape. Originally called Djajakarta, the place was re-named Batavia. In the future it was to mushroom and grow beyond all recognition.*

He was advised to use moderation, for his fiery spirit was well known in high places. Doubtless he would have taken pleasure in putting down forthwith the murmurs of revolt by the panjeram[4] of Bantam who, having welcomed the Dutch with enthusiasm — probably because he saw them as rivals to the detested Portuguese — now wanted to recover his former freedom of action and was increasing his interference in the V.O.C.'s attempts at expansion.

Mindful of this advice, Pieterszoon-the-Fearless[5] — such was the

4 Appellation given to local native chief, sometimes also called sultan.

5 Coen means "fearless" or "bold" in Dutch, and has nothing to do with the Jewish family name.

*The coat of arms of the city of Batavia.*

nickname he had been given — decided to avoid a confrontation and, giving up Bantam, left to establish his quarters beside a nearby natural harbour, on the same island of Java, at the place called Djajakarta. That was in 1619. But the disappointed kinglet took this all the more badly since his alter ego in Djajakarta was one of his hereditary enemies. The fort that the pale-skinned invader had decided to build had barely been completed when, in May of that year, he besieged it. At that particular time Coen, who had personally been on the look-out for storms throughout the building period, was away, inspecting other portions of his "kingdom". When he learned the bad news, he assembled the greater part of his forces and counter-attacked furiously, in order to inflict a resounding and definitive defeat on his presumptuous adversary. And the better to assert a supremacy that none would ever again be able to

challenge, he decided a little later to re-name the place "Batavia", a name that was to symbolize Dutch colonial power as late as the second World War.

It was from this nascent capital that Coen undertook to assert his authority over the whole Sunda archipelago and even beyond. All moderation was thrown to the winds and the erstwhile unwilling diplomat became a fierce and resolute fighter. By force of arms any who opposed his policy of territorial expansion were made, one by one, to bend the knee. A fervent enthusiast ahead of his time for the theories of Malthus, he believed that excess production of spices would inevitably result in a fall in prices and therefore took the tyrannical decision that certain islands only would be authorized henceforth to produce certain spices and in stipulated quantities.

*The fine motto of the founder of Batavia : "Despair not !"*

To achieve his aims, he immediately set a deplorable example by ordering his troops, whom no one but he was allowed to lead, to devastate all the native clove plantations on the islands of Banda, in the southern part of the Moluccas, in order to concentrate them henceforth in the island of Ambon. In the course of this wide-sweeping operation he incidentally exterminated several thousand inhabitants of this little island group, condemning the survivors to slavery. As a result, much bitterness and hate was built up against him personally which helped to introduce throughout the East Indies a climate of insidious war which was to last for many years.

In 1623, Jan Pieterszoon Coen returned to his home country, the Netherlands, to enjoy a much needed though temporary rest, to take a wife and to direct propaganda designed to awake settler ambitions among his compatriots. It was during his absence that the lieutenants whom he had trained in his merciless ways, after conducting a mockery of a trial, caused ten English merchants, suspected of commercial spying in the island of Ambon, to be executed. England, naturally, took this news very badly. The incident was all the more unfortunate in that relations between the two countries were at that time enjoying a bright spell. Urged on by the States General of the United Provinces, the *Heeren XVII* therefore had no alternative but to make their Governor General take full responsibility for the affair and officially disown him, forbidding him to return to his distant Javanese kingdom.

*Left :*
*This portrait of Jan Pieterszoon Coen dates from the middle of the 17th century — long after his death. The anonymous artist has reproduced from memory the late Governor General's features as they were when he was in his prime and the heigt of his glory*

However, after three long years in the wilderness, Coen finally regained his post in 1627, for the *Heeren XVII* had never intended to do anything but sacrifice him momentarily for reasons of state. Inwardly they still felt admiration and appreciation for the excellent trading results that his administration, cruel though it might often have been, had enabled them to achieve since he had taken up his duties.

He accordingly returned to Batavia, but the moral resilience of an extremely proud man was by then a little blunted. Moreover, though still young, his health had been much taxed by his life of battling through islands where the climate induced anaemia and malignant fevers were endemic. Yet, in this year of 1628 when the Company was preparing to launch the superb *Batavia*, the finest "retourship" ever to leave the shipyards of Amsterdam, he still had enough resilience and prestige to be feared and respected by all in the "castle of Batavia" as people at that time called the nucleus of the capital, which had grown in little more than a decade into a small prosperous township, bordered by the sea and criss-crossed by canals. It was a township that was already considerably larger than the original fortified compound, and that the crews and civilian passengers of the "retourships" on their way out from the motherland regarded rather as a promised land whose name alone was enough to make them conjure up pictures of those exotic horizons that the people of cold climates have always dreamed of discovering; and to make them forget, too, the privations and physical hardships endured in the course of an interminable crossing of oceans that were still largely unknown.

*The Grand Place, or Main
Square, at Hoorn, in the middle
of which stands the statue of the
most famous of the town's sons,
Jan Pieterszoon Coen.*

# act 2

## Francisco Pelsaert: the rosy years

Although it is an established fact that the Pelzer[1] family settled in 1605 on a rural property near Aix-la-Chapelle, in what is now the borderland between Germany and Belgium, there is no trace in the regional archives of a boy named Francisco. Nor is there any mention of his birth at Antwerp, where he may have been born, for at various times in the course of his career he claimed to be a native of that city. Inevitably, therefore, one can only make conjectures regarding the place and date of birth of the future unhappy hero of our story and, accordingly, his age at the time of the drama we are unfolding. But various pointers lead one to suppose that he was, if not still an adolescent, certainly a very young man.

There is no portrait of him either in the Netherlands where he was admittedly only a junior and, therefore, obscure, employee of the V.O.C. at the time when he first left for the East Indies in 1618 with the rank of assistant merchant. The unexpected shortness of his stay in his home country — barely five months — on his return from the Indies in 1628, when he had already been promoted to upper merchant and won an enviable reputation within the Company, would hardly have given him time, even had he been so inclined, to have his portrait painted ; thus from the point of view of history he remains for ever an invisible man, with no face and no record of his birth [2]. Regarding the rest of his life, that is to say the main stages of his career, fortunately we have plentiful information and we are thus able to form a good idea of the unusual man he was.

When Francisco Pelsaert arrived at Batavia on board the *Wapen van*

*This portrait is supposed to be of Francisco Pelsaert. It is a copy, given to Henrietta Drake-Brockman, of an engraving that was said to have been done from life, at Agra, around 1625. The subject's bearing, the line of his head, the features, hair, moustache, beard and mouth, and apparel, are so strikingly reminiscent of the well-known portrait of the famous French cardinal and statesman Richelieu, which hangs in the National Gallery, London, that one may well suspect o hoax.*

*Left :*
*The extravagant Jahangir, fourth of the Mogul dynasty, was a contemporary of Francisco Pelsaert.*

---

1 The spelling of proper names, both family names and place names, was still very little systematized at the time and thus the spelling of a person's name often differs considerably from one document to another. In the case in point however, it is clear that Pelzer and Pelsaert are one and the same family and the certificate of marriage of his sister Agniete with Hendrik Brouwer shows that this family is certainly our Francisco's.

2 His supposed portrait, discovered in India and shown to Mrs Henrietta Drake-Brockman in the 1950s, must be viewed with strong reservations as regards its authenticity, for the signature accompanying it bears no resemblance to that used by Pelsaert on various official documents that have been inspected — unless perhaps he varied his signature...

*Zeelandt*, Jan Pieterszoon Coen had just taken up his duties as Governor General of the East Indies and had begun to put some order into a house that badly needed it. Pelsaert, one amongst many other merchants, first had to undergo what today would be called a "training course" that was to take him from island to island and initiate him into the subtleties of the spice trade, this being the principal business of the V.O.C.'s commercial officers at that time. It may be assumed that his superiors approved of him, for even before his initial contract had expired it had been extended until 1624 : he had been promoted to the rank of under merchant and in December 1620 he was instructed to go to continental India to a place called Surat, situated in the northern part of the west or Malabar coast, not far from where the present-day megalopolis of Bombay lies.

Surat was at that time the main outlet onto the Arabian Sea for Agra, capital of the Mogul Empire, and hence the constant flow of people through the town included all the Muslims going on pilgrimage to Mecca or on their way back. Pelsaert journeyed to his new post from the Coromandel coast, thus crossing the Deccan peninsula, which gave him a first and enriching contact with the country in which he was henceforth to exercise his skills. The Dutch had, in fact, already set foot in India in a small way in 1606 at Surat. This gesture had greatly displeased the Portuguese, who were firmly established in the region, and they had managed by their machinations to oust the Dutch. A similar fate was planned for the English, but the maritime supremacy that had been the Portuguese preserve in this part of the world until then was soon challenged by the sons of Albion, who chased the Portuguese from Surat in 1612 with the aid of the Dutch, their allies for the occasion although they were subsequently left out of the picture.

Jan Pieterszoon Coen, seven years later, was clearly not going to accept such a situation. India, in the broadest sense of the term, having become his new realm, our enthusiast was not going to allow anyone to

outdo him. To begin with, he thought he would counter the English influence by creating a firm base at Machilipatnam, on the east coast, in order at least to rival the importance of Surat. But he soon realized that he was on the wrong tack and decided therefore to win back what had been lost at Surat itself, where the English had, of course,

*Francisco Pelsaert was largely responsible for the building of the Dutch "factory" or trading station at Agra, which looked like this towards the end of his stay in India.*

*Pieter van den Broecke, who was born in Antwerp in 1585, the year the town was sacked by the Duke of Alva's troops, began his career in Africa before being promoted to the rank of upper merchant of the V.O.C. and being sent to Surat, in India, by Jan Pieterszoon Coen. The task with which he was entrusted there was to develop a profitable commercial activity. His jurisdiction extended also to trade with the Middle East. With the efficacious support of his talented and faithful lieutenants, Francisco Pelsaert and Walter van Heuten, he achieved remarkable results. After a short stay in his native country to recover his health, he returned to India where he died in the siege of Malacca in 1629, the year of the loss of the* Batavia.

wasted no time in firmly staking a claim. Indeed, an ambassador, Sir Thomas Roe, had been accredited to the Great Mogul and a port had been built at a place named Swally, mid-way between the town, Surat, and the Gulf of Cambay, where goods could be loaded and unloaded. Promising trading relations had already begun between London and Agra, the capital situated some 850 kilometres north-east as the crow flies, far inland on the banks of the Yanuma, one of the principal affluents of the Ganges.

Thus the Dutch trading post at Surat was left more or less to stagnate until 1620, the year when Pieter van den Broecke was instructed to settle there permanently and to take in hand the destiny of the "Western quarters"[3]. It was at this time that Francisco Pelsaert joined him at Surat, before leaving again three months later to be the right hand of one van Heuten who had been instructed to get to Agra and lay the foundations there of a profitable trading relationship.

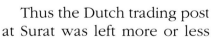

3  This should be understood as west in relation to the bridgehead that Batavia had actually become.

Agra ...The glory of the city had blossomed during the reign of Akbar, the third sovereign in the famed Mogul dynasty, who was not only a brave warrior and strategist but also a cultured man, well-versed in the arts and in theology. When he died, in 1605, the reputation of opulence and magnificence of this legendary city had for many years been known to the leading nations of Europe, whose dreams of winning a footing there were reinforced by the rumour that the late sovereign's son Jahangir [4] had inherited his father's remarkably tolerant attitude towards foreigners in general, whatever their religious persuasion. Thus it was that the Hindus' freedom of the city had never been denied by the Muslim invaders, and indeed the more talented amongst them had been from early days closely involved in the life of the Court.

Francisco Pelsaert, on arriving, discovered a fabulous city on the banks of a river, its superb palaces partially hidden by luxurious vegetation, an imposing fort, Jumna, built of ashlars that became blood-red in the rays of the setting sun, and cosmopolitan and colourful crowds. Agra was at this time the focal point of the indigo market : the leaves of the indigo plant, gathered in the neighbourhood and further to the north, produced a colouring substance that had become the vogue in Europe some years before and of which ever greater quantities were being demanded.

The English certainly had some advance over the Dutch in this area but their weakness was that they did not have much to offer the local population in exchange for what they desired. The Dutch, on the other hand, having acquired virtually absolute control of the spice trade

*The first "store-ships" came into being at Hoorn in 1585. They were soon adopted throughout the Netherlands. It was ships of this type that were used to carry amongst other things the produce gathered in India, chiefly pepper and indigo, back to Batavia. There it was transferred onto "retourships" leaving for Europe. The store-ships were smaller in size (their average length being 25 metres), and their special features were the rounded stern and pear-shaped cross section. The main qualities of these vessels were their shallow draft and very great load capacity. Being in no circumstances intended to carry passengers they had minimal fittings and decoration, and thus cost much less to build than a "retourship".*

---

4 A colourful character, much more attracted by life's pleasures than by the conduct of affairs of state. His appellation "conqueror of the world" was not very apt, for his passions were tiger-hunting and elephant fights and he delighted in a life of idle luxury. One of his other favourite pastimes was to play a cornet that the English had presented to him.

AGRA

99

It was under Babur, first of the Great Moguls, that Agra became the capital of the new Muslim empire at the beginning of the 16th century. The superb fort, which had been begun during the reign of Akbar, grandson of the first Great Mogul, existed already when Pelsaert arrived there in 1621, but work on one of the most famous monuments of the world, the Taj Mahal, was not begun until 1632, five years after he had left.

Right :
The city of Agra, seen from inland, on the eve of the 17th century. A continuous wall of ramparts protects the Great Mogul's fortified palace.

Previous spread :
Festivities at the court of the Great Mogul, within the walled city.

Far right :
There are countless portraits of Jahangir. The fine, distinguished features of the monarch conceal the reality of an unbridled pleasure seeker.

were much more interesting customers : did the Indians not consume enormous quantities of spices ? Pelsaert was quick to seize on this commercial advantage which, furthermore, fanned his ardour for his task.

Only three years after his arrival there, the man who was to become the *commandeur* of the *Batavia* felt as much at home in Agra as a fish in water. Van Heuten had just died and henceforth it was he, and he

Djehanguir
empereur Mogol de Dehli
1605 1627.

43

alone, who was responsible in the key post that he now occupied for ensuring that the interests of the Company prospered. A two-fold route supplying spices simultaneously to the west and east coasts of India? He rejected this as a tactical error, with figures in support of his argument : for the buyers in Machilipatnam found means of sending their spices across the whole country to be sold at unbeatable prices in the markets of Agra, where they competed with imports through Surat, which were easily the most profitable for the V.O.C.'s business. He compared this with the tactics of the Armenian traders who went right to the inland villages to obtain their merchandise, then organized networks to export it to Isfahan in west central Iran and thence to Aleppo in Syria.

Pelsaert, fine trader that he had become, was able to use the perfect knowledge that he had acquired of places and people to give his compatriot merchants the following advice : a musk of good quality will be

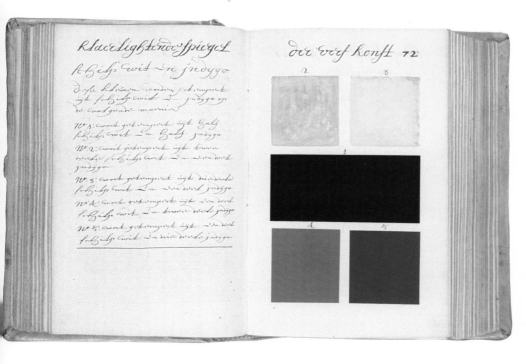

*The palette of colours that could be obtained from indigo (mixed with white in varying proportions). It was prepared at Delft in the 17th century to be used as a guide for the colouring of engravings and drawings.*

covered by a single skin and should be a yellowy-gold colour and should melt in the hand. The bezoar should be weighed, then put to soak in water for four hours, then weighed again. If it weighs less, you can be sure that your cunning vendor had covered it with lime. As for indigo, he soon knew all there was to know about this precious produce. He knew where it was to be found, how it was cultivated, the treatment process it underwent, and hence the different grades of quality. Like a modern-day fraud inspector he discovered the resourcefulness of the dishonest and was able to warn potential purchasers against the trick of covering a stock of lesser value known as *"catel"* with a thin layer of high quality indigo, called *"ziarye"*. "It is wise", he told his fellow-merchants, "to open bundles before weighing them for if you undo the strings you can tell exactly the quality of the merchandise."

*Left:*
*A Turkoman lady's robe : the weft uses threads of cotton, while the warp is silk thread that has been dyed before weaving. The colours of the background are dominated by the deep blue of the indigo.*

*45*

# Indigo: the miracle plant

Indigofera tinctoria L.

*Indigofera tinctoria is a cultivated leguminous plant, whose branches are cut when in flower about three months after the seed has been planted. The cut branches are gathered into bunches. The root left in the ground can produce as many as four growths a year.*

1. Melia azedarach. 2. Calophyllum inophyllu... coolies stir the indigo plant in water. 7. Sett...

*Blocks of indigo : the form in which the product was offered for sale in Francisco Pelsaert's day.*

plant. 4. Tank into which the indigo leaves are put. 5. Steeping trough where leaves are left to soak. 6. Beating tank, where ng vat. 9. Coolies carrying indigo to the drying place. 10. Coolies cutting the indigo plant. 11. Farmer. 12. Indigo bundles.

Before the vogue for indigo was virtually wiped out by introduction of the synthetic colouring substance, anilin, indigo was much sought after on account of the magnificent blue colouring extracted from its leaves. The branches, steeped in water, were left to ferment in a stone tank called a "steeping trough" where they were pressed and stirred from time to time. They were generally taken out after twenty-four hours, by which time the leaves would have yielded all their substance. The liquid thus obtained was then transferred, by gravity, into a second, smaller tank, called the "beating tank", where a little fish oil was added and for two or three hours it was vigorously stirred by hand, using a sort of long paddle. This operation, giving off a foul smell, was considered the most important one where "the indigo manufacturer who did not know his job could be found out" for if the operation went wrong the colour became black : then the indigo was said to be "burnt". Following this second treatment, density caused the liquid to separate, depositing a bluish sediment on the floor of the tank. When the liquid floating on top had been drawn off, the sediment was transferred to the "settling vat" before being put into sacks to drain off the remaining liquid. Lastly it was spread out on racks to dry and then cut into small blocks, which were the saleable product. There is at the present time a resurgence of interest in this natural colouring substance, and indeed the makers of the famous Persian carpets have never used anything else. Indigo gives a superb range of deep blues, some verging on violet or purple.

47

*One of Jahangir's favourite pastimes was to watch elephant fights, their ardour in battle stimulated by all sorts of cruel artifices. It will be noticed that the tips of the animals' tusks have been sawn off.*

But Pelsaert was not only a trader, far from it. Indeed, his remarkable gift for observation, coupled with an insatiable natural curiosity, has given us an exciting picture of the life of the peoples of North India in this first quarter of the 17th century, and more particularly in the capital of the Great Mogul. In point of fact he had little sympathy for Jahangir, whom he considered a misguided sovereign, an unworthy successor to his father, interested only in futile pleasures and totally devoid of any sense of justice, indifferent to the suffering of the people whom he, Francisco Pelsaert, a truly humane observer, viewed with compassionate sympathy. While the sovereign watched elephant fights from the windows of his palace, the walls of which were rough-cast with a mixture of lime, milk and sugar, then agate-polished, his subjects squat-

ted in pitiable hovels, where there was no fire-place, no bed, no furniture at all and only a few clay pots for household use, the air smelling foully from the open fire on which burned a few pieces of cow-dung.

The very peculiar customs of the rich and powerful who gravitated towards the Emperor attracted his attention a great deal : while he admired their dwellings for their comfort and cleanliness, which he found far in advance of any he knew in Holland, he noted at the same time that they were at the mercy of the least report made to the prince. Their buildings and their palaces lasted little more than a man's life. He commiserated too with their wives, for though their clothes were the most beautiful in the world, they were so unhappy that "not one of them would not have changed places with the poorest of our Dutch women". There is no denying that they were most often regarded as mere objects, who were kept together in *zenanas* or *mahals* where the atmosphere was one of extreme sensuality, not to say lasciviousness, and where their lives were ruled by tyrannical eunuchs[5]. Wives were

*Tiger-hunting was second only to elephant fights in entertaining the Great Mogul, who watched the scene from the incomparable observation post afforded by the back of an elephant. Here a mahout is leading the animal while a servant provides shade for the monarch, whose head appears ringed by light. Behind them comes the monarch's retinue made up of an army of huntsmen carrying guns, pikes and clubs. A wounded animal was often trampled to death by the elephant.*

---

5 In this connection it is interesting to note that, contrary to what is generally assumed, removal of the testicles does not necessarily result in inability to achieve an erection, provided that the mutilation is performed

constantly treated with scorn, having to endure without protest the spectacle of their husbands sprawled on a luxurious couch, indulging without restraint and to the point of intoxication in aphrodisiac or alcoholic drinks before coupling, quite unabashed and in full view of all present, with any beautiful passing slave who happened just then to whet their appetite... Unfortunate members of the so-called weaker sex, they were also often obliged, in communities that practised monogamy such as the Rajputs [6], to be burned alive when their husbands died prematurely.

Francisco Pelsaert certainly possessed the gifts that make a great journalist, judging by his account, laced with racy anecdotes, of the expeditions on which the Great Mogul and his Court would set out at the beginning of summer, travelling to the mountains in the north of the country by a very dangerous road that was "costly" in life and limb. Referring to the peoples of the "Cassamir" region (present day Kashmir), in the foothills of the immense snowy chain of the Himalayas, Pelsaert says he was struck both by the poverty and dirt in which they lived and by their natural gentleness of disposition and their fervent faith.

In 1626 he had the excellent idea of setting down in writing his comments on the Company's commercial strategy in the Indies and also his observations on the world to which he had devoted so much energy throughout six well-filled years, in a document he called *Remonstrantie*[7].

The "High and Mighty" naturally did not become aware of the *Remonstrantie* — on account of the time it would have taken to reach

*Eunuchs played an important role within the* zenanas, *where their intrigues ruled the life of the wives of the Muslim dignitaries who gravitated towards the Great Mogul. Resigned to the polygamy practised by their lords and masters, these unfortunate women were condemned to live in a cloistered world where slaves of the fair sex were at their service.*

*Right :
It was this report, entitled* Remonstrantie, *written by Pelsaert after he had spent six years in India, that was to earn him a reputation as a shrewd and enterprising man and suddenly accelerate his career.*

after puberty. But it should be added that actual castration was sometimes replaced by merely crushing the spermatic cord, that is to say, the testicles' "alimentary" cord. In some cases, this practice involved only stopping the *vas deferens*, the canal through which the spermatozoons are evacuated. In that case, provided there remained a little testicular tissue to fabricate the hormone, the male could, without being fertile, attain a satisfactory erection. Many eunuchs of both types were thus able to have clandestine sexual relations with certain more or less willing inmates of harems, relations that would have been all the more appreciated in that they entailed no risk of conception.

6 The Rajputs settled in India in the 7th century A.D. They were Brahmins and the Muslims gradually forced them back into the mountainous areas of the country. Their area of cultural influence today constitutes the State of Rajasthan.

7 This word, now obsolete, was probably borrowed from the English "remonstrance". Contemporary Dutch would probably use "vertoog" or "betoog", which mean "demonstration", "discourse" or "exposition". The latter is perhaps the most appropriate translation. Pelsaert's *Remonstrantie* was thus an exposition (that is to say, of the commercial and political aspects of life in the Mogul Empire at the beginning of the 17th century), addressed to the *Heeren XVII*. His drafting of the *Remonstrantie* was completed on 15th February 1627 "at the Factory of the Dutch Company at Agra".

# Remonstrantie

Van 't geene door my Francisco Pelsaert, Coopman eende[...] deser Landts handel, naer 't nauw[...] rich ondersoeck, ende Sekere ondervindinge der tijt berwijl ick gevonden, In 3 Jaeren datse wegen der Vereenich[...] [...] Indische Compag: op 't Comp. Agra als ander plaatsen haer uijt gethof drie t[...] soeck, onder de directie vanden Commandeur Pieter van brocke, ende hebbe het Int cort beschreven, als volc[...]

Eerstelijck vand' Stadt Agra die geleghen op der hooghte van 28 graeden 45 minuten, des uijtter maten groote maer [...] oper, en onbemuert de Stadt, Ongeordentelijck inden Tratz der huijsen betimmert, hebbende wel vele groote Fraeie ende Heerl. gebouwde[...] haer ra[...] in 't Egijp ende Doorkenwerken, vert dat onder[...] op ganck vande Stadt want daer te voorden maer den Dorp Bas. raende onder de Jurisdictie van Bajana, maer omdat d' Co. achabar, Int Jaer 1566 daer synne Sidentie naems [...]r [...]lijck dat [...]ll Liet bouwen op de riviere Zemena die hier voor Bij [...]roomt Brdof, dedum[...] [...] schoot ende ondevrijck[...]t van het gebo[...]mte, die 't rontom hem hiet [...], gelijck[...] [...]der des hoff als dese Stadt soo hdet [...], door [...]t aende genoms en[...] [...] ocht dat hem [...] [...] vondt onder gelegen[...] [...]
der dalun[...] gelden uijtbu[...] plaatsen van marchtes of [...] besaten, gelijck In Lahoor Barampoer, [...]bat of [...] au[...] [...]g maer alles dicht be[...]t en bewoont den beijden onder den moors den rijck rond[...] en armen [...]dijt, ende soo dat Coninck hier syn zidt plaats gebonden hadde, gelijck syn vader, soo soude dit des wonder des werelts adv[...]t tebbe, want de poort onder dese Coninck [...]bap 'tot verschejdingh vande Stadt laten maken hadd', als m[...] [...]trase, 't art[...]dewrase, nijnderwase, Puttendewrase. [...]ry [...] wete Taer m[...] Int midden vande Stadt uut t'bant de [...] [...] vingh wel drijmael Int ronde groot[...] is

Het Begrijp vande Stadt belijst wel [...]elien bred[...]t niet als wel lemet [...] doet, omdat de verbl[...]socht het [...]don[...]ier kant nae[...] 't be wesen de halvehei't op 't water lanck [...] [...]roy [...] met alle groote beiden van na[...] harde Galleijset bebont [...] [...]der[...] tr[...]de praecktich laet a[...] als, [...] lengte van 6 [...] of te 3 l hollant mijl, darbonnen wel de voornaem [...] hael h[...] haer ve[...]de ad[...]ichem, begunnend' vand [...] [...]t bij [...] daet Taat het hoff van Badorea die Coninck van het [...] [...]le [...]hasteen gewes[...] [...]s dat [...] Cos van Barampoer Leijt daer aij het hoff

van

51

them — until the following year and then there is no doubt that its author's arguments, backed by the good results he had obtained, immediately went home and led Hendrik Brouwer[8], one of the powers behind the throne in the V.O.C., to propose to his distinguished colleagues that the author be invited to play a more important role in the life of the Company — to which they readily agreed.

When his contract terminated at the end of 1627, Francisco Pelsaert turned down the offer made to him by the ever-active Van den Broecke to sign another. Sated with the exotic, his health undermined by an indefinable illness[9], he had in fact resigned himself to returning to his native Flanders to stay there. He took passage homeward on board the *Dordrecht*, a vessel captained by one Adriaen Jacobsz. The two men met for the first time in the port of Swally, on 15th December 1627, and almost immediately a violent dispute broke out between them, witnessed by other people. According to some, it would appear that Pelsaert had chanced upon the personal commerce that the ship's captain was carrying on and had reproached him in no uncertain terms. This is undoubtly the most plausible version but of course we shall never know exactly what happened.

How could the author of the *Remonstrantie*, a work that was so appreciated by his masters, have suspected on returning to Amsterdam

*An engraving dating from 1645 which shows the imposing building of the V.O.C. "factory" at Surat. All the goods collected in different places up-country were assembled here.*

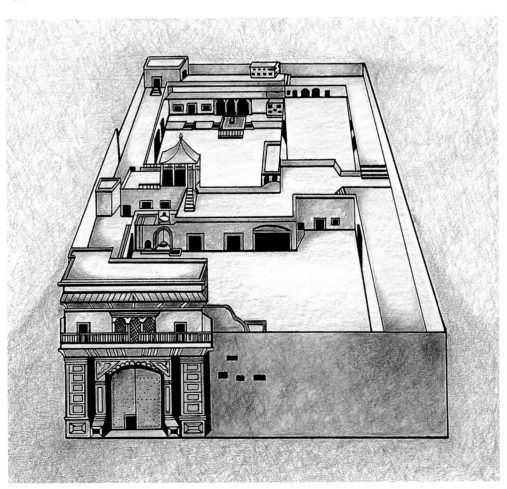

six months later, after ten long years' absence, that the very success of his mission in the Indies and the perspicacity that he had displayed throughout his writings, would serve him ill? He barely had time to renew ties with his loved ones, to view the familiar skyline of the towers and belfries of Amsterdam and Antwerp, to become accustomed again to the inimitable flavour of herrings from the North Sea, before the V.O.C. offered him the promotion that one does not turn down : immediately to return to the far-off colonies of the East, to the East Indies this time, with the prestigious title of *commandeur* [10] of a fleet of seven ships. What was more, he would sail in the finest ship ever to leave the shipyards of the Amsterdam Chamber, a vessel whose name alone was a cry of national pride : *Batavia* ! All this and the news too, divulged to him in private by his brother-in-law, that it had been decided in principle to appoint him in the very near future to a post of the greatest prestige : Councillor of the East Indies [11]. Intoxicated by so much sudden esteem, Pelsaert hesitated only a few days and then, ignoring his deteriorating health, gave his answer to the "High and Mighty" Gentlemen : it was yes, they could count on his diligence and on his habitual devotion to duty.

On Amsterdam's Peperwerf — the "Spice quay" — in the populous district of Rapenburg [12], the "scheepsbouwers" of the V.O.C. were busy putting the finishing touches to the superb and imposing *Batavia* before her departure, which had just been set for the end of October in this year of grace 1628.

*The authentic signature of Pelsaert-the-Fleming.*

---

8  He had married one of Pelsaert's sisters, Agniete, and was thus his brother-in-law.

9  Most likely malaria.

10  An honorary title giving its holder no power at all regarding the technical operations of sailing a ship, these being entrusted to the professional sailors, but on the other hand giving him prerogatives that were his alone in all other matters.

11  The council had eight members, whose task was to assist the Governor General in carrying out his mission. Francisco Pelsaert was raised to this rank by a decision of the *Heeren XVII* adopted in the month of June 1629, but his letter of accreditation did not reach Batavia until after Coen's death and after the *Batavia* disaster, not long before his own death.

12  Rapenburg was an island district of Amsterdam. The town having grown considerably since then, by filling in and building on what was formerly water, the name now belongs only to a street, a square and a canal.

# act 3

## The Batavia in her day

The exact details of the *Batavia*'s construction will never be fully known for the simple reason that the V.O.C. did not keep a detailed record of each ship leaving its shipyards. Nor have any drawings of the fine "Indiaman" survived to the present day. Nevertheless one can form a good idea of its main characteristics from various sketches and paintings of the period and also from the specifications drawn up by the *Heeren XVII* at their assembly held in Amsterdam on 29th March 1626. These read as follows :

"In compliance with the terms of the contract for construction, the dimensions of a "retourship" shall henceforth conform to the following specifications :

| | |
|---|---|
| - length on deck | : 160. Amsterdam feet [1] |
| - depth of hold | : 12.5 - - |
| - height 'tween decks | : 5.5 - - |
| - beam | : 36. - - |

Should the shipbuilder fail to comply with the foregoing, penalties shall be payable by the person responsible for execution of this contract (based on the regulations of August 1616). In such case, the said person shall pay a fine of 1,000 Flemish pounds which sum shall be given to the poor. The two new vessels [2] shall be built by the Amsterdam Chamber".

These specifications are in fact tantamount to the "birth certificate" of a new generation of "retourships", larger, faster and more handsome than those built before this year of 1626. The supreme authority of the V.O.C. had at last realized the need for planning the Company's shipbuilding and standardizing dimensions so as to form a homogeneous fleet, composed mainly of yachts, store-ships and "retourships",

*The Dutch flag, with the V.O.C. emblem.*

*Left :*
*This is how the Batavia might have looked, sailing in thick weather under shortened canvas.*

---

1 This measurement relates only to the hull itself, and does not include the beakhead and the bowsprit or jib-boom. The Amsterdam foot, a unit of measurement later abandoned, was equal to 0.28325 metres.

2 One of which was the *Batavia*.

designed respectively for coastal traffic in Indian and East Indies waters, for inter-island traffic, and for the outward and return voyages between the mother country and the distant colonies.

Needless to say it was the Amsterdam shipyard, belonging as it did to the most powerful and most influential Chamber and situated within the country's best-equipped and most frequented port, that was the principal purveyor of new ships to the V.O.C.

The various shipyards that had been grouped together in Lastage, a district which had by tradition been dedicated to ship-building but was overtaken by the growth of the town from 1585 onwards, moved out to the islands of Marken, Uilenburg and Rapenburg. Ever since the creation of the V.O.C., the Company had made Rapenburg its own preserve and by 1608, six years later, its Peperwerf[3] shipyard had largely

*Until 1660 when the shipyards moved to Oostenburg island, Rapenburg having become too small for the task, all the V.O.C.'s fine Indiamen were built on the Peperwerf at Rapenburg.*

replaced all the others in the neighbourhood. This immense area, particularly well-situated near the Company's warehouses beside the Ij, an arm of the Zuider Zee, gave the V.O.C. the means to match its ambitions.

There, two workshops operated side by side under the direction of Jan Rijksen, who at nearly seventy years of age still ruled his teams with a rod of iron. With the help of the standardization of design described above, extraordinary feats of production were accomplished. Thus no more than eighteen months ever lapsed between the decision by the "High and Mighty" to start construction of another vessel and delivery of

---

3 Literally, this means "Pepper Wharf", a reference to the "queen of spices" that was stored in nearby warehouses.

the latter to its owner. With time and experience, they reached the stage where some "retourships" were built in just six months, starting from scratch. Even in our day this would constitute a major technical feat.

This result was achieved by means of organizing the work in a manner foreshadowing what was to become, some three centuries later, assembly-line production. No sooner had the oak planking [4] fastened to the frames risen above the water line, than the vessel was launched and towed into a nearby enclosure, fenced in by wooden posts. These enclosures, situated right in front of the shipyard, were known as "cages" and inside them teams of workmen specializing in the various tasks of ship-building were busily employed on the next stages of construction. Thus there was room on the sloping area of the Peperwerf for assembling the framework of another vessel. At this rate, the

*Jan Rijksen, marine engineer, and his wife Griet. He used to supervise the building of the V.O.C. ships on Amsterdam's Peperwerf. He was 66 at the time of the launching of the Batavia.*

V.O.C. was to produce some 1,500 vessels in the course of the 17th century, more than half of which were made in the Amsterdam yard alone.

Although today she would be fairly dwarfed by any of the giant merchant vessels that ply the oceans, the *Batavia* and her sister-ships were among the largest vessels of their time. With their 600 gross tons, these "retourships" were three times the size of the caravels that had borne Christopher Columbus towards the mysterious shores of the West Indies in 1492. As for Captain Bligh's notorious *Bounty* that was to arouse such passion a century and a half later, she was no more than half the size of the *Batavia* ! Despite the fact that it was a very new design, her pronounced sheer still gave the *Batavia* the air of an Iberian

---

4 The oak planking was sometimes covered by a sacrificial planking of pine to protect the high quality oak from the wood borers that proliferate in warm seas.

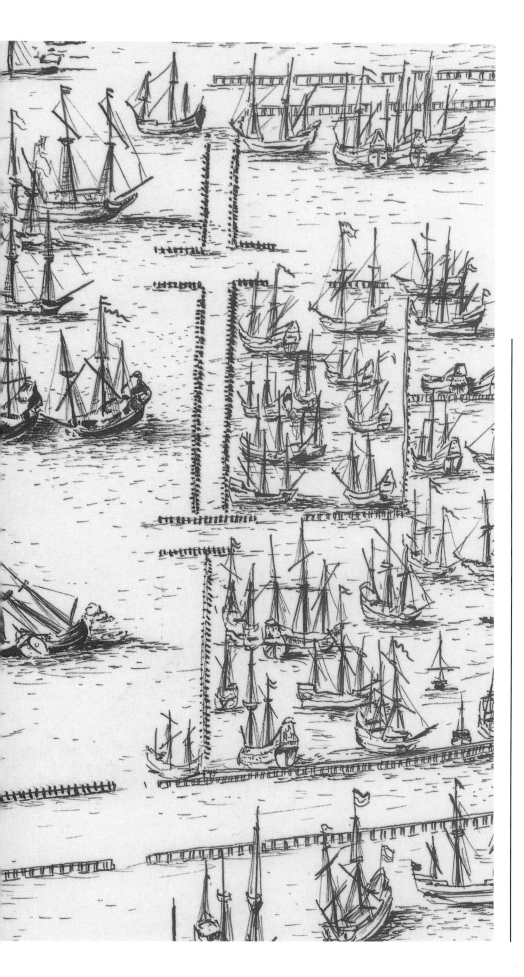

*The small island of Rapenburg
(marked A) which at the time of
the construction of the
Batavia was outside the town
of Amsterdam, to the east,
served from 1585 to 1660 as
headquarters for the V.O.C.
One can see the Company's two
shipyards. The neighbouring
island of Marken (marked B)
concentrated on building barges.
It also specialized in caulking
work and the manufacture of
hemp rope.
Shipbuilding for private
customers was done on the
island of Uilenburg
(marked C).  The three islands
were connected by bridges and
in the middle of each was a deck
that could be raised to allow
passage to the shipping in this
busy part of the Ij.*

*A shipwright at work dressing timbers on one of the Peperwerf shipyards.*

carack. On account of the flat slope of the lower part of the stern, forming at either side a sharp angle with the hull, this part came to be known as the "mirror". It was the part above this "mirror" that artists were engaged to embellish with a variety of carved figures, usually painted green and gold, these two colours being used also on the painted trims along the length of the hull. Only the figurehead, the Lion of Holland, was coloured red. When one remembers that the very name Batavia was full of symbolism [5], one may be sure that very special care would have been taken with the ship's decoration.

Rigged as a three-master, with a bowsprit, the handsome vessel could spread more than 1,100 square metres of canvas to the breeze when all her ten sails were set. These, being for the most part square, did not give ships of her generation much ability to go to windward and thus they were often obliged to go far out of their way in search of

---

5 The Batavians were people of Germanic stock who had settled at the mouth of the Rhine river, and from whom the Dutch have always claimed descent. They put up heroic resistance, under the leadership of their undisputed chief Claudius Civilis, against Julius Caesar and his legions.

*The launching of a ship was always a festive occasion. The two vessels shown here are far from complete as yet. Each will be towed to a floating enclosure where the finishing work will be done.*

favourable winds. The required height of the spars, made possible by jointing several lengths of timber by means of "sleeves", made it necessary to set water-sails to improve course stability and to help balance hull windage[6]. These water-sails were additional sprit-sails set at the forwardmost point of the ship, fastened to the bowsprit, which helped to lower the centre of effort and thus improve the stability of the ship. The drawback of this type of rig was the multitude of ropes and blocks required for the handling of so much canvas, making the work of the crew as complex as it was gruelling.

---

6 The resistance to the wind of the built-up portions of the ship's hull and superstructures.

61

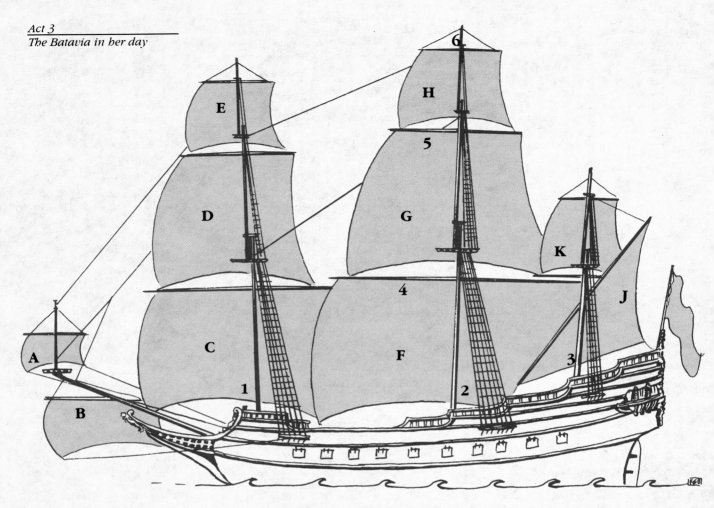

## The rigging of the Batavia

The rigging of the Batavia

1  Fore mast
2  Main mast
3  Mizzen mast
4  Main yard
5  Main topsail yard
6  Main topgallant yard

A  Spritsail topsail
B  Spritsail
C  Fore course
D  Fore topsail
E  Fore topgallant
F  Main course
G  Main topsail
H  Main topgallant
J  Lateen mizzen (or spanker)
K  Mizzen topsail

Cross section of the Batavia

I    Hold
II   Orlop deck
III  Gun deck
IV   Upper deck

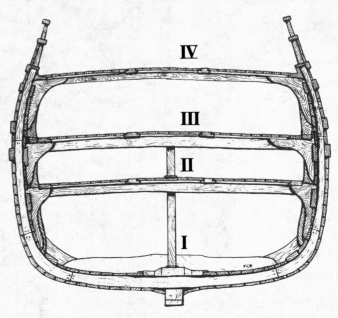

## Cross section of the Batavia

*It is partly thanks to its impressive "retourships", technically vastly superior to the merchant vessels of other European nations, that the V.O.C was able to establish its colonial power in the East Indies.*

During the first half of the 17th century, the "retourships", which put to sea two or three times a year accompanied by a small flotilla of merchant vessels of different types, became the spearhead of Dutch colonial expansion.  To carry to the other side of the world, as they did on each voyage, between two and three hundred people, sometimes more, on board a single ship, was no mean feat from many points of view. The directors of the V.O.C. had countless problems to contend with : the ships' safety at sea when confronted by foreign powers' covetousness or the sudden apparition of pirates, provisioning of the ships, the health of all on board, maintenance of discipline — not to speak of all the risks involved in sailing a sea route on which countless technical obstacles had to be circumvented, in particular the risks of protracted calms or on the contrary, violent storms in the higher latitudes of the Atlantic and the Indian Ocean.  In these various respects the first "retourships", acting rather as scouts, had supplied much valuable information to the Company which enabled it as time went by to conceive the means of coping with the main hazards encountered.

As regards her internal geometry, the *Batavia* comprised three main levels : the hold, the orlop-deck and the gun-deck.  In addition to these there were partial decks, stepped to form the quarterdeck and the superstructures of the poop.

The hold (*ruim* in Dutch) was the lowest part of the ship. As it was essential to carry heavy ballast in vessels of such shallow draft¯, various suitable cargoes were stowed there including sand, gravel, bricks, blocks of stone (such was the case for the *Batavia*, as we shall see), metals, canon balls, spare anchors, barrels of powder, timber for repairs to the ship, etc. In the hold were also stored barrels of fresh water, each holding 600 litres, and the foodstuffs that were supposedly non-perishable. There being little ventilation in the hold, fermentation of all kinds was facilitated and the water intended for human consumption, for instance, quickly stagnated and became virtually undrinkable.

The *orlop* deck or "cow deck" (*koebrug* in Dutch), which was theoretically intended for storing the spice cargo, was used on the outward voyage to house the soldiers. The experience of the first voyages had shown that in fact these mercenaries, of whom there may have been as many as a hundred on board a single "retourship", very rarely got on well with the sailors. The Company therefore decided to segregate them, with the result that the soldiers came off by far the worst, for they found themselves confined in a closed area within which it was difficult even to stand upright. On the other hand, they were not required to do any of the heavy work on board and of course played no part in the ship's handling.

*The Salamander, a ship of the same generation as the Batavia, was launched in 1638. Apart from a few minor details, the two were identical.*

As for the gun-deck or *overloop*, this was a world of its own. It carried an impressive number of guns⁸, positioned opposite gun-ports that could be closed by movable panels of wood and it was divided into two parts separated at the main mast. The forward part was allocated to the

De Salemander een Ooſtindis Vaerder,

sailors and to the few civilians who embarked as ordinary passengers. It was here too that the store-room or pantry and the galley were situated, the latter providing only a minimum of hot meals.

The hapless sailors, who alone represented at least half the number

*Another artist's impression featuring the elegant Batavia under full sail.*

---

7  Indeed, as a "retourship", fully laden, drew over 5 metres of water, there was difficulty in negotiating certain parts of the channel in the Zuider Zee leading to the North Sea, where there were shallows no deeper than 3.80 metres, including the dreaded "Pampus" sandbank : accordingly, passengers and goods had to be assembled on the Friesian island of Texel, bordering on the North Sea.  However, in the last quarter of the 17th century, a means of overcoming this difficulty was found : a ship was fastened to two enormous wooden pontoons, known as "camels", the inner side of each of which had exactly the same contour as that of the hull of the ship to be raised.  The pontoons were made of watertight compartments and the operation consisted in pumping water into these until the weight began to make them sink and the two contours, of pontoon and hull, fitted each other exactly.  This done, the two "camels" were clamped to the ship on port and starboard and maintained in position by slings or lines passed under the ship's keel and tightened with a windlass.  All that remained to be done then was to pump the water out of the pontoons to raise the whole structure.  The ship was as it were carried by the "camels" and her draft accordingly lessened considerably ; thus it was possible to embark freight and passengers in the port of Amsterdam and no longer at Texel.  Each "camel" had a rudder, and the whole structure could be set in motion by the use of sails or, more often, small rowing-boats which towed it through the Zuider Zee.  The Marken fishermen made such manoeuvres their speciality.  Use of "camels" was discontinued in 1825 after the North channel was cut.

8  The *Batavia* was armed with twenty-four iron, six bronze and two composite guns.

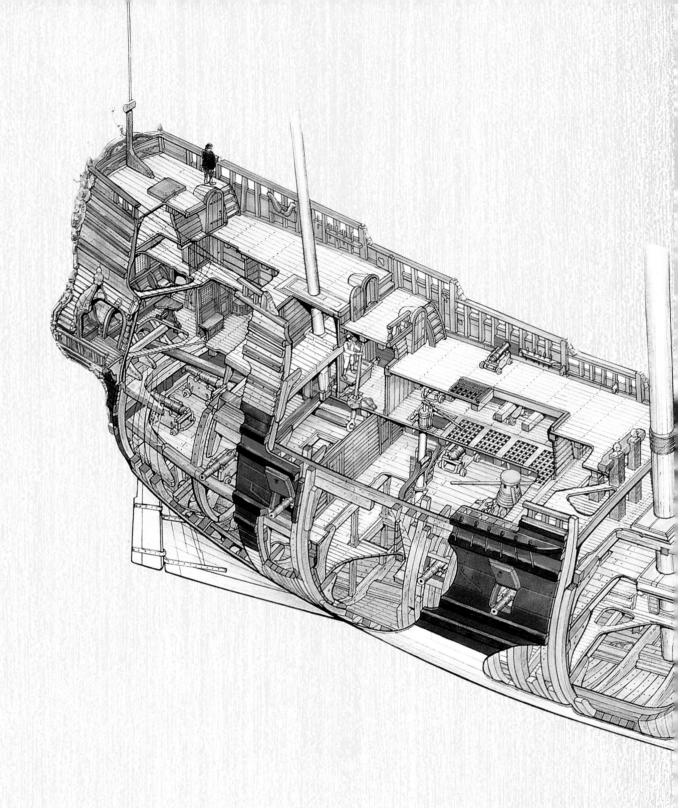

*Exploded view showing the interio
lay-out of the Batavia:*

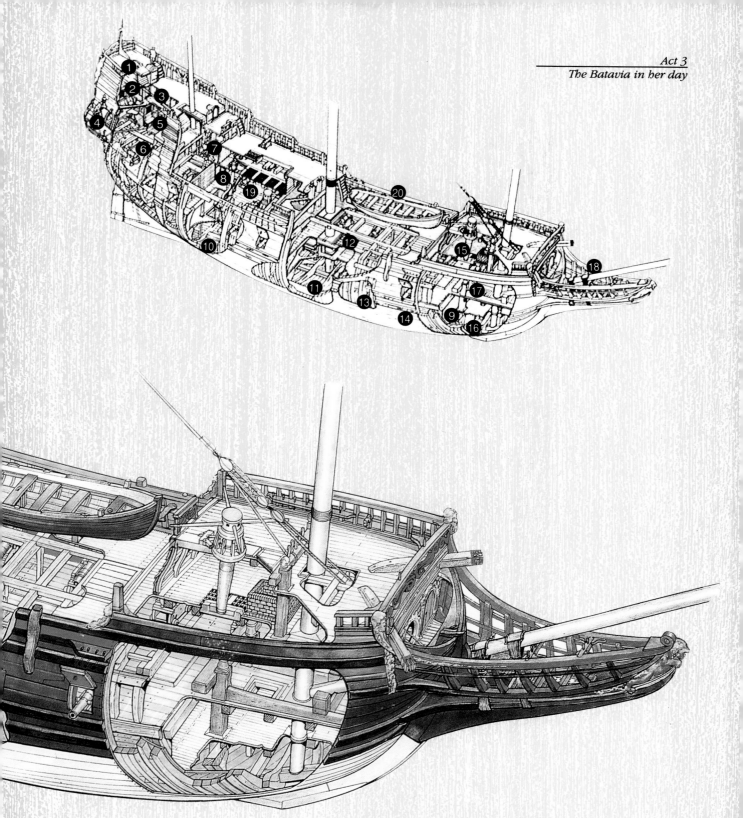

| 1 Commandeur's cabin | 7 Helmsman | 14 Pine planking |
| 2 Master's cabin | 8 Bilge pumps | 15 Windlass |
| 3 Officers' cabins | 9 Orlop deck | 16 Tweendeck ceiling |
| 4 Accommodations for the V.O.C. merchants | 10 Hold | 17 Bitt head |
| 5 Saloon | 11 Floor timbers | 18 Gammon lashings |
| 6 Armoury | 12 Hatch coaming | 19 Capstan |
|  | 13 Oak frames | 20 Longboat |

of persons on board (the extra large proportion of sailors was to provide against the risk of their being suddenly decimated by an epidemic), had to establish their quarters as best they could — between the guns. Each was allowed to bring with him a sea-chest in which to keep personal effects, mainly utilitarian, and also some provisions to eat during the first weeks of the voyage. A sailor provided his own kit, consisting of a hammock or palliasse in its cover, something to serve as a pillow and blankets.

The midshipmen, the cook, the bo'sun and the ship's carpenter were housed aft of the main mast, which was a privilege in that they were thus spared too close proximity to the rather strong-smelling ordinary seamen. Far aft, separated from the rest by a timber bulkhead, was the domain of the "constable", an important person if ever there were one, since he was in charge of all the artillery on board, and directly responsible for the defence of the ship, under the direction of the *commandeur* and the officers. It is interesting to note that, in appearance at least, there was nothing to distinguish a "retourship" from a man-of-war. The main characteristic of the latter was that they were less heavily loaded, which made them much handier, and carried far fewer men, whose only task was to defend the ship and the convoy of which it was part, in the event of an attack by an adversary.

*Daily life aboard a "retourship" at sea. We are on the gundeck, and the seamen enjoy a few moments' rest between watches.*

The upper decks — right at the top was a cabin known as the "roost", reserved for the *commandeur* — occupied only a small part of the ship's stern and were the exclusive domain of the ship's officers and of people entrusted with official duties (including the chaplain and the "surgeon", who often acted also as barber !). Passengers who were persons of distinction, rarely more than twenty-five or so on any one voyage, also had the freedom of this privileged portion of the ship and they too were accommodated in cabins. Naturally they were exempted from all fatigue-duties — Heaven knows there were many in a floating village such as this — and they took their meals in a small dining room, at a table laid with a linen cloth and pewter implements. They also had the very considerable privilege of being allowed to use the two lavatories with wooden seats, that were built projecting from the stern.

Life on board was for the most part sadly monotonous, punctuated only by changes of watch, which were called out ceremoniously by the "marshall" (whose other functions were to supervise any prisoners there might be and to mete out punishment), and by meal-times. Food was issued to seamen and soldiers in wooden bowls, each holding six men's portions. Rations were generous, but the fare exceedingly plain and often unappetising. The V.O.C. authorities — dieticians before their time — endeavoured, however, to provide for all eventualities ; amongst others they tried to guard against the problem of constipation by inflicting on their enlisted personnel a twice-daily intake (breakfast and supper) of gruel in which was mixed a large quantity of prunes. Woe to anyone who turned up his nose at this dish ! For the mere refusal to eat, even once in a while, without a valid reason, constituted a serious and punishable offence. At midday the meal invariably consisted of dried vegetables with some salted provision — sometimes meat, sometimes salted pork or smoked herring. Bread and sea-biscuit were issued weekly, five pounds to each man, with half a pound of fat. To drink, there was water and beer, of which everyone was entitled to a litre a day, and a small pitcher of wine was served with the midday meal. The quality of the drinking-water deteriorated rapidly, as we have seen, and towards the fourth month at sea, swarming with larvae, it would begin to give off a fetid smell, so that one had to close one's eyes and hold one's nose to drink. When the ship carried live poultry and pigs, these served only as an occasional supplement to the meals of the officers and passengers of distinction, as did the produce of the little shipboard garden where a few cabbages, onions and carrots struggled to survive the very sudden and disconcerting changes of climate.

The smell in the orlop deck and the gun-deck was quite appalling. The two hundred or so men packed into the latter had nowhere else to go during their eight hours' rest between watches. Bodily secretions — naturally there was no question of being able to wash, or even to take a shower — and the stench of bedding impregnated with sweat and filth and of the vomit of the many who were not good sailors, all combined to make a cocktail of suffocating odours. In addition there would sometimes be the stench of urine when some undisciplined man, taking

*Typical costume of a Dutch sailor in the 17th century.*

*Next spread :*
*Rest and relaxation : Gathered together in one of Batavia's taverns, these V.O.C. captains can forget for a time the hardships of their profession while enjoying the pleasures of good food and drink, and the gentle euphoria of tobacco, which at the time was smoked in long-stemmed clay pipes.*

*To reach safe haven : the dream of every sailor ... It was here, a stone's throw from the citadel of Batavia, whose walls can be seen in the background, that seamen in transit came to buy a stock of exotic goods before undertaking the long passage home. On the opposite bank of the canal, the artist has depicted the Governor General's troop engaged in a tour of inspection.*

advantage of his companions' or the supervisors' momentary distraction, chose to relieve himself surreptitiously in a dark corner, rather than climb to the upper deck and make his way right to the "heads", a pair of plank seats with a hole cut in them cantilevered over the bow of the ship, which had to serve for the whole population of seamen and soldiers. But of course, there was no question of going up onto the upper deck at will, as this could have interfered with the ship's handling, and a man had to await permission to go out, and then it would be in successive groups, at specified intervals, under the supervision of a petty officer. Woe to any who were plagued by a colic and who could not wait : the only recourse for them was the pewter chamber-pots that were normally kept for female passengers.

With laudable concern for the prevention of epidemics, the V.O.C. had made it a rule that all bedding must be regularly aired and the sleeping quarters scoured. From time to time they were fumigated to kill vermin, after which floor and walls were sprinkled with vinegar. The only evil for which the Company had found absolutely no remedy was scurvy, whose cause remained a mystery in an age which knew nothing of vitamins. And if, by ill luck, an epidemic (of dysentery, typhus or typhoid fever, or even a particularly virulent 'flu) broke out on board a "retourship" at sea, it sometimes happened, in severe cases, that half a ship's company perished within a few days...

The most severely punished offences, after the crime of murder, were mutiny, sodomy, blasphemy and drunkenness. The shipboard court could, in extreme cases, hand down the death sentence, which was carried out on the spot, the condemned man generally being thrown overboard alive, hands bound and feet heavily weighted. There was a wide variety of other forms of punishment, ranging from imprisonment in "hell", a dark, noisome hole in which a man could neither stand nor lie without bending double, to stoppage of wages, and including loss of bread and water rations and various kinds of corporal punishment, the principal one being flogging. Activities that were forbidden on board were gambling, and even ordinary card games ! Chess or chequers was however permitted.

All the same, the Company was concerned to be benevolent in its treatment of the men in its service to the extent that it could, and accordingly offered them some pastimes. Thus a library was constantly available to them, though needless to say it did not include anything such as comic strips or titillating fiction, but was composed entirely of morally uplifting works extolling good over evil, recounting the tenets of the Christian faith and the martyrdom suffered by the Dutch people under the iron rule of Spain. In certain circumstances, trolling for fish was allowed, any catch being taken to improve the men's daily fare. But it goes without saying that the best of the catch went to the officers' table. "Crossing the line" was invariably accompanied by colourful ceremonies. On this famous occasion, the sailors were exceptionally allowed to sing the drinking songs and bawdy choruses that were banned from their usual repertoire by order of the prudes responsible for ensuring morale and discipline on board. Men who were crossing the Equator for the first time had to prostrate themselves before King Neptune and were then thrown into the sea at the end of a rope and after being hauled back on deck were tarred and feathered. Sometimes a group of seamen would improvise comic sketches, which delighted the less demanding among the spectators. And then those who had any musical talent were always ready to entertain their shipmates on fiddle or flute.

A sailor who survived all the hazards of the voyage and reached Batavia in good health could there recover from the fatigue and hardships he had suffered, discover the fortress and its surroundings and indulge in "treasure hunting". For the Company magnanimously allowed each of its employees, even the most humble, to bring home a few exotic objects or some merchandise, though in strictly limited quantities of course. Such articles always fetched a good price in Amsterdam and thus allowed their seller to enjoy a few days or even, if he was thrifty, a few weeks of comparative luxury before he sank back into the greyness and semi-poverty that were the lot of the lower orders of that time, unless the call of the sea induced him soon to sign on again for another voyage. Then, who cared about the deprivations and hardships that would have to be endured ! All that counted was the prospect of new adventures and the lure of the distant Orient, with its myriad scents and unfamiliar flavours, its copper-skinned beauties and their black silk tresses, its vast sun-drenched shores...

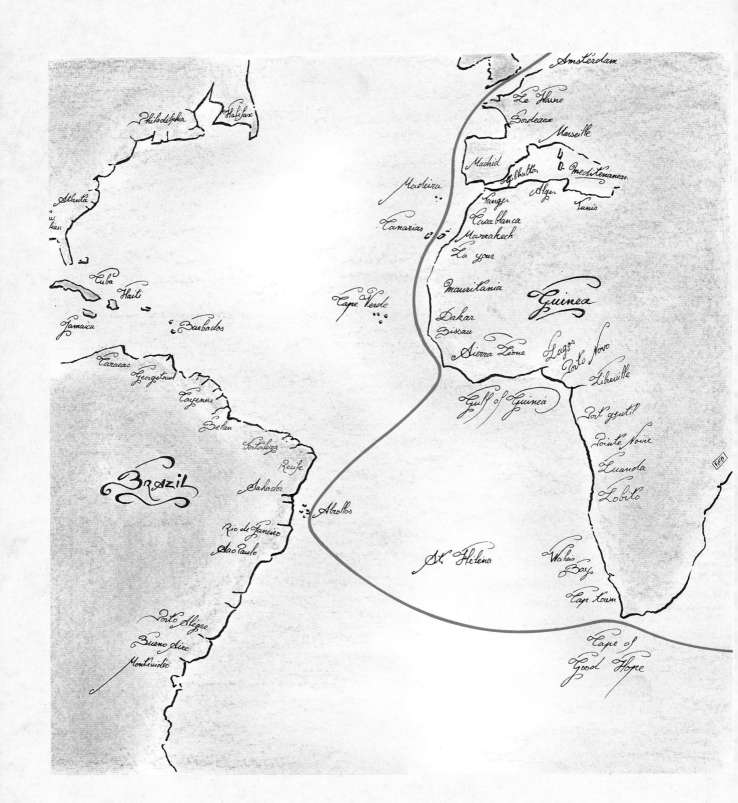

# act 4

## *En route for the East Indies*

On 29th October 1628, the *Batavia*, leaving behind her the immense pouch of the Zuider Zee with the port of Amsterdam at its far end, entered the Marsdiep channel that separates the mainland from Texel, last and largest of the islands of Western Friesland. Officially, there were three hundred and forty-one[1] people on board. That at least is the figure in the ship's articles, but a few last-minute desertions were noted, as was relatively common at the time. Of those who actually embarked, slightly more than two-thirds were the officers and men sailing the vessel. The remaining number was made up of soldiers, about a hundred, and civilian passengers, by far the smallest group, who were going, or in some cases returning, to the distant Dutch colony of the East Indies and especially to its very new capital, Batavia, situated in the north-

*Left :*
*The route of the Batavia and her consorts during the first part of their voyage to the East Indies.*

*This engraving dates from 1614, but the town of Amsterdam had changed very little between that date and 1628 when the spanking-new ship Batavia sailed from the harbour one fine October day. The dynamic and prosperous city, which already contained several proud and fine monuments, had a population at that time of some 25,000.*

1 This is the figure stated by Francisco Pelsaert in a letter addressed to the *Heeren Bewindhebbers* giving an account of the tragedy (see Act 13). This letter is in the V.O.C. sector of the National Archives at The Hague. The figure of 316 crew and passengers, quoted in Henrietta Drake-Brockman's well-known "Voyage to Disaster" and reproduced by various authors subsequently, is thus an under-estimate.

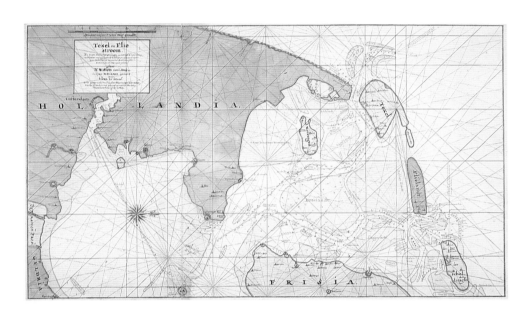

*A chart of the Zuider Zee, showing the winding channel that ships had to negotiate in order to go from Amsterdam to the Friesian island of Texel, the last stage before the open sea.*

western tip of the island of Java. This explains the presence on board, among the passengers, of women and children.

And what an ordeal such a voyage would be — one that on average would take eight months, in a ship that pitched and rolled abominably, living in conditions of promiscuity and lack of hygiene such as have been described. And yet the *Batavia* was a floating palace compared with some of the "Indiamen" of the line. No fewer than seven other vessels were sailing in convoy with her. First there was a man-of-war, the *Buren*, to provide cover for the convoy, for the risk to merchant vessels of encountering corsairs[2] or pirates of various origins was very real. Three "retourships" were also making the voyage, the *Dordrecht*, the *Galiasse* and the *s'-Gravenhage*, two store-ships, the *Assendelft* and the *Zaandam*[3], and lastly a yacht, the *Kleine David*. It was not by chance that the convoy was leaving the mother country at this time of

2 Mainly English and French.

3 Called the *Sardam* by earlier authors. This vessel, which belonged to the Amsterdam Chamber, was called after a town whose name is today written "Zaandam" and which, like Assendelft, is situated north of the beautiful city of canals. We have adopted this spelling, as did J.R. Bruijn, F.S. Gastra and I. Scheffer, authors of the book "Dutch-Asiatic Shipping" (Vol. 2, Outward-bound voyages from the Netherlands to Asia and the Cape (1595-1794) - Den Haag 1979), which recapitulates all the V.O.C. ships' movements during nearly two hundred years of the Company's existence. Thus we use the contemporary version of both towns' names : Zaandam and Assendelft.

*"Indiamen" of the 17th century setting out for Asia. They are shown going through the Marsdiep, the principal channel connecting the Zuider Zee to the North Sea.*

year, for experience had shown that the most favourable period for setting out from Europe for the East Indies was between October and January. During these four months the climatic conditions in the northern hemisphere were of course very difficult, with storms and freezing cold, but as soon as ships crossed the Equator they were able to benefit to the maximum from the winds that would carry them towards the Cape [4].

However, the convoy had barely entered the North Sea, and was not yet in the Channel when it was assailed by an extraordinarily violent storm and most of the ships lost sight of each other. The *Batavia* herself on this occasion just escaped disaster, running aground on a sandbank from which she was able however to free herself, but the less fortunate *s'-Gravenhage*, to which the same thing happened, was so severely damaged that she had to limp into the port of Middelburg for repairs, and did not leave again until September 1629 ! Then with calmer weather, the dismembered convoy, now reduced to the *Batavia*, the *Assendelft* and the *Buren*, rounded Cape Finisterre and were out of sight of land until they were off the Lusitanian coast. From there, descending in latitude in order to benefit from the Canaries current, the

---

4 Certain convoys left the Netherlands at Easter (the "Easter fleets"). In that case, the conditions were the opposite : propitious in the northern hemisphere, and hostile in the south.

77

convoy set course for the Cape Verde Islands (taking the risk of sailing wide of them) and thence to sight the coast of Sierra Leone[5] before veering westward : a course that was tempting on account of speed but which also courted danger as it entailed a strong risk of being caught in a ferocious coastal current running from west to east. Certain V.O.C. ships had in fact been caught in this hidden snare and had been swept into the Gulf of Guinea, and thus found their voyage considerably lengthened.

Happily all went well and the three ships were able without difficulty to resume the course recommended by experience, a course that was to take them far into the Atlantic Ocean, almost to the Brazilian coast, turning anti-clockwise in order to take advantage of the high pressure regime that generates the trade winds and the marine currents. Finally, they reached the Cape of Good Hope, completing the first leg of their voyage, on 14th April 1629[6], one month ahead of the estimated date, to the great joy of crew and passengers alike .

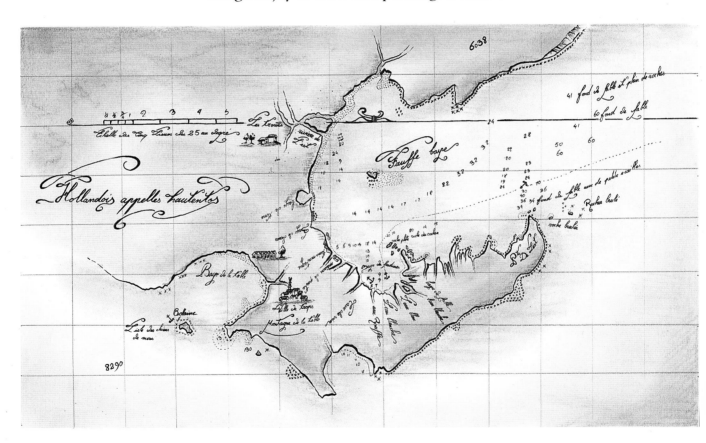

*This cartographic representation (one of the very first) of Table Bay and False Bay is the work of a Frenchman, Laborie. The berths where the Dutch ships were accustomed to lie are shown. But experience proved these moorings to be somewhat insecure, especially the one in False Bay.*

5 Some authors, misunderstanding a passage in the famous letter by the predikant Gijsbert Bastiaensz, have claimed that the *Batavia* made a port-call here, but this is not so. The Dutch had no settlement in Sierra Leone and their ships never called in there. On the other hand, it sometimes happened that they called in at the Cape Verde Islands (Sao Vicente) and at Saint Helena.

6 In "Dutch-Asiatic Shipping" - see note 3 above.

7 Disregarding the Company's instructions recommending them not to stay longer than a week, captains often chose to stop there as much as a month, in order that sick people on board might recuperate. It was not until April 1652, following a very favourable report by the survivors of the wreck of another V.O.C. vessel, the *Haarlem*, who described the country's agricultural and pastoral possibilities, that the *Heeren XVII*

Unfortunately, the week[8] the ships stopped in the bay at the foot of the Table Mountain was to be punctuated by unpleasant incidents. As *commandeur*, Pelsaert was frequently obliged to go ashore to negotiate with the Hottentot population the purchase of fresh supplies of foodstuffs. On his return from one such absence, earlier than foreseen — this time he had been inland on a hunting trip — he discovered a situation that, to put it mildly, displeased him greatly. Adriaen Jacobsz, the ship's captain, had taken advantage of the *commandeur*'s absence to induce the under merchant[9] to accompany him on a drinking spree visiting the other two ships of the convoy moored a few cable-lengths from the *Batavia*. Having drunk more than was reasonable, he and a few companions picked a quarrel with members of the *Buren*'s crew, which

led to a violent fight and some broken heads. When Pelsaert returned on board, the captain was still tipsy, but sufficiently lucid to recognize the contempt in the dressing-down that the *commandeur* gave him in

decided to lay the foundations, in the shadow of the Table Mountain, of a settlement that was to include quarters for troops, a hospital, warehouses, fruit and vegetable gardens, cattle-pens and a rudimentary aqueduct to facilitate supplying fresh water to the ships that called there.

8 The *Batavia* was to put to sea again on 22nd April 1629.

9 Who, in this case, acted as supercargo also.

public : "Worthless fool that you are, you can't conduct yourself with the dignity that your rank merits ! You've behaved like the lowest of ordinary seamen. Take a look at yourself in the mirror — repulsive with your glassy stare, your red and puffy face and your unkempt hair. Get out of my sight ! Go to your cabin and sleep off your gin. You're confined on board until we sail !" The ill-feeling between the two men that had existed since the end of the year 1627 when the storm of abuse that we have already witnessed first set them at loggerheads was naturally exacerbated by the terrible disgrace of this public reproach.

But already the *Batavia* was setting out to face the ordeal of the formidable "roaring forties". Since 1611, at the instigation of Hendrik Brouwer, the former route which cut diagonally across the Indian Ocean had been abandoned. Henceforth the Company's ships followed the much more rapid one that, according to the Company's instructions, was "to progress eastward between 36° south and 39° south,

*Previous page right and right : A pen and pencil drawing by Cornelis de Mooy's, dating from the end of the 17th century. It stresses the majesty of Table Bay, thus named in 1601 by the Dutchman Joris van Spilbergen with reference to the mountain rising in the background. The former name of this haven, given by the Portuguese, was "Aguada da Saldanha". Judging by the fact that there is a military fort, "Die Kasteel", beside the sea, this drawing must have been done many years after the Batavia stopped here. A small fort was first built in 1647 by the survivors of the wreck of the Nieuw Haarlem, but it was not until after the arrival in 1652 of the first Governor of the Colony, Jan van Riebeeck, that the building depicted above, which still exists today, was added to the new town on the Cape. The construction was done in two stages : the fortifications were begun in 1656 and the fort itself in 1678.*

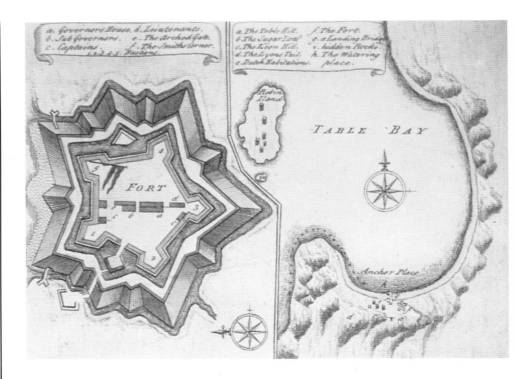

to run 3,500 miles, then steer north-east until 30° latitude south, and you sight Eendracht's land [10] before sailing on to Java".

Unfortunately, only a short while after putting to sea, the convoy was to encounter another storm in the course of which the *Batavia* lost all contact with her consorts. Pelsaert was very vexed by this turn of events and doubtless it provoked, in private this time, a further heated exchange with Adriaen Jacobsz. In any event, from this point on the atmosphere on board the ship, now sailing alone, became distinctly disagreeable.

10 "Land of Concord" in Dutch : the former name, no longer used, for the central part of the west coast of the Australian continent.

Engraved for MILLAR's *New Complete & Universal* SYSTEM *of* GEOGRAPHY

*Habits of the* HOTTENTOT *Men & Women*

*Perspective View of the Cape of Good Hope*

*Francisco Pelsaert doubtless had ample opportunity to contemplate the Hottentots' festive attire during the Batavia's stop in Table Bay in April 1629. However, the embryo of the future Capetown, as it appears in this engraving done in the second half of the 17th century, did not yet exist at the time of his visit.*

Pelsaert, who had become seriously ill — the price paid for a delicate constitution and his recent lengthy spell in the heart of India and in various miasma-infested islands — was obliged more often than not to remain in his cabin, with the result that discipline on board began imperceptibly to slacken. Nevertheless, this situation should not be interpreted as some authors have done, who see in it the seeds of a dramatic plot and attach too much importance to the rumour that a conspiracy had been fomented by the captain, the supercargo, the bo'sun,

*The Dutch were the first to establish successful trade with the Hottentots who lived in the Cape region. They supplied ships on the outward voyage to Batavia and on their return with fish, beef and milk, in exchange for tools, metals (mainly lead) and a variety of "mariner's venture", i.e. small articles and trinkets.*

*The history of bovine species in the African continent is closely associated with that of human settlement. It is known for certain that there were ruminants in the southern extremity of the continent five hundred years before Christ. They were probably introduced from the north by nomadic tribes and taken over from them by the Hottentots. During these lengthy migrations, the three original strains would have become crossed. Experts believe that these original strains were the "hamatic longhorn", the "shorthorn" with no hump and the humped zebu. The result was a very particular type known as "sanga", which has for a long time cohabited with the zebu in South African tribal herds. Therefore the meat procured by European ships calling at Table Bay during the 17th century would have been from one or other of these animals.*

some disloyal officers and a few bad lots among the ordinary seamen. Likewise the confessions later extracted under torture should be regarded with the greatest circumspection. If some "conspirators" had really wanted to seize the *Batavia*, as certain authors maintain, the proximity of the African coast and the illness of Pelsaert offered excel-

*Hendrik Brouwer was a very skilled navigator who was later appointed a "Councillor of the East Indies" in 1617 and subsequently raised to the dignity of Governor General of the East Indies (1632-1636). He was also Francisco Pelsaert's brother-in-law, and this family bond explains his readiness at all times to use his influence to encourage Pelsaert's promotion within the Company.*

lent opportunities for getting rid of him in absolute secrecy, whereas in fact he was allowed to recover a semblance of health on board a ship that was steadily nearing Batavia.

On the other hand, what is certain is that the *commandeur's* temporary absence from the scene was enough to encourage some, beginning with the captain, to give free rein to their lowest instincts. Jacobsz, who was a sailor of undeniable experience and acknowledged intellectual qualities, was regrettably also what is commonly called a "big mouth" and at the same time a sensualist very fond of the pleasures of the flesh and of the table. Furthermore, he was short-tempered and proud. Physically, he was an imposing figure, of handsome appearance, with a high-pitched voice. The *Batavia* had scarcely left Amsterdam when he began making advances to the beautiful Lucretia, a 27-year old lady of good social standing who was going to Batavia to join her husband, Boudewijn[11] van den Mylen, a V.O.C. under merchant, to whom she had been married for eight years. In consideration of her social rank, she had been given a private alcove and was accompanied by a maid, named Zwaantie Hendrix. For a while Jacobsz had dreamed of obtaining the favours of this aristocratic lady but her haughty attitude left him little hope and while the *Batavia* was off the Sierra Leone coast, he resigned himself to addressing his attentions to the servant, amongst whose assets was — if certain witnesses are to be believed — a superb bust and other enticing curves. Zwaantie having succumbed to the first assault, it was no secret that Jacobsz became her lover, and

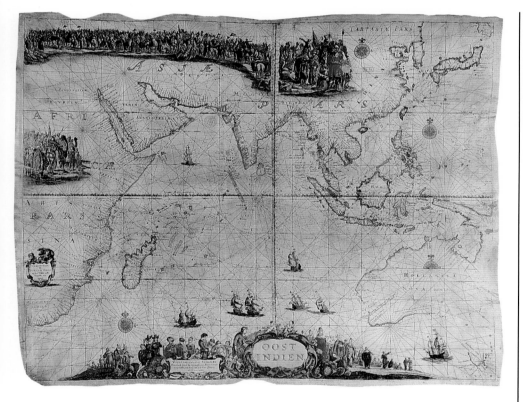

*A convoy of "Indiamen" sailing the famous "Brouwer's route". On the return voyage, with the aid of the prevailing winds, they reached the Cape of Good Hope by cutting across the Indian Ocean.*

his passion for this sensuous woman merely increased with time. The resulting clash was inevitable. Lucretia could no longer stand the constant indiscretions of a servant whom Jacobsz was encouraging to escape from bondage, going so far as to discredit the beautiful Madame van den Mylen, claiming that she was a high-class prostitute who was selling her charms to Francisco Pelsaert. The poor *commandeur*, though in reality a puritanical and austere Protestant, thus slandered, found himself losing his prestige and also becoming an object of dislike and even of jealousy !

---

11 The Flemish form of Baudouin, the Christian name of the former King of the Belgians.

*The famous Rijksmuseum of Amsterdam contains a single work by Torrentius, the spiritual leader of Jeronimus Cornelisz. It is called "Emblematic still-life with flagon, glass, jug and bridle" and shows the artist's unquestionable talent and mastery of technique.*

It must be admitted that during these interminable voyages the continence forced on so many young men, arousing unhealthy tensions, posed a problem. Notwithstanding the presence on board of the marshall, who was responsible for maintaining discipline in general, and of the chaplain (often replaced by a simple predikant), the mere sight of a petticoat provoked lewd conversation and salacious comment. So the unfortunate women passengers scarcely knew what attitude to adopt and if they chose to preserve a haughty distance as in the case of Lucretia, they were repaid by becoming the subject of the most ignominious calumny.

The third most important person on board after the *commandeur*

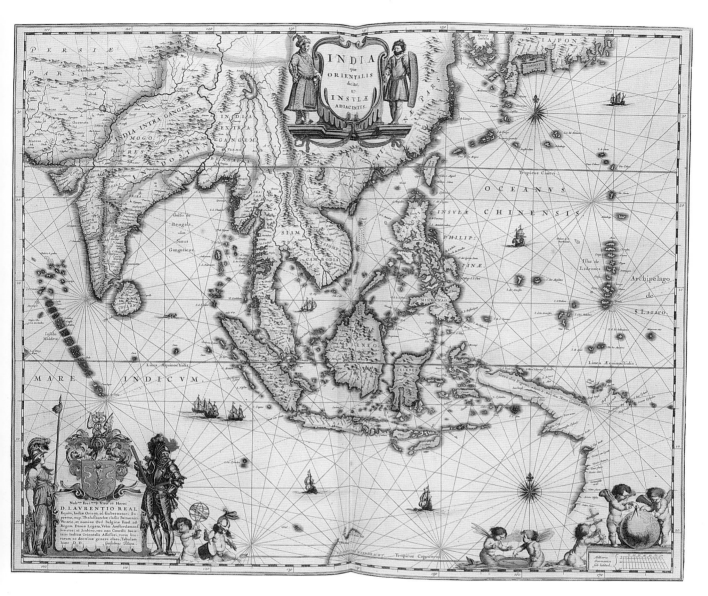

and the captain was Jeronimus Cornelisz, an under merchant, who had a complex personality and was a real Dr. Jekyll. A cultured and discriminating man in appearance, this thirty-year old former apothecary from Haarlem seemed to have an attractive manner. But the dormant Mr. Hyde was ever ready to emerge. Then the former follower of Torrentius [12], the talented painter whose philosophy was summed up in a biting formula : "All religions restrict pleasure. In doing so they are contrary to the will of God, who put us on earth that we might, during our brief existence, enjoy without hindrance everything that might give us pleasure". Needless to say, such a doctrine was rapidly to lead to great difficulties for its author who, having survived the rack and escaped the gallows by a miracle, found himself forced to seek refuge in

12  His real name was Jan Simonsz van der Beeck, and he was born in Amsterdam in 1589. Having won a very flattering reputation as an artist in his home town (still-life and miniatures) he moved to Leiden and then Haarlem. It was there that his polemical talk and his dissolute ways attracted the wrath of the law. He underwent torture without flinching and was given a prison sentence of twenty years in 1628. But the admirers of his artistic work, chief amongst whom were Prince Frederik Hendrik of Orange-Nassau and King Charles I of England, interceded for clemency for the artist. He was released in 1630, and went into exile, living in England until 1642. He died two years later in Amsterdam.

*The map of the celebrated "East Indies" included in "The Theatre of the World", an atlas published in 1635, is still far from a model of accuracy. Seeing this, one can imagine what hazards navigation must have involved for vessels that sailed the seas of the East Indies in those days.*

*Next page :*
*The attack on the beautiful Lucretia van den Mylen, while the Batavia was crossing the Indian Ocean, was subsequently to be exploited by Francisco Pelsaert's enemies, who blamed him for his grave lack of firmness on this occasion and for having allowed a "satanic" atmosphere to develop on board the ship.*

England, while his disciples, hunted down as henchmen of the devil, prudently scattered in all directions... Doubtless Cornelisz was not the only one to covet the beautiful Lucretia and to regret that fate had not bestowed on him sufficient fortune to enable him to aspire to a place in the existence of such a captivating creature.

It was when Pelsaert's illness was at its worst and the ship was somewhere in the empty vastness of the Indian Ocean that an incident occurred that was subsequently to entail most severe consequences for its presumed authors. A group of masked men attacked and proceeded to "hang overboard by her feet the lady van den Mylen and indecently maltreat her body".

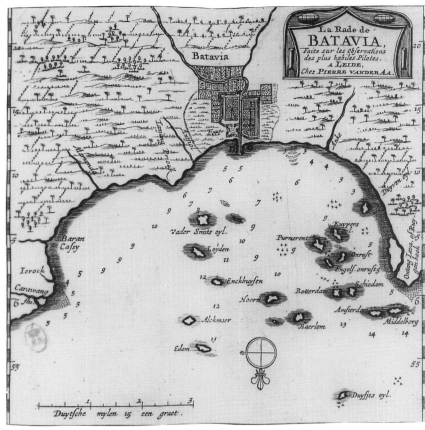

Rape ? The account is ambiguous. According to other sources, the unfortunate lady was "undressed, half stifled with her hair-ribbon and then plastered with excrement and tar". And it was in this terribly humiliating situation that she was found by the officer of the watch, in a dark corner of the deck. Later the victim claimed to have recognized the voice of Jan Evertsz, a man devoted to the captain who himself was on the best of terms with Jeronimus Cornelisz. But that is a far cry from claiming that the two men were the true instigators of the plot...

A captain's savage resentment of his *commandeur* and of a distinguished passenger, his own repressed debauchery, the ill-controlled sexual appetites of a batch of anonymous individuals who would stop at nothing, as they had just demonstrated — the *Batavia*, which was going to take a little more than five weeks to cross one of the planet's largest expanses of water, was certainly sailing under disastrously sombre auspices.

*This map is undated but, judging by the extent of the small township, one can assume that is was probably drawn about 1625. It bears the following legend :*
*"The roadstead of Batavia drawn according to the observations of the most skilled pilots".*
*It will be noticed that all the islets in the bay are named after Dutch cities.*

# act 5

# The Houtman Abrolhos

The average distance between the islands of the Abrolhos archipelago and the west coast of the continent of Australia is a mere sixty kilometres. The islands and islets, none higher than fifteen metres, are spread out over some eighty kilometres between 28°15.5' and 29°00.5' latitude south.

Three groups of islands — clusters would be a more appropriate description — form the archipelago; following the detailed reconnaissance carried out in 1840 by Lieutenant-Commander Stokes of H.M.S. *Beagle* they were named, from north to south, Wallabi, Easter and Pelsaert.

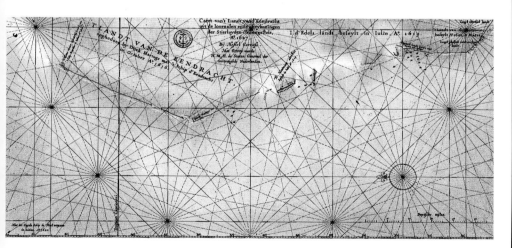

*The first reference to the Abrolhos archipelago appeared in this portolan, dated 1622. It was the work of Hessel Gerritsz, the V.O.C. official cartographer, who also drew the following one, five years later. Neither is very close to reality.*

Apart from North Island, situated rather like a sentinel north of the archipelago, the only islands worthy of the name are in the northern group : West Wallabi and East Wallabi. They are covered with bushy vegetation and beside them are some very low islets named Little and Great Pigeon islands — the latter being the focal point of the present-day lobster fisheries — Goss Island, Long (or Seals) Island, Beacon Island, and a number of insignificant islets. In the Easter group, in the middle of the archipelago, the main islands are Suomi Island, Wooded Island, Rat Island, Leo Island and Serventy Island. And then in the

*Sclerophyllous vegetation,*
*typical of the Wallabi islands.*

south, in the misnamed[1] Pelsaert group, the more note-worthy among the emerged lands are called Gun Island, Square Island, Middle Island, Newman Island, Post Office Island and Pelsaert Island the last of which unwinds a fine trail of coral nearly ten kilometres long.

These low-lying lands result from a combination of alga sedimentation and coral growth on a shallow pedestal that the geologists call the "Rottnest continental shelf". This shelf or plateau is on average seventy kilometres wide and extends roughly from Perth to Geraldton.

The earliest coral structures probably appeared here in the Pleistocene period, 100,000 years ago, thanks to the concurrence of two factors : the high temperature of the water and its shallowness. The debris of the corals' calcareous skeletons, mixed with smaller amounts of shells, in time came to form the sedimentary mass that constitutes what is now the emerged land.

When the last phase of the Quaternary glaciations began, about 30,000 years ago, this continental shelf was completely uncovered, and the old, emerged coral structures appeared as low hills or hillocks scattered over an immense plain.

1 This appellation is due to the fact that the survivors of the *Zeewyck*, another V.O.C. vessel that was wrecked in the southern group of islands in June 1727, had found on the south-western tip of the island on which they had taken refuge the remains of a large vessel that they thought must be the *Batavia*. Hence the name Pelsaert given to the island and to the group to which it belonged.

This was the time when New Guinea and Tasmania were joined to Australia, the period during which terrestrial animals and plants of the continent established colonies on the new lands. But when a gradual warming of the climate began some 11,000 years ago, the glaciers of the northern hemisphere began to melt and the seas to reclaim their former territory. The rise in temperature, and in particular the temperature of

*Unlike its twin,*
*West Wallabi, whose coasts*
*are entirely rocky, the island*
*of East Wallabi has one*
*of the most perfect*
*beaches imaginable.*

the water, also encouraged the corals to resume their slow growth. The little protuberances breaking the monotony of the plain were to become islands again, doubtless to the delight of the birds[2] that came there in large numbers to nest and in doing so, laid a thick layer of guano[3]. As for the land animals that survived the cataclysm by taking refuge on the highest of the islands, they were to remain there, unable to leave. The only ones amongst them that managed to settle and reproduce were those for which fresh water was not vital to their survival. Such are the tammar-wallaby[4] whose system can adjust to sea-water, lizards, a large python[5] and insects.

---

2 Ornithologists have noted 40 species of seabirds — silver gulls, caspian, crested, bridled, fairy, sooty and roseate terns, pied cormorants, wedge-tailed and little shearwaters, common and lesser noddies, white-faced petrels, gulls, ospreys, white-breasted sea eagles, red-tailed tropic-birds (to mention only the principal species), 22 land-birds — rails, owls, brush bronzewings, kingfishers, swallows, pipits, wrens, white-eyes, etc. — and 33 species of shorebirds — reef herons, oystercatchers, plovers, stints, sandpipers, turnstones, curlews, whimbrels, etc.

3 56,900 tons of this fertilizer were taken from the Abrolhos in the years between 1847 and 1885, and a further 10,900 tons between 1943 and 1946.

4 *Macropus eugenii*, also found on Kangaroo Island (South Australia) in the south-western horn of the continent and in certain islands in the Port Lincoln region.

5 *Morelia spilota imbricata* which may grow to more than six feet in length and which leads a lazy life on the island, feeding on the eggs and chicks of seabirds (petrels) or, unusually, on baby tammars. It is common also on Garden Island (off the coast of Perth). On the other hand, it has become very rare on the continent, where it is confined to the south-west part of Western Australia (Dryandra forest, Jarrah forest and the neighbourhood of Collie, Yanchep and Wanneroo), for the young of this oviparous animal are eaten by the foxes that were unfortunately imported from England in the 19th century.

# The birds' world

*1-2 : The tern, whose graceful flight makes it the real queen of heaven of the Abrolhos.*

*3 : The majestic movement of the white-breasted sea eagle (Haliaetus leucogaster), gliding through the skies in search of food. This bird of prey, like the osprey, is amongst the most commonly found birds in the archipelago, where it nests.*

*4 : The elegant pied cormorant is one of the most frequently seen seabirds for there is a large population throughout the archipelago.*

# Cracks and bushes are their home

## The Wallabis' python (1-2)

It may not look very lovable, but the Wallabis' python, which can grow to as much as two metres in length, is nevertheless quite harmless. It slumbers throughout the day, curled up in a deep cavity in the coral, as dark and humid as possible. Except during its periods of prolonged digestion, it leaves its nest at night-time to go in search of prey.

## Lizards and geckos (3 to 6)

The spiny-tailed skink, *Egernia stokesii*, is very common on the two main islands of the Wallabi group. It is dark in colour, with light brownish patches, and may reach fifteen centimetres in length. Despite its alarming aspect, it is quite harmless.

Three other species of lizard and two geckos cohabit with it. Shown here are :
- *Pogona minor minimus*, **the bearded dragon** (4).
- *Diplodactylus spinigerus*, **the spiny-tailed gecko** (5).
- *Lialis burtonis*, **Burton's legless lizard** (6).

2

5

6

# The tammar-wallaby (7)

A prisoner of the Abrolhos since the level of the ocean last rose, a little more than ten thousand years ago, the tammar-wallaby has had to adapt as best it could to an inhospitable habitat. Although men, beginning with the survivors of the *Batavia* shipwreck, have occasionally hunted it for food, or simply for sport, its main predators have always been birds of prey and pythons both of which covet its young.

"There is also on these islands a large quantity of cats of an incredible aspect, being as large as hares ; the head is similar to a civet's, the front legs are short, about the length of a man's finger, on which grow five small nails like monkeys have. The two hind legs measure at least half an **ell** and these cats run on the flat part between the median joint and the extremity of the leg, with the result that they cannot move very fast.

"The tail is very long, similar to that of a **meerkat**. When they eat, they sit up on their hind limbs and hold their food in their forepaws, as monkeys and squirrels do. Their manner of procreation is little short of miraculous and is certainly well worth narrating. Under her belly, the female has a pouch

...... is large enough to slue one's hand into and inside this are her dugs. We have observed that the young remain there, growing, the teats in their mouths, and we have found some that were no larger than a pea but were yet perfectly formed.

"It is clear therefore that they are born in this pouch and develop there, feeding on milk from the mother's dugs, until they are big enough to leave this shelter and to run on their own. Even when they are grown, they frequently take refuge in this snug hiding place when they are afraid and the mother can perfectly well move around by leaps and bounds carrying this heavy load underneath her".                    *Francisco Pelsaert*

*This description is historically the first information we have about a marsupial, and it is for this reason that it is so fascinating. Although the details given here by Pelsaert are in general very precise, his speculations concerning the manner of reproduction of the species are erroneous. Deeply interested and attentive observer though he was, the commandeur of the* Batavia *unfortunately never had an opportunity to witness the birth of the animal which, as soon as it emerges from the mother's cloaca, immediately makes its own way, with difficulty, up into the pouch which of course is not the actual "hatching" place.*

*Girella, pliant as the fingers of a creeper, a flash of turquoise shot through with mauve iridescence.*

*Coral cod dressed in sombre purple livery, superbly spotted with blue.*

# underwater world

*Light sparkles through the lacy filaments of the lion fish, reminiscent of the raiment of a dancer.*

*Neatypes in gold-striped vests, like footballers descending on their adversary's goal.*

*1 : A nautical ballet by sea-lions who have chosen to make their home on Long Island, sometimes called Seals' Island because of their presence.*

*2 : A couple of rock lobsters of the* Panulirus cygnus *species at the entrance to their home. This species constitutes the great wealth of the archipelago : by careful management — at present the fishing season is open every year exclusively from 15 March to 30 June — the population of these crustaceans is regularly replenished and contributes to the region's prosperity.*

*3-4 : The incredible range of colours of the* Panulirus versicolor, *a rock lobster that is found only rarely in the waters of the archipelago whereas it is fairly*

In our day, the islands are noted as the most southerly coral reefs of the southern hemisphere and of the Indian Ocean.

These corals, of which there are as many as eighty species — Acropora and Montipora being the most common — on certain particularly favourably exposed reefs, are an aberration explained by the presence of a warm current, known as Leeuwin's current, which comes from the North, bringing with it coral larvae and also a profusion of tropical fishes — more than 130 species, that cohabit with those commonly found in similar latitudes of the southern hemisphere.

The presence here of sea-lions[6], generally found in much lower latitudes, adds to the uniqueness of the archipelago and completes the picture of a world that is a meeting-point of others, the like of which does not exist anywhere else throughout the seas and oceans of our planet.

*What a pity diving was not practised as a pastime in 1629 for it would have allowed Wiebbe Hayes and his faithful soldiers to make up for their sad daily lot by contemplating the splendour of the underwater gardens of madrepores and the beds of multi-coloured sponges that surround the two "Islands of the Cats".*

It is a world of strange beauty also, seen from the sky, with its countless shallows of opalescent colours, its overlapping foam-fringed reefs, its sinuous channels that sometimes come to an abrupt end, and its "chimneys" of deep blue, dotted here and there on the reef-flats that the sea covers at high tide, and that were formed by rain-water, locally acidified by contact with certain plants, percolating through pockets of soft limestone at the time of the land-bridge.

6 *Neophoca cinerea*, a species endemic to Australia, where it is the sole representative of the pinniped family on the coasts of the continent. It is found on the islands of the continental shelf, from the Abrolhos (the most northern population) to Kangaroo Island, and there is one other colony established on the edge of the continent at La Batt Point (South Australia). Its present population, which remains remarkably stable in the absence of predators, is estimated at 4,000 individuals.

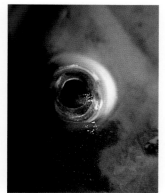

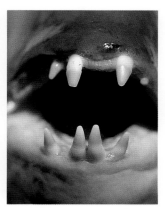

*The multi-coloured eye and sharp-pointed teeth of the blue bones groper.*

It was this out of the ordinary archipelago that Frederik, the younger brother of Cornelis de Houtman, discovered on 29th July 1619 when, following Brouwer's route with the *Dordrecht*[7], which originally had been leading a small flotilla of V.O.C. ships, he came quite by chance upon what he described as "a string of low islands with a slight relief surrounded by reefs". This immense and formidable trap for sailing

---

7 Having lost touch with the *Eendracht*, the *Mauritius* and the *Leeuwin* for some time, the *Dordrecht* was sailing alone with the *Amsterdam*, her only remaining consort. The two ships' first sight of the continent was at 32°20' latitude south, i.e. slightly below the mouth of the Swan River. In following the coast northward intermittently they came upon the notorious Abrolhos.

*HOLLANDIA*

*G F de Wit landt. detecta 1628*

*Willems Riviere*
*Jacot Remens Riviere*

*Tropic of Capricorn.*

*Landt Dirck Hartogs Ree*
*Cap. d' Eendragt*

*Hautmans Abralhos*

*I. de Edels landt beseylt Anno 1619*

*Turtel duyf*

*NOVA*

*detecta 1644.*

*Landt van P Nuijts, opgedaan met het gulder 16 Ianuarÿ Anno 1627.*

*Landt van de Leuwin anno 1622 aangedaan*

**When this second edition (redrawn here) of Thévenot's map was published in 1665, the Batavia had already been lying in her coral grave for many years, but both the position and the configuration of the archipelago are still very approximate.**

ships that he escaped by a miracle was to be named after him : Frederik Houtman's Abrolhos[8].

Abrolhos... there is still controversy about the origin of the name. What is clear, however, is that this term, used by Portuguese navigators, was given to any group of reefs that constituted a danger to navigation, whatever part of the world it was situated in. The first such group to have been named thus lies off the coast of Brazil, between Rio de Janeiro and Bahia, and some authors have asserted that the original name came from one Frederico de Abrolhos, a mysterious 15th century Portuguese nobleman of whom there is unfortunately no trace in Lusitanian

*Left :*
*Frederik de Houtman dressed in the fine uniform of Governor of the Moluccas. It was he who discovered the Abrolhos archipelago in 1619.*

8  Frederik de Houtman (1571-1627) who was born in Gouda, accompanied his elder brother during his first, famous voyage to the Indies under the colours of the Republic of the Seven United Provinces, in 1595. Four years later, he took part in another expedition, this time to Sumatra. It was during this that Cornelis was killed in a battle against the troops of the Sultan of Atjeh. Frederik himself, having been taken prisoner, took advantage of this period to learn to speak Malay and on his return to his home country for a while in 1602 he wrote and published the first Malay-Dutch dictionary. He was Governor of the Island of Ambon from 1605 to 1611 and was later appointed Governor of the whole Moluccas group of islands, from 1621 to 1623. He died a natural death in the charming city of Alkmaar, famous for its picturesque cheese market, eight years after the discovery of the Abrolhos to which he had given his name.

archives. It must be said too that Abrolhos is not known as a family name in Portugal... so the explanation does not seem very convincing.

The generally accepted theory therefore seems the most likely : it suggests that the word "Abrolhos" is a contraction of the Portuguese expression "Abri vossos olhos", literally meaning "Open your eyes", a warning to sailors who would understand it as "Watch out for danger !". Cornelis de Houtman, it will be recalled, had for a long time been in Portuguese service as a maritime pilot and, whatever its real origin, the term Abrolhos was doubtless familiar to him, and to his brother, and so it is not surprising that the latter should make use of it.

*The second known portrait of Cornelis' younger brother with his authentic signature.*

The archipelago appeared for the first time on a map, or more precisely in the portolan drawn up by Hessel Gerritsz, the V.O.C. cartographer, in 1622. It was simply an approximate indication in the form of a group of small circles that were supposed to represent the islands and were situated too near to Eendracht's land, whose coastline was still shown only intermittently. The next map to be drawn was dated 1627. It is on roughly the same scale as the earlier one and portrays the same sector of coast of the mysterious continent, but though it is a little more exact regarding the general position of Frederik Houtman's Abrolhos it is just as hazy regarding their outline. On the other hand, it shows Dirk Hartog island correctly drawn and positioned.

To think that the captain of the *Batavia*, Adriaen Jacobsz, setting sail from Texel one fine day in October 1628, had nothing more than these two maps, so approximate, to guide him ! How was he to suspect that at such distance from the civilized world, far away on the edge of the planet's largest ocean, as yet scarcely defined, fate had decreed for him a tragic encounter with those treacherous Abrolhos ? Strips of land virtually always swept by southerlies and lying so low on the horizon that even those who "keep their eyes wide open" had little chance of perceiving them at the time of day when darkness veils the ocean with its black shroud.

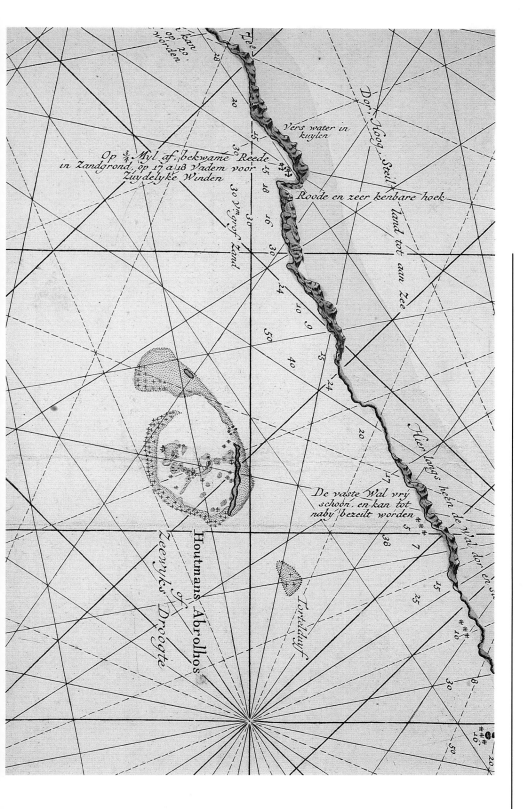

*Another representation of the archipelago, dated 1753, by Johannes van Keulen, who has endeavoured to indicate the exact position of the various islands, but this is still very far from reality.*

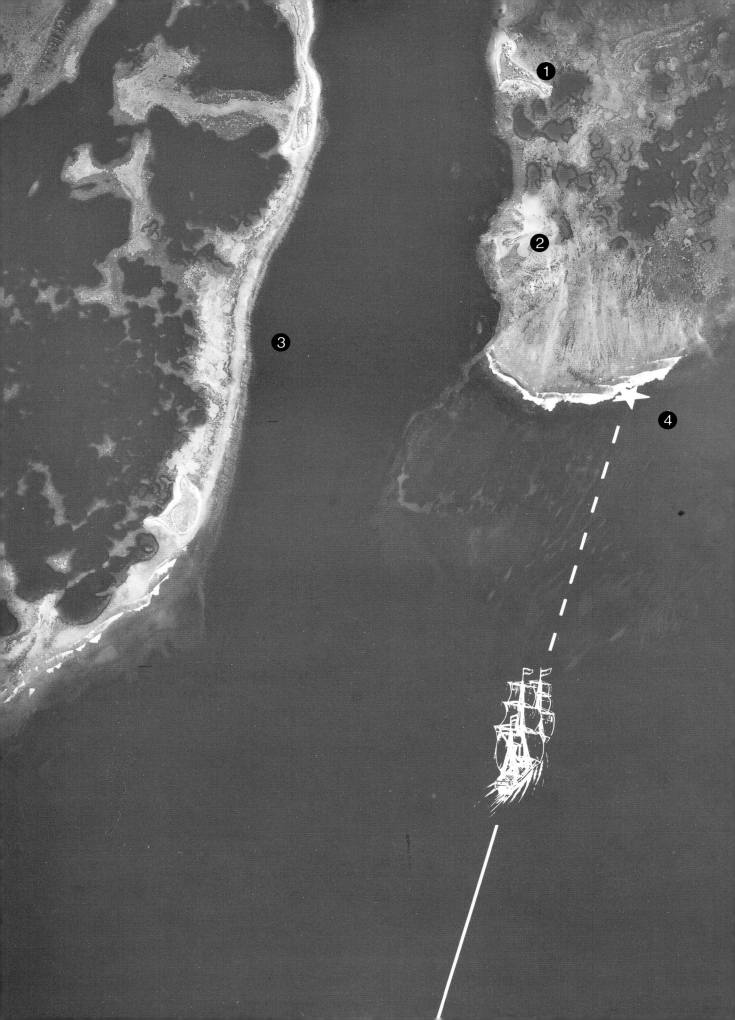

# act 6

## Shipwreck !

4th June 1629 — It is two hours before daybreak and the moon's wan light still glimmers on the ocean. Carried forward by the southerlies, the *Batavia* is carving her way through the slight swell, all sails set. Her captain, Adriaen Jacobsz, is on watch and Hans Bosschieter, the gunner, is standing beside him serving more or less as lookout. Meanwhile, Francisco Pelsaert, still convalescent, is dozing in his cabin. The vessel, on a north-east by north course, is now some 1,550 nautical miles from Batavia and her longitude by dead reckoning places her a long way yet from Eendracht's land (thus named, as we have seen above, thirteen years earlier by Dirk Hartog, another V.O.C. captain). So the watch is fairly relaxed. The dreaded Houtman Abrolhos — so the master of the ship, second only to God on board, is convinced —

*Left :*
*What a superb sight, this series of "blue holes" (probably the evidence of a former forest) punctuating the immense coral plateau encompassed by the reef. On this photograph one can see :*
- *Beacon Island (alias "the Batavia graveyard") (1)*
- *Traitors' Island ( 2)*
- *Long Island (or Seals' Island) (3)*
- *Morning Reef (4)*

*Among the many treasures that are connected in some way or another with the most famous of Australian shipwrecks is this very interesting painting (in Max Cramer's collection) done between 1930 and 1940 by A. Wakefield Bassett, who had won a fine reputation throughout Western Australia. The painting shows the tragic moment when the Batavia strikes the reef and becomes history...*

lie as yet at a respectable distance to the east. Thus the way ahead should be perfectly clear.

Suddenly, a sharp blow followed by a series of violent tremors leaves no doubt : the *Batavia* has run smack into a reef and her momentum has carried her on and pinned her onto it. Immediately the proud wounded vessel begins to heel over slightly to starboard and Jacobsz shouts at Bosschieter : "I told you I thought I saw breakers but you swore it was only an optical illusion, no more than moonlight reflecting

*It was here, right in the middle of the light-coloured area, that the Batavia was to end her brief career.*

on the ocean. Now see what a mess we're in !" The situation does indeed appear rather dramatic. The *commandeur*, thrown out of his bunk by the violence of the impact, has rushed up on deck in his night-shirt and in this rather ridiculous attire is found hurling abuse at his captain as the dazed passengers appear on all sides and assail the crew with questions.

But this is no time for reprimand or comment. They must act, and act quickly. Pelsaert sends for the sounding leads kept in the helmsman's cabin. Aft of the vessel the bottom is eighteen feet deep, forward it is just below the surface.

Jacobsz, who knows that his career is finished and that even his life may be at stake, the Company's directors being little given to forgiving such errors, starts shouting that he hopes the tide is low and that as it rises it will refloat the vessel after she has been lightened. All the ship's guns are thrown overboard, then the *commandeur* orders that the dinghy and the longboat, the only small boats carried on board, be launched in order to sound the depth around the *Batavia*. Thirteen metres is found aft, within bowshot, which allows some hope... A kedge anchor is prepared, ready to be cast from the stern. Thus, provided the tide is really on the ebb now, the vessel will be able eventually to swing round this fixed point and refloat herself without the crew's intervention.

But with the dawn a short while later the terrible truth becomes clear : the *Batavia* has run aground at high tide and there is therefore no chance that the vessel will be able to float herself as had been hoped. Worse, the sea is getting rougher and causing the keel to strike

constantly against what is now revealed as the southern fringe of an immense coral reef flat that is gradually emerging[1]. The blows are so violent that it has become practically impossible to keep one's balance on deck without holding on to a rope or some part of the upper works.

"What if the heel of the main mast were to pierce the hull !" In view of this danger, it is decided that the main mast must be cut down for there is the added risk that the rocking motion and its great weight could lock the *Batavia* yet more firmly into her coral prison. Adriaen

*Twenty-seven years after making the "discovery of a life-time", Max Cramer points to the site of the wreck on the edge of Morning Reef. One can easily imagine that such a slight fringe of foam might have escaped the vigilance of gunner Hans Bosschieter, on night watch at the time of the tragedy. In the distance can be seen Beacon Island, the sight of which when dawn broke gave the survivors some hope.*

1 The *Batavia* had thus miraculously missed the central "nebula" of the archipelago, having very probably skirted its north-west fringe. Only a few hundred yards more, and this miracle would have continued, enabling her to leave the Wallabis to port and missing the fatal Morning Reef. Thus she would have sailed over one of the worst ships' graveyards of our planet without her captain realizing it !

*Rescuing survivors in the ship's two boats in the early morning of 4th June 1629.*

*A view of
Morning Reef with a long line
of waves breaking on the coral
reef flat. The site
of the wreck is marked X.*

Jacobsz, the only person empowered to perform this task, so fraught with consequence, is to strike the first blow of the axe. But in falling the great shaft gets caught up in the rigging and it becomes impossible subsequently to heave it overboard. The vessel is thus in an even more perilous position than before. The inextricably tangled sails and ropes form insurmountable obstacles all over the place and the list is accentuated to such a degree that the waves now wash over part of the deck, which will render the passengers' evacuation vastly more complicated.

About ten o'clock a small leak appears on the starboard side ; the holds are partially flooded and imperceptibly the stern of the *Batavia* begins to sink. How many passengers and crew were to drown thus ?

All vestiges of discipline having of course vanished by now, some ne'er do wells among the soldiers and crew get together forward, in the parts of the ship that are still dry and, doubtless considering that it is high time they snatch a few last moments of happiness, gorge them-selves with wine, and also with the schnaps so parsimoniously rationed since their departure from Amsterdam. They begin to lose all self-control. Following the example of two hysterical men who have just thrown the log-book and all the *commandeur's* papers overboard, a French soldier, Jean Thiriou, gets hold of one of the dozen chests containing silver coins, and plunging both hands into the treasure, flings handfuls towards his hilarious companions, as if he were sowing seed ! The atmosphere has become quite hallucinating : drunken roars and shouts from the belly of the sinking ship mingle with the screams of women and children who, clustered on the deck over which waves are washing, despair of ever being able to climb into the life-boat.

*The story of the proud vessel still inspires many artists who love the sea and are aware of the tragedies that it sometimes engenders.*

# act 7

## A providential islet

In the morning of the 4th of June 1629, after Adriaen Jacobsz had made a first reconnaissance, the longboat managed to make several voyages to and fro between the sinking ship and the nearest island. This rescue operation was rendered particularly difficult by the *Batavia*'s list and by the panic-stricken fighting among people who wanted to get into the longboat. Its destination was a little less than two kilometres away, as the crow flies, and measured barely 350 metres in the longest part and on average seventy-five metres across.

The first contingent of survivors was landed there in three successive journeys and included all the women and children, the sick and the psychologically weaker men. Thus ended a night of terror for these unhappy people who felt death prowling around them ; exhaustion and anxiety could be read in every line of their bearing.

Soon about a hundred and eighty people were crowded onto a sort of large, roughly triangular platform of coral rubble. Here they tried as best they could to make a camp, some in the shade of spindly bushes, some beside two little coral beaches where, with fragments of canvas and whatever they could find to serve as stakes, more and more of them tried to make rudimentary tents. It had been possible to get out of the store enough bread for the foreseeable future, and this had been

*Opposite left :*
*The "Batavia graveyard" as seen from the sky. Its configuration has probably changed very little since 1629, except for a few huts and landing-stages built by the lobster-fishermen of our century. In the background, Morning Reef where the Batavia was wrecked.*

*Next spread :*
*Another aspect of an islet that does not seem a likely decor for a tragedy of such magnitude as it actually witnessed. On the other side of the pass whose dark blue colour shows that the water must be fairly deep, Long Island can be seen with its unending trail of coral broken here and there by little hillocks of white sand.*

*Left and pp 124-125 (bottom) : Naive 17th century engravings describing the tale of the shipwreck and its immediate consequences. Despite his lack of documents, the artist has represented fairly accurately the position of the wrecked ship and the islets respectively. Only their height is a little exaggerated.*

121

*The tiny Traitors' Island is surrounded by impressive "blue holes". It was on this thumbnail-sized piece of terra firma that Francisco Pelsaert decided to establish his base after the shipwreck, far from the agitation on the islet that was much later to be given the sinister name " Batavia graveyard".*

brought over in the ship's boat, but fresh water was sorely lacking, for the water butts were in the holds and these were partially flooded. Furthermore, the drunks on board threatened anyone who tried to approach the precious casks.

Francisco Pelsaert, for his part, remained in the background. He chose to make his quarters, with forty other survivors, including the captain, on a small islet half-way between the wreck and the island serving as refuge for the larger crowd ; onto this islet he had managed to bring the most precious objects from the ship, some provisions and two or three small barrels of water containing in all some eighty litres,

*A dozen plant species, all able to withstand the winds, have colonized the islet. Amongst them is a succulent plant (Mesembryanthemum sp. of the Aizoaceae family) commonly called "ice plant", that forms great purple carpets contrasting attractively with the blinding whiteness of patches of coral skeletons. In some places there are tiny piles of broken corals that make a curious little musical sound if one stubs them with one's foot when walking.*

he only ones that it had so far been possible to extract.

The sea was rising gradually all through the afternoon of 4th June. The *Batavia*, still heeled over on the reef, threatened to start breaking up at any moment. Of the seventy men who had not yet been able to leave, most were by now so drunk that they did not realize their danger. Jeronimus Cornelisz, the under merchant, was amongst them, though it was not the prospect of drinking that had made him hold back, but rather fear : for he did not know how to swim and the incredible fighting amongst those who wanted at any cost to pile into the ship's boat made him afraid that its heavy and agitated load would cause it to

capsize as the sea became increasingly rough, hour by hour.

The *commandeur*, having recovered the longboat, that could carry forty people, and the dinghy, meant for ten, attempted to approach his unfortunate ship, now lying on her side, but the waves were breaking so strongly against the hull that he had to give up his efforts. He did, however, manage to get a message to the men captive on the wreck, through a ship's carpenter who was brave enough to leap into the sea when he saw him coming, to ask for instructions : *"Make some rafts and leave the ship as quickly as you can"*, Pelsaert told him, *"and God help you"* !

On the mid-way islet that the survivors on the larger island had already begun to call "Traitors' Island", everybody coveted the provisions and the small stock of fresh water to such an extent that the *commandeur* was obliged to lose his temper and to appoint soldiers to mount guard over the "treasure".

On 5th June, in the morning, a heated argument broke out between

*Disputing every inch of her domain with the men who invade it each season, the* Sterna fuscata *is the only year-round inhabitant of Beacon Island. Her nest is hidden in the heart of impenetrable thorn bushes where she watches vigilantly over her brood, uttering a plaintive little cry at the approach of an intruder, and leaving the nest only at the very last moment. Her flesh is quite inedible but her eggs when fresh can, if need be, make an omelette.*

*This little beach near the landing-stage must be the one that Gijsbert Bastiaensz, the predikant, refers to in his famous letter written to his family and his dear ones, in which he said : "I spent most of my time reading the Bible, sitting on the beach".*

Pelsaert and Jacobsz.  The previous day, some much larger islands had been spotted on the horizon and Jacobsz proposed to go there alone to investigate.  The *commandeur* did not agree with this at all and in the end was able to impose his point of view : that he would take part in the expedition and furthermore, if they were unlucky in their search the two men would simply have to look to the coast of the neighbouring continent — this mysterious continent that the Portuguese, and following them the Dutch, had so far barely sighted.  However, conscious of his responsibilities as supreme commander of the ship, he decided to inform the thirst-enraged people on the larger island of his decision. There were now more than two hundred people there, for in the course of the preceding day some of the Traitors' Island refugees had joined them.

As the longboat approached, the sight of so many people congregating on the beach, desperate to snatch at the slightest hope, alarmed Pelsaert — who claimed later that he had wanted to jump into the water to go to them but that his companions had held him back — and he therefore yielded to the urging of Jan Evertsz, the bo'sun, who predicted that if he set foot on the shore he would become a kind of hostage and would no longer be able to leave.  The longboat, therefore, turned back and with a bad conscience Pelsaert, on returning to Traitors' Island, drafted a letter in which he tried to exculpate himself,

*The southern part of the island is bordered by this sombre shore onto which the sea throws bunches of sea-weed. From here, the survivors would have been able to see the upperworks of the* Batavia *until the waves gradually smashed them and they disappeared into the depths.*

*A providential islet*

explaining that it was imperative that he keep full freedom of movement if he were to have any chance of finding water. Then he set off in the direction of the two islands that could be perceived like a single long dark streak on the horizon to the north-west. On the islet which was only later to be called "the *Batavia* graveyard", anger and despair raged among the survivors. Dire thirst, aggravated by the blazing sun, soon began to wreak havoc, inducing madness in some, followed by death. Some drank their urine, others placed themselves in the hands of the Lord and tried to lose themselves in prayer. Then at last their prayers were heard and on the fifth day, miraculously the skies opened and poured down on the survivors, affording them a short-lived respite.

In the course of the following days, others who were able to escape from the wreck, now slowly breaking up under the staggering blows of the waves, and who did not drown, as did some forty of their unfortunate companions, were to swell the number of desperate people on the island of refuge. Jeronimus Cornelisz himself reached there on 12th June, worn-out after taking two days to cover the distance between the wreck and the islet, sitting astride a part of the bowsprit, with a little piece of a plank to serve as a paddle. He was greeted with the attention due to his rank and offered what comfort there was.

Exhausted though he was then, the man who was a wolf in sheep's clothing was soon to reveal his true and terrifying self...

*Until his dying day Pelsaert was to regret his indecision at the pathetic moment when the privileged people who were with him in the longboat urged him not to go ashore on the islet of refuge, where he was awaited like the Messiah.*

# act 8

## Cornelisz' webb of treachery

Thus Jeronimus Cornelisz reached land safe and sound and within a few hours he had recovered from his fright and was beginning to reflect on the precarity of his situation. That is to say, his situation and his alone, for he was so extremely egocentric that the existence of his companions in distress carried very little weight with him.

His reflections quickly led him to a two-fold conclusion. First, it was evident that with so many mouths to be fed, the horrendous spectre of famine would very soon rear its head. Hence the absolutely vital need to reduce the number of survivors at any cost to a very small group of hand-picked individuals. Secondly, the prolonged absence of the *commandeur* and the captain meant that their search for water on the higher islands or on the coast of the neighbouring continent had proved unsuccessful and unless something untoward had happened to them, they were heading for the distant fortress of Batavia. And what were their chances of reaching it ? Knowing the skill of the old sea-dog Jacobsz and the well-tried sturdiness of the longboat, Cornelisz considered that they were at least reasonable and that it was therefore not totally impossible that they might one fine day reappear on a big ship to recover the *Batavia*'s precious cargo and to rescue the survivors, if any, which was less certain.

This might then be a marvellous opportunity to seize the relief ship by guile and steal away with it to become a buccaneer somewhere off the coast of Madagascar or elsewhere... And if no such ship ever appeared, all that remained was to invoke the devil's help in building a strong boat of the timbers that could be recovered from the wreck of the *Batavia*, strong enough to carry him and his faithful followers to some haven before supplies ran out completely. After all, the V.O.C. had nothing to reproach him with save a few minor offences, for the present at any rate. But, if for some reason or other a long drawn-out agony appeared unavoidable, then, as preached by Torrentius, at least this last period of life on earth could be one of sensual pleasures !

*Jeronimus had transformed into a charnel-house the islet that today is called Beacon Island. The first lobster-fishermen to go there found shallow graves containing skeletons with smashed skulls which three centuries later confirmed the terrifying accounts given by survivors of the massacre.*

*Left :*
*A psycho-morpho-graphic study – the expression used by the artist himself – produced this portrait of the former apothecary of Haarlem. A truthful reconstitution of features in which perfidy, sensuality and greedy lewdness can be detected yet also a certain charm on account of the elegant lines and natural distinction of the face.*

Meanwhile a council had been set up to watch over the interests of the community and to mete out punishment if there were any misdeeds. Cornelisz, who had not arrived on the island at the time of the council's election, was not a member and showed no inclination to be co-opted onto it. During periods of fine weather many more visits had been made to the wreck of the *Batavia* since Pelsaert's departure with his companions, and enough pieces of timber, tools, nails and ropes had been torn from the dismembered ship to build rafts and even one or two rough boats. Provisions and drink were also stocked on the island in sufficient quantities to meet the needs of the immediate future. All the precious goods were assembled in a safe place, including the *objets d'art* that had been intended for high level barter, and the rich materials, brocades, gold braid, fine apparel, the boots of best leather and hats of finest felt.

**As the days passed, Jeronimus Cornelisz was to transform the islet of refuge into a harrowing field of death.**

Cornelisz saw few ways of laying his hands on all this wealth and also increasing his own chances of survival. But being quite devoid of any scruples and having no conscience to worry him, he quickly worked out his strategy : he would get together a nucleus of men as greedy and as little imbued with compassion as he, not more than forty all told.

The others would all have to be physically eliminated.  It would scarcely be possible, however to run a sword through such a large number of individuals, many of whom were armed soldiers, without producing a strong reaction.  Cunning ways would therefore have to be devised and, in that respect, Cornelisz was never short of ideas.

The curtain soon rose on the tragedy.  The former supercargo had little difficulty in asserting his hold on a few ambitious men to whom he promised the moon.  From the outset he proposed to be their leader and they blindly agreed to follow him.  Among the new followers, some were  immediately detailed to take a raft to investigate the nearest island, a thin spit of land on which could be seen a few clumps of vegetation and some hillocks of sand. On their return, they of course reported their findings only to their attentive leader : not the least drop of fresh water, as was to be expected, though there were a few depressions with brackish and stagnant water, fringed with pale green moss,

*Misinformation, carefully arranged by Cornelisz, made Seals' Island appear like the Garden of Eden.  Many of the survivors, congregated on the islet of first refuge, fell for the trick and agreed to be taken there by raft : they found an island that was certainly much larger than the one they had just left, but equally inhospitable and bereft of fresh water.*

*Previous spread :*
*The sky, playground of white-*
*plumed birds,*

*Right :*
*Pale moss green, a comfort to*
*the eye and the soul in a harsh*
*world,*

*The waves lapping shores where*
*the foul smell of horror seems to*
*linger have an*
*out-of-this-world tone,*

*The dunes' dazzling brightness,*
*the turquoise ocean and the*
*fresh green of the swamps,*

*A world of solitude*
*and strangeness...*

beside which seals[1] were basking ! Regardless of this, our Machiavelli let it be known that Seals' Island, as it was forthwith named, had plenty of fresh water. Those misguided fools who wished to go there therefore gathered on the shore and forty-five of them, men, women and children, were promptly embarked, after being promised that they would receive regular supplies of provisions. And that was that many less who would die without making trouble and who would no longer take any of the precious rations !

Meanwhile, a commando of soldiers led by one Wiebbe Hayes was instructed to go and explore the "high islands" that could be seen on the horizon, the very ones that Pelsaert, Jabobsz and Evertsz had inspected hastily before changing course for the continent. Their instructions were to look there for "other" sources of drinking water. Cunning Cornelisz took care to confiscate their arms just as they were leaving,

*Time seems to have stood still on Seals' Island where sea-lions have for centuries frequented the brackish water-holes beside the chaplet of dunes.*

claiming that they would only be a hindrance to them in the task they had to carry out. The valiant explorers were instructed to light fires as a signal if their search proved fruitful. And their raft soon disappeared over the horizon...

But a few soldiers still remained. Some of them had already joined Cornelisz, but they were a minority. The tyrant, however, wanted to have a completely free hand, so he conceived the idea of quickly getting rid of them by simply drowning them at sea. To this end, he sent them off on other rafts in small groups charged with futile missions, and with them went the strongest of his accomplices to carry out this evil deed.

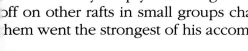

[1] They were in fact, as we have seen, sea-lions.

Having thus got rid of the majority of his potential opponents slaughter could begin. The first step taken by the new authority was to dissolve the existing council and institute his own. Since he now had control of all the arms and was fully supported by henchmen who were quite as cruel and megalomaniac as he, Cornelisz was able to give free rein to his fantasies. And his were worthy of a Nero.

*Displeased at being disturbed in his siesta, this sea-lion, who had been dozing in a pool of brackish water surrounded by an attractive fringe of succulent plants of the Halosarcia halocnemoides species (Chenopodiaceae family), has drawn himself up and is giving a roar of warning. These animals, so graceful and light of movement in water, appear clumsy on land, for being very heavy, they move with difficulty. In the distance a few fishermen's huts and a coral cairn break the smooth line of Beacon Island's silhouette.*

138

Hedonist that he was, the first action of this sovereign of a new Lilliputian kingdom was to take to bed the beautiful Lucretia van den Mylen. Realizing that her life depended only on the tyrant's will, she yielded, if not with good grace, at least without letting her revulsion be too obvious, to all the perverse whims of her torturer ; her tent was surrounded day and night by watchful guards, no one being allowed to approach it without having first shown his credentials.

Not only were the desires of the flesh to be satisfied but also their sartorial desires : the members of the new style of government, inebriated by their unaccustomed wealth, dug into the chests and clothed themselves like princes. Cornelisz was the first to parade up and down the islet attired in a manner producing an utterly surrealistic effect in such a setting : scarlet tunic bright with gold braid, great silver buckles on his shoes and a hat with an ostrich feather ! At times he liked to fin-

ger and caress the treasures, of which he had drawn up a meticulous inventory : a marvellous antique cameo in onyx and a finely carved vase of agate[2], fine pieces of ivory, precious stones, dishes and receptacles in solid gold or silver and a variety of valuable curios. Having some psychological sense too, he did not forget to distribute largesse to his faithful followers. His generosity did not, of course, go so far as sharing with them the favours of Boudewijn van den Mylen's wife, but three other married women, also very desirable, became the prey to the whims of his accomplices.

But the worst was yet to come. Starting on 5th July, a wave of bloody madness swept through the islet, with one murder after another in quick succession, the defenceless victims being shot down by musket-fire at point-blank range, or run through with a sharpened rapier, while others had their throats slit, not to mention successive drownings, skulls

*The long white line of Beacon Island as it appears from the southern extremity of Long Island. The small distance between the two enabled the pitiless Jeronimus Cornelisz to keep an eye on those whom he thought he had got rid of for good.*

___
2 It will be seen below (Act 12) that the presence of this incomparable collector's piece on the *Batavia* is subject to controversy.

smashed in with an axe, stranglings... and even pregnant women and children were not spared.

When it was found that the people who had been banished to Seals' Island were surviving longer than expected (for their skeletal silhouettes could be seen through a glass as they wandered on the shore) Cornelisz sent his knights of death to despatch them. They were chased over beaches, dunes and swamps and savagely massacred, except for three young boys who were too nimble for their pursuers but who were eventually captured. Only one of them survived, however, having agreed to assist the murderers of his young companions.

On 20th July, the day after smoke had been seen in the fresh morning air rising from the shore of one of the high islands clearly indicating that Wiebbe Hayes' soldiers had discovered water, Cornelisz decided to try poison. But as the child to whom it was administered did not die quickly enough for his liking, he sought the assistance of one of his lieutenants to strangle the victim. He and his followers thus proved themselves to be the first advocates of euthanasia, by assisting the sick — and Heaven knows there were many — to pass quickly over to the other world.

Gijsbert Bastiaensz, the predikant, witnessed these hellish goings-on, horrified, but had too colourless a personality to carry any moral weight and to intervene.  All he could do was pray, but he himself was not spared the most terrible trial.  To his distress, he found that his eldest daughter Judick was coveted by Conrad van Huyssen, a young nobleman who was nevertheless one of the twenty-six conspirators who had sworn allegiance to Cornelisz.  In the evening of 21st July, the

*"What cruelty !  Oh horror of horrors !"*

messenger of Christ, who had until then been spared, was surprised to receive an invitation together with his eldest daughter to dine in the tyrant's tent. Oddly, his wife and his five other children were not invited. But to refuse on a pretext of form was tantamount to signing his death-warrant. The unfortunate man therefore accepted the invitation from the mutineers' chief, not doubting that the sentimental fate of Judick hung in the balance. And of course Conrad van Huyssen was there, literally devouring with his eyes the woman of his dreams. At the very moment when Cornelisz was filling his guests' glasses with his best wine, a few men on his instructions were smashing the skulls of Maria, the predikant's wife, and the five

*What horrible feasting the gulls must have enjoyed when Jeronimus and his acolytes found the ground too hard to dig and therefore offered the birds their many corpses to feed on.*

children, two girls and three boys, who had remained with her. The unhappy man whose task it was to console human suffering could do no more to relieve his own pain than to utter a harrowing cry : "What cruelty ! Oh horror of horrors !"

But Cornelisz the sadist was far from sated with strong emotions. On 16th August, doubtless wishing to vary the monotony of his daily fare of bloodiness, he proposed to gouge out the eyes of a little child, drawing brief excitement from the child's cries of terror and the look of unbearable suffering that his face portrayed at the fatal moment. To finish it off, he decapitated the child alive.

The islet had become a place of carnage. Some hundred and twenty innocent people had been put to death and the survivors had the air o hunted animals. At the least movement in any direction, they would be threatened by Cornelisz' men. To begin with, the corpses of those who had been killed were simply dumped without ceremony into graves dug in the coral sand, but the task soon became too demanding, and it was judged both easier and more practical to throw the corpses into the sea where they stirred up the sharks whose sinister fins could be seen momentarily on the surface of the water. From time to time, some blood-tinged viscera would be washed up on the shore, to the satisfaction of gulls and terns, heedless of the fetid odour of their feast. Without doubt the island's sad name, "the *Batavia* graveyard", that it was to bear henceforth was already fully justified.

On the 20th of August Cornelisz proceeded dictatorially to reorganize his government and proclaimed himself Captain General. To mark the occasion, he had a new pact signed, this time by thirty-six men, amongst whom was the predikant who, traumatized, was acting like an automaton.

Still no sign of a sail on the horizon. Supposing now that the only chance of lasting survival lay, after all, over there on the farther of the great high islands where Wiebbe Hayes and his men were perhaps leading a life that could not but be better than the one to which the recluses of the tiny island-cemetery were condemned ? Cornelisz was furious that he knew nothing of what was happening over there.

His decision was taken : he must know...

*One of the five skeletons discovered to date on "the Batavia graveyard" (Beacon Island) where systematic digs would doubtless uncover a vast charnel-house. In various parts of the skeleton, particularly the skull, one can see the marks of violent blows that would have been made by Jeronimus Cornelisz' cruel henchmen.*

# act 9

## A legendary maritime feat

As soon as they reached the nearer of the high islands[1], Pelsaert and his companions divided into several small groups each of which went in a different direction in search of fresh water. But not a drop was to be found either by digging holes in soft ground or in the small depressions scattered all over the rocky hard-pan that covered a large part of the island. The terrain on which they had set foot, though covered with vegetation which from a distance gave a false impression of greenness, turned out to be very unprepossessing when seen close to, for it was no more than a pedestal of greyish limestone seamed with numerous cracks into which thorn bushes and spindly little trees, bent double by

*The strange and inhospitable world of East Wallabi. Pelsaert and his companions in distress sought in vain any sign of water on this broken crust of limestone on which were scattered a few thorn bushes.*

---

[1] Today named East Wallabi, this island is the most hilly of the archipelago and is the only one to have a beautiful beach of white sand.

the wind, had thrust their roots. The only pleasing surprise was the discovery of a very large number of curious little furry, jumping animals, relatively easy to catch for they were not very fierce. Cooked on an improvised barbecue, their meat was found to be excellent and this unexpected reserve of food did a great deal to increase prospects of survival. But the problem of lack of water remained, a truly obsessing problem.

Aware that time was running out, Francisco Pelsaert soon ordered their withdrawal and the *Batavia*'s longboat put out to sea with the high tide to make for the second high island, which was larger in area than the first but not very different as regards its aspect and its resources. A few pockets of brackish or stagnant water were certainly discovered here and there, but none with which the water-barrels could be refilled : despite the fact that water was severely rationed, the level was going down hour by hour.

The *commandeur* therefore decided to play his last card and to make for the coast of Eendracht's land without further delay and to try, cost what it might, to set foot there. The devil take it if this continent, which everyone had the greatest difficulty in picturing, did not have at least some streams of running water, or at worst, some ponds of stagnant water. In this regard, the reports brought back by the rare countrymen of theirs who had approached it, admittedly in more northern latitudes, gave grounds for real hope.

There was no question of undertaking a journey that might last several days in an open boat, permanently exposed to sea spray and burning sun, and accordingly it was decided that a shelter deck should be constructed. The far-sighted Adriaen Jacobsz had in fact already thought of this when they set out and the few planks floating near the wreck of the *Batavia* had been recuperated and stored on board the longboat. The carpenters set to work on these forthwith. Everyone was aware now that his fate would be played out in the very near future — his own and also that of all those unfortunate people, who could be seen through a telescope crowded together on those few yards of bare coral, their hearts full of despair.

*Yet it did exist, though it was very difficult to find, this natural well full of drinking water that was situated in the western part of the island. Had the thirsty passengers of the Batavia's longboat happened upon it, the tragedy would perhaps not have reached the proportions that it did.*

The sun was low on the horizon when the dinghy appeared. Ten men landed from it, following Gillis Fransz, one of the *Batavia*'s former assistant helmsmen, who had had no more luck than the others in their search for fresh water. As soon as he learned of the *commandeur*'s plans, he urged him to allow him and his men to go with them. His main argument carried weight : if the longboat could take in tow the

dinghy, much easier to manoeuvre than the former, it could prove very useful when they attempted a landing. Pelsaert hesitated a moment and then agreed.

*Hunting tammars through the scrub on West Wallabi Island.*

Night had fallen by now. Forty-five[2] people crouched round two fires on which were cooking some of these strange little animals with the atrophied fore-paws and a pouch under the belly in which they kept their young. Before the animals were skinned and cleaned ready for grilling, Pelsaert spent some time studying them and compared their build to a hare in size, a civet or a large cat in appearance. The sky was studded with stars and not the least cloud was to be seen. There were certainly more clouds over that flat country of theirs which had never seemed so far away. Here, it was the beginning of the southern winter, the night wind roared and was glacial, and many began to shiver. Zwaantie moved closer to Adriaen Jacobsz who tried to avoid the eye of the *commandeur*, full of bitterness. The other woman in the group

2 This is the figure given by Pelsaert himself in the report of the shipwreck that he drew up for the Company. On the other hand, Antonio van Diemen reported in a letter to Pieter de Carpentier that 48 passengers had reached Java on board the longboat.

147

*Cliffs reminiscent of those of Dover ! Here we are on the portion of the continental coast between Port Gregory and Kalbarri and it is evident that the overloaded longboat would have had no possibility of landing here.*
*As for fresh water...*

hugged a sleeping baby to her breast[3] and gazed ahead with a vacant stare. The succession of incredible events she had just lived through had, as it were, drained her. The night ahead would be long, and few amongst them would manage to sleep...

The dawn had barely broken when Pelsaert read out a solemn resolution which he asked everyone to approve and to sign, and then the order was given to leave. Very carefully the longboat, propelled only by rowing, made its way through the maze of reefs and reef-flats, the dinghy in tow. Less than an hour later the way ahead was clear and the two little sails were raised and immediately filled by the wind that had grown even stronger during the night. The boats moved smoothly ahead in a north-easterly direction. The continent did not appear until the early afternoon, as yet much too far away for there to be any chance

of approaching it while visibility was good before nightfall. Adriaen Jacobsz, who was in charge of navigation, therefore preferred to lower the sails and wait at a distance in order not to run the risk of being driven ashore.

*The continental shelf in the same area : "But the land here appeared to be arid and cursed, with not the least vestige of grass or leaves of any kind." (Francisco Pelsaert)*

---

3 According to the abovementioned letter from Van Diemen to Carpentier, this child was three months old when he arrived at Batavia, which means without doubt that he was born on board the *Batavia*, somewhere between the Cape of Good Hope and the Houtman Abrolhos !

The following morning, land appeared again after less than an hour's sailing. It came nearer rapidly, for even before midday Pelsaert was able to observe and to memorize every detail of it : a flat, bare land apparently totally devoid of any vegetation and ending abruptly in cliffs that were somewhat similar to those of Dover and against which enormous waves were crashing.

The longboat was now moving forward more slowly, alongside the coast in a northerly direction. All on board were scrutinizing this mysterious world passing before them, attentively and somewhat fearfully. A little further on they came to a sort of bay, but on approaching, found that there would be no question of dropping anchor there. Furthermore the weather was getting worse and the sea rougher as the wind rose rapidly, with sudden squalls. They therefore prudently made for the open sea, under a sky heavy with great black clouds stretching to the horizon on all sides. Would they fulfil their promise ? The answer soon came as the sky suddenly poured cataracts onto the longboat and its passengers who burst into cries of joy. To drink until they were no longer thirsty ! A dream that none had dared entertain...

The *commandeur* whose bad conscience was plaguing him more than ever was not the least satisfied at this providential downpour. It seemed evident that it was not simply a local squall and that therefore their companions abandoned on the Abrolhos must be enjoying the same relief.

In the morning of 10th June the rain had stopped but the sea, on the other hand, was rising so strongly that the situation soon became critical. Despite the deck that was supposed to protect it, the overloaded boat[4] was beginning to ship water and, but for the desperate efforts of all on board to bail out, she would already have gone to the bottom. Suddenly the great voice of Adriaen Jacobsz, the only one who could make himself heard above the wild roaring of wind and waves, thundered : "I said cut the dinghy's painter ! Will you do what I say, in the name of God... Go on, throw everything overboard, lighten her, lighten her ! Yes, even the bread, too bad, everything... Don't look back, it's

*The breakers, that almost everywhere on the stretches of coast alongside which the longboat sailed between the 8th and the 16th June 1629, prevented all attempts to land.*

everything overboard, that or we perish." Thus lightened, the longboat was able without too much damage to get through the terrible hours, lasting part of the night as well, until the elements gradually calmed the following day. In the morning of 12th June 1629, close observation of the coast could resume. All along it, foam-capped breakers mounted guard and made it impossible to approach what Pelsaert was later to describe as "a dastardly dry land, with neither beach nor cove, as there are in any other country of the globe". The same day, with the return of fine weather, it was possible to take bearings which situated the longboat at 27° latitude south. The following day, at the same time, she was at 25°40', but the coast still appeared just as unwelcoming and desert-

---

4 It will be remembered that it was intended to carry a maximum of 40 passengers.

like[5]. And indeed, the wind blowing from the desert, drying the air, soon brought back the dread of thirst...

A first glimmer of hope appeared in the morning of 14th June when, rounding a small promontory, they saw a column of smoke rising into the morning air. Smoke means humans and human presence means fresh water... But great waves breaking on a shore strewn with rocks made the approach very dangerous. However, six sailors agreed to

5 The longboat was at this time sailing alongside the vertiginous cliffs of the western coast of Dirk Hartog Island. It is surprising that Pelsaert makes no mention of the compatriot who had preceded him here. If he and his men had gone ashore on the northern tip of the island, they would have seen, clearly placed on the summit of the cliffs, the engraved pewter plate fixed onto a pole and left there thirteen years earlier by the captain of the *Eendracht*. The plate was not discovered and reclaimed until February 1697, when another Dutch navigator, Willem de Vlamingh, found it.

eap into the sea and swim with all their strength towards the shore, which they reached safe and sound[6]. Meanwhile, the longboat had anchored in twenty-five fathoms and those aboard her spent the day feverishly waiting for news of their brave companions, soon lost to sight. Towards evening panic seized them momentarily when they saw bounding towards the shore, four black and hairy men, about whom their companions, who reached the boat a little later exhausted and with cuts and bruises here and there, were to furnish most interesting details : "We were approaching the fire from which we had seen smoke rising, when these four suddenly appeared. On seeing us, they came towards us on all fours. Their skin was black, their hair wild and their

*The western coast of Dirk Hartog Island. Although some plants do manage to put down roots in an occasional spot on the island, there are few places on earth more forbidding and desperately dry than this.*

This spot would be approximately on the latitude of Minilya station, north of Lake McLeod.

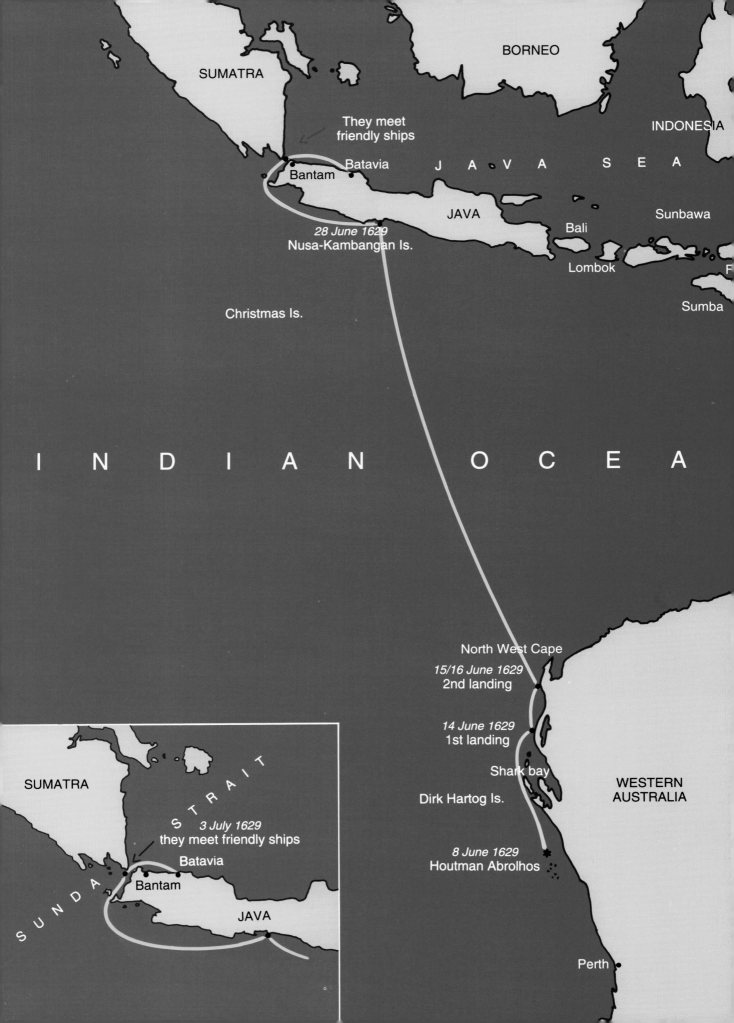

imbs were thin ; they were not wearing the least clothing, not even a loin-cloth. We were just wondering whether they were an unknown species of primate or whether they were really human beings when, one of us having frightened them, we saw them stand up and then run away". This first anthropological finding did nothing, alas, to drive out their obsession with their burning thirst.

Adriaen Jacobsz, loud-mouthed as ever, made no secret of the fact that he was all in favour of stopping this hopeless search for water and setting course as quickly as possible for the island of Java which he declared they could reach in under ten days provided the wind did not slacken and that his companions in distress agreed to a further reduction of their meagre daily ration of water. But Pelsaert did not share this view and decided to persevere with his attempts to find water.

On 15th June, the longboat managed with considerable difficulty to circumnavigate a chain of reefs and to anchor a short distance from the coast. This was to be their last attempt. The *commandeur*, keen to go ashore, made the following detailed report of the experience : "As soon as we set foot on the shore I had holes dug in the sand, but the water we found was as salt as the sea-water. However, a little later we discovered some rain water in a crevice in the rocks, which was a great relief for we had been allowed only a quarter of a pint for several days now. I ordered some of our men to continue the search throughout the night and I stayed with them. We were thus able to collect sixty pints more. I found traces of humans' presence near the shore in the form of ashes of fires amongst which there were the remains of shells of sea snails and crabs".

*The famous engraved pewter plate, commemorating the landing of Dirk Hartog and his companions. This was in 1616, on the northern tip of the large island that today bears the name of the captain of the Eendracht. Not having set foot on the coast in this sector, the passengers of the Batavia's longboat were unaware of it.*

The hope of adding to their stock of water led them to stop a day more ; it was thus possible for those who had remained on board in order to guard the boat, to go ashore in turn. The *commandeur* described this longer contact with the mysterious, desert-like continent in the following terms : "Sadly, everything was dry, even the deepest openings in the rocks. Inland from the coast we were unable to find any traces of water either. The land there was flat and bare, with neither grass nor trees, and all we could see were anthills or rather a sort of hive that the termites build to shelter in. Most of them are so large that one would take them for Indians' huts. The flies were so numerous everywhere in the area that we had great difficulty in ridding ourselves of them. In the course of our excursion which alas, was fruitless as regards finding water, we perceived, within range of our muskets, a group of eight savages, each of whom was holding a stick in his hand. They ran away as we approached. We were at that point at 28°17' latitude south[7] and

---

[7] The reference to a chain of reefs together with the latitude makes it possible to situate quite definitely their landing place at a point a little below the southern border of the Cape Range National Park. This region is indeed bordered by the immense Ningaloo Reef, broken here and there by channels, which is now a divers' paradise. The hinterland is still full of anthills and of the exasperating little flies that are the scourge of the warm regions of Western Australia.

we were thus too far from the river reported by Jacob Remmessens[8] ; we were too far also from the islands of the shipwreck. I therefore decided that we must continue to Batavia".

Adriaen Jacobsz' proposal thus prevailed in the end and leaving behind them the hostile world they had been skirting round for a week with so little success, Pelsaert and his thirsty and hungry band set out to cover the 900-odd nautical miles[9] that still lay between them and the island of Java.

It was not until 27th June in the evening, after twelve days of sailing without particular incident, that the longboat's haggard passengers stepped ashore onto the island of Nusa Kambangan[10] where they found, hidden

8  The latitude given by Pelsaert (22°17') does indeed suggest, as Henrietta Drake-Brockman thought, the watercourse that is now known as Yardie Creek, the only one in the area that is never dry on account of the embankments on either side of the river bed formed by immense and spectacular vermilion-coloured cliffs that make it look like a gorge, and of a sand-bar near its mouth that encloses its green water. The Ashburton and Fortescue rivers, situated a little further north, beyond Exmouth Gulf, certainly would not appear so striking seen from the sea, even though each is distinctly wider. As for Jacob Remmessens (some maps also mention Jacob Remens or Remmissen), he was a bo'sun on the *Leeuwin*, which moored in 1622 within sight of the estuary of the small watercourse to which his name was given (this detail is indicated in the legend of a manuscript map that the Austrian National Library has at Vienna). Other maps of the period also mention a "Willems river" situated a little further north than Yardie Creek, which might be what is today called Mandu Mandu creek, although this runs only in the rainy season.

9  This is the orthodromic distance, but it goes without saying that the boat's inevitable drift would have caused it actually to cover a greater number of miles.

10  Today Nusa Kambangan is no longer an island, a causeway having been built through the swamps at the

under exotic ferns, a waterfall of cool, pure water of which they drank to repletion before also filling the two small casks that were practically empty. Francisco Pelsaert was the first to kneel on the ground to thank God for his mercy.

With renewed vigour, as one can well imagine, the survivors now had only one idea in mind : to get to Batavia as quickly as possible.

This was not so easy however, for it was another seven days before they reached the entry to the Sunda Strait, through which all vessels going to the citadel had to pass. During this time they made no further attempt to go ashore anywhere for the island of Java was then still far from pacified and the people in the longboat were justifiably wary of the possible hostility of indigenous populations.

The longboat was off the island of Sangiang[11] on 3rd July towards the end of the afternoon when three sails appeared astern. It being hardly likely that they would encounter an enemy ship in these waters, Pelsaert resolved to go to meet them. With what astonishment he recognized the first of the three vessels — the *Zaandam*, the store-ship that had been accompanying them when they left Texel and from which the *Batavia* had become separated by a storm !

He was the first to be hoisted aboard, and was welcomed by upper merchant Van Dommelen who had difficulty in putting a name to the gaunt face before him, yet more in realizing that here was the author of

*Next spread :*
*Anthills in the area of Cape Le Grand. Although this scenery is not without a certain beauty, with these strange mounds of red earth rising out of a layer of spinifex, it does not promise springs and waterfalls and one can easily understand that the people on board the longboat, discouraged by so much dryness and irritated by the terrible little flies that are the scourge of this region, decided to turn their backs for ever on this hostile and unknown world and to set sail for verdant Java.*

mouth of the rivers Daman, Dangal and Oedjoeng which meet at this point. For today's citizens of the Republic of Indonesia the name Nusa Kambangan has a sinister connotation because on the peninsula is a prison of very bad reputation ; it is a heritage of Dutch colonialism which today houses prisoners serving long sentences.

11 Before the Indonesians renamed it with its native name, this island was known as "Dwars in den Weg" by the Dutch and "Thwart the Way" by the English, for it does indeed lie right in the middle of the Strait thus obstructing passage through it in a straight line.

the *Remonstrantie*. The waxy pallor, the fever-bright eyes, the face half hidden by a hermit's beard : the former *commandeur* of the *Batavia* looked like a living ghost as he began recounting his lamentable adventure to his compatriot, speaking in a hollow voice, his hands trembling convulsively. But his interlocutor quickly interrupted him, urging him to eat — and to wash — first. When Pelsaert finished his tale an hour later, Van Dommelen was overwhelmed by a profound compassion for this man so sad at heart that he was unable to rejoice in the fact that his fantastic maritime expedition had at last come to a happy end. For over there, on the Houtman Abrolhos, men, women and children had been left to their vile fate and were doubtless slowly dying, one by one, if they were not already all dead. And he, Francisco Pelsaert, who had done his utmost to find for them the water on which their life depended and who, though weak with illness, had pushed himself to the extreme limit of his strength, did he not now risk being accused of desertion ? Van Dommelen did all he could to dispel his fears and suggested also that he should without further delay cross onto the *Frederik Hendrik* which was at that time quite near the *Zaandam* and on board which was a high official of the V.O.C., Crijn Raembruch, Councillor of the East Indies [12]. Pelsaert readily agreed to this suggestion and the crew of the store-ship prepared immediately to transfer him.

The man who had survived so much and had done what he could to make himself presentable spent the next four days, from 4th to 7th July, the time that it took the *Frederik Hendrik* to reach Batavia, unburdening himself to Raembruch, telling his whole story and making no secret of his bad conscience and his apprehension. But no one could have been more receptive to his arguments than the Councillor who, far from blaming him, tried on the contrary to persuade him that his doubts were groundless, that he had acted well and honestly and that his comportment merited nothing but praise : "You can count on me, at all events, to argue your case, if there were any need to do so, with Governor General Coen. He has acquired a reputation of being heartless, but believe me, Pelsaert, I have spent much time with the man and I can assure you that he is never indifferent to the misfortune of others, and he is always deeply concerned to be fair. Furthermore, he has voyaged even more than you and he knows full well that accidents at sea can happen to anyone. ... No, you really must stop blaming yourself. Rather than penitence which is out of place, it would be more appropriate to pray that the Abrolhos survivors may have been blessed with the same divine mercy that has enabled you to overcome a thousand dangers and to reach us safe and sound".

Despite these kindly and understanding comments, Francisco Pelsaert did not feel very reassured when on Sunday, 8th July 1629, one month to the day after he had left the Abrolhos, he found himself before the dreaded founder of Batavia. For a moment, the Governor's piercing look seemed to bore right into him, as if to read the deepest

*The island of Nusa Kambangan seemed particularly welcoming to the longboat's passengers for they were able to assuage their thirst and fill their water-barrels here, in a delightful setting.*

---

12 Pelsaert had no inkling that, at that very time, he had been raised to the same dignity and that he was in fact talking with one of his peers.

recesses of his soul and then, already informed of the broad lines of the tragedy, he asked Pelsaert a series of specific questions. He was certainly not indifferent to the fate of so many people left to themselves in the most hostile environment imaginable, but at the same time, scrupulous administrator of the Company's interests in this part of the world that he was, Coen was also concerned about the possibilities of recovering the goods that the *Batavia* had been carrying. There was no trace of hostility in his attitude but, quite the contrary, his discreetly expressed sympathy restored Pelsaert's peace of mind as he told him : "Be present tomorrow morning at the meeting of the Extraordinary Council that I shall convene to determine the action to be taken and, in any event, however great your exhaustion, make ready to go to sea immediately. Only you can direct the relief expedition. You may go now. God protect you".

Not surprisingly, the following day when the members of the Council had heard Pelsaert's detailed account, they officially instructed him to return to the Abrolhos with the *Zaandam*, to recover the goods belonging to the Company and, what was much less certain, to rescue any survivors of the tragedy that there might possibly yet be. All that remained was for the ship to be fitted out for the specific mission to which it was assigned and for divers to be recruited for the task of searching the wreck in order to extract from it the buried treasures.

On 15th July, Jan Pieterszoon Coen gave his instructions personally to Pelsaert, proposing that he should set sail the very next day. But Pelsaert showed how keen he was to start by ordering the captain of the *Zaandam* to weigh anchor on the hour. By a quirk of fate, the captain's name was Jacob Jacobsz but he was no relation of big Adriaen Jacobsz who, as soon as they arrived, had been thrown into one of the citadel's dungeons, charged with negligence while in command of the *Batavia*. His fate was much more enviable than that of the bo'sun Jan Evertsz, who was charged with indecent assault on Lucretia van den Mylen and who had undergone all the sufferings of their voyage of 1,200 sea miles only to be condemned to death by a specially convened court and immediately handed over to the executioner.

Pelsaert thus set out on a long voyage again. Although the physical

*Francisco Pelsaert dreaded most of all what Jan Pieterszoon Coen would think of how he had acted in the time immediately following the shipwreck. In the event, he was immensely relieved to find the much-feared Governor General an attentive and sympathetic listener as he expounded his distressing tale, and inclined to support him. The founder of Batavia, whose furrowed features are seen in this portrait, done in Holland in the intermission in his career, was at this time nearing the end of his life and indeed did not even have the satisfaction of learning that the Zaandam had been more successful in her mission than they had dared hope and had brought home safely a group of miraculously saved survivors and the greater part of the Company's precious goods.*

conditions in which he was travelling on the *Zaandam* were more than adequate, they could not remedy his extreme weakness, tantamount to utter exhaustion. No one has ever said enough of the heroism displayed by this man of weak constitution, still undermined by the effects of lengthy illness as much as by the privations he had recently undergone. Furthermore, he was haunted by the idea that perhaps, indeed probably, he would find nothing but corpses ripped to shreds by the cruel beaks of sea-birds or turned to parchment by the implacable sun of the Abrolhos. In such circumstances, peace of mind was unattainable.

Held back by constant winds, the *Zaandam* did not come within sight of the breakers that mount guard north of the Abrolhos until 10th September, that is nearly two months after her departure from Batavia. The lengthy voyage reinforced the despair felt by the former *commandeur* and put an end to any vestiges of hope that he might have had of finding his former companions alive. Taking enormous risks, the ship threaded her way right through the northern breakers of the fateful archipelago, so that she might approach her objective from the east. It took nine interminable days before she could at last come in sight of an island that Pelsaert recognized straight away as the first of the high islands, the one he had crossed again and again throughout that day, the 6th of June, that already seemed so far off...

On 17th September, the *Zaandam* finally found a safe mooring, near that same island, which was the smaller of the two "Cats' Islands", and Francisco Pelsaert, who had begun to hope again since he had seen wisps of smoke rising from an islet near the site of the wreck, and also from one of the two high islands, climbed at last into a dinghy and was rowed ashore. How was he to guess that, within a few minutes, he would find himself suddenly plunged into a world of unimaginable nightmare...

*It was perhaps here, on this beach at the western tip of East Wallabi, that Francisco Pelsaert learned of the tragic crimes that had been perpetrated during his absence.*

# act 10

# The "Cats' Island" besieged

On 16th July, one of the men banished to Seals' Island, a sailor by the name of Pieter Lambertsz, guessing that he had fallen into a trap, found a means of escaping by clinging onto a piece of floating wood, and gradually progressing from one emerged point to the next he had managed to get to the farther of the high islands, where he informed Wiebbe Hayes of the situation on the islet of refuge. What he had to tell aroused justifiable suspicions — which were proved terribly true when, on 21st July, the second barber Aris Jansz, having managed to escape the vigilance of Cornelisz' lieutenants, also joined the men on the "Cats' Island" with the aid of a makeshift boat[1].

Wiebbe Hayes therefore knew what he must now be prepared for and the first thing he did was hastily to pile up as many flat stones as possible to make rudimentary fortified emplacements, one near the shore, the other further inland. Though minimal, these structures would at least provide protection for him and his men (the majority of whom were French soldiers[2]) against musket-fire, provided of course that it came from some distance. But these rough retreats, being covered with pieces of canvas and branches collected from all over the island, also served as dwelling places.

For West Wallabi — as the island was later named — bore no resemblance, the Lord be praised, to the minute islet of refuge, already known as "the *Batavia* graveyard"[3]. To their great surprise the survivors found the island fairly rich in animal life. First, there were plentiful sea-birds whose eggs could be used to make omelettes, then there were wild fowl — sandpipers, turnstones, curlews — several species of lizard, a large placid snake of the boa family, not very attractive at first sight, and especially, these curious little hopping animals that

*It is difficult to believe that this simple edifice of piled-up stones might be the oldest evidence of the presence of white men in Australia !*

---

1  Several survivors were subsequently to escape in turn from the cursed island and two months later there were more than forty people, including Wiebbe Hayes and his men, to repel Cornelisz' attacks on the island of West Wallabi.

2  Jean Hongar, Jean Reynoult de Mombry, Thomas de Villiers, Jean Bonivert, Edouard Cout, and others.

3  It was not until the 20th century that the island was named Beacon Island (see Act 14).

were not identified until much later as belonging to the order of marsupials and then named tammar-wallabies. They were found in large numbers in the little copses where they took shelter in the hottest part of the day and were not too difficult to catch. As for their meat, the newcomers found that its taste had a suggestion of venison and they enjoyed it as had Pelsaert and his companions a few days earlier. On the shore, mainly at low tide, fish were found imprisoned in little ponds, and the large quantities of crustaceans and shell-fish of different species added flavour to their daily fare. There was no risk here of going hungry, with such abundance all around.

And then of course, more precious than anything else, there was fresh water. Admittedly, it had not been easy to find. For the first few days, they searched desperately everywhere on the surface of the island, under a burning sun whose heat was scarcely tempered by the

*Plentiful meat from tammars and water-fowl, sea-birds' eggs, fish, shell-fish and crustaceans, not to mention the fresh water from the wells that Bastiaensz the minister described, perhaps with some exaggeration, as being "sweet as milk", meant that the men exiled on West Wallabi lacked virtually nothing. There were even various kinds of wild berries, that were perfectly edible and added flavour to their daily diet as well as providing the vitamins that they needed.*

continuously blowing southerlies. Then they thought of looking below the surface and there, wonderful !, they found a few water-holes hidden under slabs of limestone and supplied through fissures in the rock, deep within which was clear water, only slightly brackish, in quantities sufficient to allow all the *Batavia*'s survivors and more to drink their fill. This discovery was greeted with shouts of joy and the good news was immediately signalled to Cornelisz by sending up smoke from rough fire-places built hastily on top of the little cliff overlooking the sea, on the south-western edge of the island.

One can imagine Wiebbe Hayes' consternation when he received no response to his signal. Could it be that something dreadful had happened to the people on that islet separated from them by a few twisting channels, interspersed with coral outcrops that were barely covered at low tide ? Could it be that all were dead ? He was to ask himself these questions for only a few days, before he knew the answer — and confrontation seemed inevitable.

*One cannot view this structure without some emotion, for it was here that the soldiers who remained faithful to the Company spent days of terrible anxiety. Fortunately the Abrolhos islands have been little visited, otherwise these stones of incomparable historical significance might have been scattered by vandals or people not realizing what they represented.*

*A view from above that shows clearly that the structure comprised two parts : they are roughly the same size and would certainly have been covered by branches and bits of sail-cloth.*

On 23rd July, an emissary from Cornelisz appeared with a letter, translated into French by an assistant merchant, Daniel Cornelisz, and secretly addressed to the French soldiers, for it was apparently supposed that, being mercenaries, they would have no particular sympathy for one camp or the other. Cornelisz simply proposed that they enter into a pact with him, in return for which they would be given special

treatment. The emissary having been taken prisoner, the sender of the letter received no reply and was accordingly greatly displeased. The kind way having failed to produce the required result, the only alternative was to use force. After all, did he not hold all the arms ?

On 27th July, a first detachment was sent to attack what was already regarded as the enemy position. It was composed of seasoned soldiers armed to the teeth. But they had not allowed for the difficulty of approach. The keels of their two boats were soon scraping the bottom and they therefore had to continue on foot. Thus they proceeded, in full view, the water to mid-thigh and their feet sticking and sliding on a mud bottom slippery as soap, to wade towards the shore of the verdant "Cats' Island", where a tough reception committee was awaiting them. A hail of large stones, some of them hurled by rudimentary catapults, rained down on them. Trying to avoid them, they slipped and fell into the water with their muskets which thereupon became useless, and to complete their defeat they were given a sound beating. They returned, feeling very sorry for themselves, to report their misadventure to Cornelisz who flew into a rage at the news. How could men who had no arms, no food and whose clothing must now be in rags, people who had water, perhaps, but neither bread nor wine — how could they put up such resistance and not succumb to temptation ? It was quite unbelievable. There must be some way of bringing them to heel !

The bloodthirsty tyrant studied the lesson of this defeat and came to the conclusion that he would have to take the matter in hand himself. Doubtless the emissary had not had the right manner. He, Jeronimus, Captain General, would know how to present all the advantages of joining his cause. Immediate advantages, in the form of distribution of wine, liqueurs and warm clothing, but also long-term advantages with the prospect of reaching by some means or other, a welcoming land

The immediate approach to West Wallabi by sea poses insoluble problems. Those who wish to set foot on the island must therefore wait for low tide and walk there. But the muddy bottom, covered by a thin layer of sticky sea-weed, makes this exercise very difficult : one can see how it was that the mutineers who came to attack Wiebbe Hayes' positions suffered so many rebuffs.

Opposite left :
This splendid aerial view gives a fair idea of the difficulty of navigating in the immediate surroundings of the two Wallabi Islands, East and West, on account of the labyrinth of shallows around them. And this explains why the Zaandam, though her goal was in view, took so many days to find a safe mooring. During this time of course Francisco Pelsaert's nerves must have been painfully on edge as he urged his captain to be doubly vigilant. The assumed position of the mooring is shown by a cross while that of the two fortlets built by Wiebbe Hayes is shown by red circles.

where the cream of the cargo would serve to win the favour of some petty king. And if Pelsaert were to return, there would be a fine opportunity to put on an act and grab his ship by guile. Was it a premonition? Perhaps; in any event, the prospect of the *commandeur*'s return was beginning to haunt the Captain General's dreams increasingly.

A little more than a month had elapsed since the repelled attack when Cornelisz, in turn, embarked for the voyage to the more western of the high islands. Little more than an hour at sea: his physical courage would stand the test. The predikant was in the team and had promised, if not sworn, that he would be an intermediary and would plead the cause of the abominable instigator of the murder of his family. Playing their own game, Wiebbe Hayes pretended to listen with interest to his visitor's propositions. Wine and warm clothes in return for their submission? The proposal seemed worth considering... but he must

*The second emplacement, consisting of a single rectangular room, is much less well-situated, from the strategic point of view, being towards the centre of West Wallabi Island. It is on a slight incline, on ground of hard limestone, with no vegetation at all. It is clear, from the lack of patina on its stones, that this shelter has been patched up, which may have been done by people who came here to scrape the surface for guano in the 19th century. The fact that there is a minute excavation in the form of a well containing a little fresh water (there are two others, both larger, on the island) not far from its walls, and that there is a cairn half-way between it and the first structure, support the notion that it might well have been Wiebbe Hayes' principal dwelling-place and also a fall-back position in the event of a large-scale attack.*

first talk it over with his men whom it would probably not be difficult to persuade. Cornelisz should return the following day, and to demonstrate his peaceful intentions, would he please come unarmed, those with him likewise. Secretly, his evil adversary was already savouring the morrow's victory. So it was all, as he had thought, a matter of talking persuasively. The idiots who had gone before him had not had the right manner, that's all. The following day, for he must strike while the iron was hot, when they saw all the good things he would lay out before them, this soldiery would soon find their every scruple vanishing ; then, once the dead weight remaining amongst those on the islet of refuge had been summarily disposed of, the others, who were of the same kind and spoke the same language would gather here on the big island... The minister requested the favour of remaining with Wiebbe Hayes in order to have time quietly to draft the reconciliation pact while awaiting the return of Cornelisz. His request was granted.

But when Jeronimus returned the following day accompanied by five of his most faithful lieutenants, among them Conrad van Huyssen — not without leaving a squad of armed men on a neighbouring islet, for one can never be too mistrustful — he was quickly dealt with. He was taken prisoner, tied up and thrown like a bundle of dirty linen into the nearest fortlet, as were four of the five men[4] accompanying him. The mutineers who were to provide cover for their leader quickly realized that things had gone wrong for him and downcast, they took back the bad news to their companions, the reserve force, who were already preparing to make the move from the small islet. That very evening, in view of the difficulty of guarding his prisoners effectively in the event of an-

---

[4] Jacob Pietersz, soldier (1st class), was able to make a last-minute get-away with the dinghy they had used for the attack.

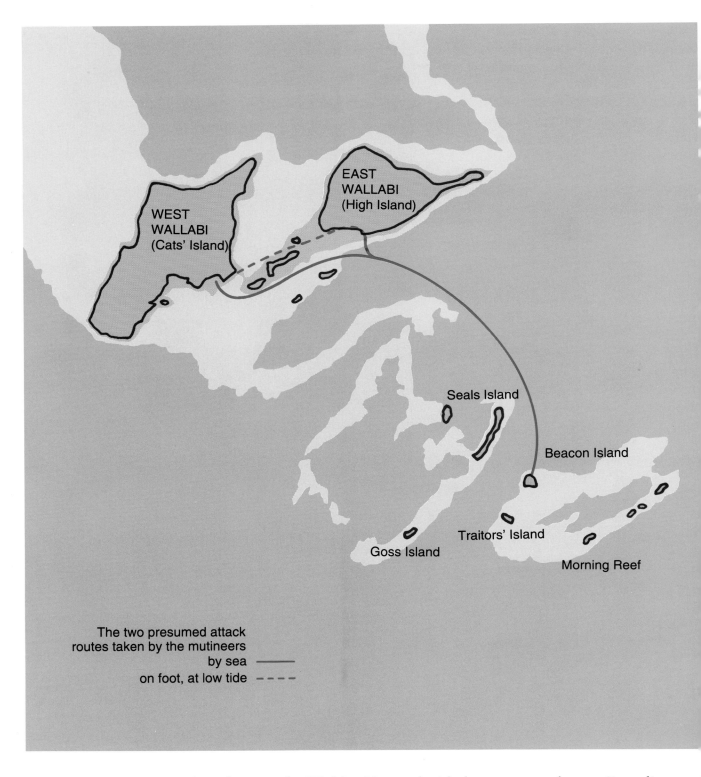

WEST
WALLABI
(Cats' Island)

EAST
WALLABI
(High Island)

Seals Island

Beacon Island

Traitors' Island

Goss Island

Morning Reef

The two presumed attack
routes taken by the mutineers
by sea ———
on foot, at low tide - - - -

other attack, Wiebbe Hayes decided to execute them. Cornelisz was
the only one spared for the time being, for reasons of strategy.

However, amongst the remaining conspirators there was still some
will to fight and the bad soldier Wouter Loos proposed to his confeder-
ates of "the *Batavia* graveyard", who were still desperately short of
drinking water, that he should himself take over from their captured
chief and that they should launch a counter-attack, throwing into the

battle this time everything they had. On 8th September, the last batch of rebels solemnly swore allegiance to him. Little did the newly promoted leader imagine that at that very moment Pelsaert was not far off, on board the *Zaandam*, trying to find a way through the labyrinth of shallows that hampered access to the two "Cats' Islands", gradually nearing the island that he was virtually certain was the very one from which he had departed almost exactly three months earlier.

Then came that incredible day, the 17th of September, when events came tumbling one after another at vertiginous speed. At dawn, Wouter Loos put to sea with his small team in the direction of the island where Wiebbe Hayes was in control. His declared intention was to free Cornelisz and his accomplices, not knowing of course that the latter were dead, and to chop into little pieces those who had so cunningly tricked him. The attack had been under way for some two hours, and it would have been about nine in the morning, when the *Zaandam* appeared on the horizon. This put the rebel leader in a terrible dilemma : should he continue an action which it looked as if he was going to win, since four of the enemy had already been wounded, one fatally ? Or should he on the contrary quit, running the risk of giving Wiebbe Hayes freedom of movement which could prove dangerous, in order to set up as quickly as possible his piratical strategy to attack the vessel that had appeared with, surely, the *commandeur* of the *Batavia* on board ? He quickly chose the latter course of action.

Just on midday, the *Zaandam* was at last in in operational position, near the island of East Wallabi. Francisco Pelsaert's journal tells us the chronology of events from that moment on : "As soon as we had dropped anchor,

*This copper coin was found a short while after the wreck was discovered, buried under several centimetres of silt right beside the emplacement nearest the shore. It is a duit, the smallest currency in circulation in the Batavia's day. The Republic of the Seven United Provinces had decreed that all its members' currencies should be unified, an exception being made for Western Friesland, part of the province of Holland, which enjoyed the privilege of being allowed to continue issuing its own money. The three cities of Hoorn, Enkhuizen and Medemblick also enjoyed, in turn and for periods of ten years, the considerable advantages of issuing currency. The first coins of this type came into circulation in 1604. The one shown here bears the identification mark of Hoorn. On the obverse can be seen, in the centre, the two lions that appear on the coat of arms of Western Friesland (in other words the countries situated north of Amsterdam) while around it is the inscription, partly effaced :*

*DEUS FORTI. ET SP. NOS (God is our strength and our hope)*
*The reverse reads only :*
*Western Friesland*
*1626*

*At the time, 8 duits made one stuiver (sou), and 20 stuivers made one guilder or florin. Considering that the daily wage of a sailor was one florin, i.e. 160 duits, this coin was scarcely a fortune in those days...*

I embarked in the ship's boat and set out for the higher of the islands[5], which was also the nearer, taking with me two barrels, one containing fresh water, the other bread and also a cask of wine. On reaching my destination, I saw no one, which surprised me. But almost at the same moment as I stepped ashore, I perceived a little boat, with four men on board, rounding the point north of the spot where I was. One of the occupants, Wiebbe Hayes, leaped ashore and began running towards me. I heard him shouting from afar : "Welcome, welcome, but return on board as quickly as you can, for there is a band of villains on the islands near the wreck of the *Batavia*. They have two bigger boats and they intend to seize your vessel !"[6]

Realizing the danger, the *commandeur* straight away hurried back to the *Zaandam*. It was fortunate that he did so, for no sooner had he alerted his crew than the mutineers' boat was alongside the *Zaandam*. Not knowing that their ploy had been discovered, the mutineers appeared, all dressed up for the occasion in a manner that was bizarre in such a setting and in such circumstances and, only slightly surprised that they were asked to lay down their arms, they excitedly climbed the ladder to the deck. Needless to say their expectation was short-lived, for they were immobilized on the spot, searched and put in irons in the depth of the hold where an immediate interrogation informed Pelsaert of all the intricacies of the plot. Later in the day, Wiebbe Hayes, who was already regarded as a hero, accompanied the predikant and Jeronimus Cornelisz on board, the latter tied up like a sausage, looking daggers and hurling abuse at all around him.

All that remained was to deal with the handful of mutineers left on the island of tragedy. After embarking Wiebbe Hayes and the forty-odd companions in arms who remained and who doubtless looked their last with strong feelings on the island where they had spent twelve interminable weeks, the *Zaandam* set sail for her objective. The remaining group of rebels soon realized that the game was up and surrendered without resistance. The mutiny was over. The survivors of the abominable carnage could not refrain from weeping with joy, while

*Right :*
*The last of the attacks made by the Cornelisz faction was murderous : one of Wiebbe Hayes' soldiers was killed and three others seriously wounded by the attackers' fire.*

---

5 He was certainly thinking of East Wallabi which is, in fact, higher than the neighbouring island.

6 In actual fact Pelsaert's journal is rather contradictory on this point, for a little further on one reads : "At the very moment when the battle was on (i.e. the fighting between Wiebbe Hayes' men and those with Wouter Loos) we appeared on the *Zaandam*, which provoked an explosion of joy amongst the besieged people, while on the contrary the attackers were overcome by despair, realizing that they had missed their chance and that their plans had come to nothing."
However, the two versions can be reconciled if it is assumed that events actually occurred as follows :
- Wouter Loos attacks at dawn ;
- Fighting has been going on for two hours when the *Zaandam* appears, causing the attackers to desist ;
- Instead of making directly for the slowly-moving vessel, which is still a fair distance from the "Cats' Islands", the mutineers decide quickly to return to "the *Batavia* graveyard" to assemble reinforcements, stock up on munitions and hold a brief council of war ;
- Towards midday, the *Zaandam* finally comes to a halt off the island of East Wallabi, while Wouter Loos, who has now determined his strategy, has already left his base and is urging his oarsmen to row as hard as they can towards the *Zaandam* ;
- At the same time, Wiebbe Hayes leaves his stone fortlets and he too makes for the *Zaandam*, now riding at anchor, and thus a race begins between the two opponents, without their being aware of it ;
- Wiebbe Hayes is met by Francisco Pelsaert whom he informs forthwith of the plot ;
- Pelsaert hurries back on board and arranges a "reception committee" ;
- The mutineers, who had planned to seize the ship by guile, themselves fall into a trap and are disarmed and overpowered.

he more pious among them fell on their knees on the coral shore and ands joined in prayer, their faces turned to heaven, gave thanks to the ord. Needless to say, Lucretia van den Mylen and Judick Bastiaensz hed no tears when they learned the fate of their forced lovers, one a risoner, the other executed.

Good had finally triumphed over evil, and for Jeronimus and what emained of his followers, the time for settling accounts had begun.

# act II

## *The monsters' retribution*

Once all the evil elements had been reduced to impotence, Pelsaert could at last turn his attention to the Company's material interests. It was found that none of the precious objects was missing, save a simple gold chain, which was a great source of satisfaction to him. But efforts still had to be made to recover the various casks of valuable merchand-ise, including three casks of cochineal[1], and in particular a number of chests of money lying on the bottom, amongst the remains of the *Batavia*. For this purpose four Indian divers from Gujarat[2], who were renowned as deep divers, had been especially recruited and were on board the *Zaandam*. They had now to prove their skills. But the conditions had to be right for diving. For the moment this was not so : the wind was so strong that enormous waves were breaking on the reef and making any approach to it impossible.

The last mutineers captured on "the *Batavia* graveyard" had been transported forthwith, under close guard, to Seals' Island. Pelsaert remained very wary for he knew that it was not impossible that all these bandits might cook up some plot if they were allowed to get together.

*How cruel those days were ! Cornelisz's judges sentenced him not only to be "hanged by the neck" but also, before that, to have both hands amputated. However, Gijsbert Bastiaensz, the minister, stated in his famous letter, in which there is a wealth of fascinating detail, that the mutineers' "damned spirit" had only one hand cut off, like the other four condemned with him. The illustrator is slightly mistaken in showing bodies hanging from the gallows in the background. In fact, Jeronimus Cornelisz was the first of the condemned men to be executed.*

---

[1] The first-known cochineal had come from Central America. It is a small insect which lives as a parasite on a species of cactus originating in Mexico ; before she lays, the female secretes carminic acid. As its name indicates, this substance is bright red in colour, verging on violet. The Spanish were the first to import cochineal from the New World in the 16th century. At that time it was the most precious product after silver and pearls. It was obtained simply by sun-drying the insects gathered by hand (it took 140,000 females to produce one kilo of colouring matter !). Sometimes the latter was mixed with curcuma to obtain a scarlet mingled with flame colour known as "Holland scarlet". Other species of cochineal exist throughout the world. Amongst the most important are those known as "kermes" that develop on the cork oak trees of the Mediterranean basin, and another that is found in Poland where it is a parasite of a herbaceous plant called "German sanguinaria". The dye-stuff obtained from the latter produces a crim-son colour. The cochineal that was being carried on board the *Batavia*, like all that was used by the 17th century Dutch, was the first type and had been supplied from the little town of Oaseaca in south west Mexico, by Dutch commercial agents based in the West Indies. This species had a colouring strength eleven times greater than that of kermes. Cochineal was one of the export products that was most sought after at that time in Asian countries. In India, in particular, it was used for dying wool and silk bright red. Its golden age was in the 19th century in the Canaries, where production reached the fantastic figure of 2,720 tonnes in 1875, but thereafter, like most natural colouring substances, cochineal gradually fell into disuse.

[2] A large state situated in the west central part of India and giving onto the sea of Arabia. Gujarat, whose capital is Gandhinagar, shares a border with Pakistan.

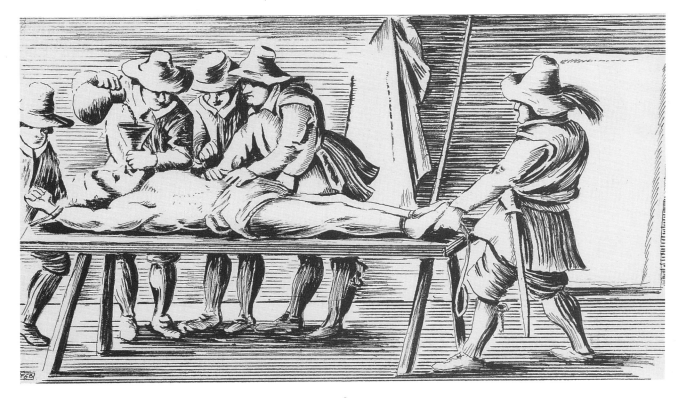

*Hy werdt ter Examen voor den Hooft-officier geprefenteert half naeckt, fyn handen op fyn rugge gebonden op een ladder gdeydt, met tevoren aen fyn voeten geftrickt utgereckt, dus eerfelingh achter overleggende, water te mondt ingegoten, tot groote opfwellingh van fyn Lichaem.*

Those who were imprisoned on the *Zaandam* were on the whole a lesser threat, for they were in irons.

The preliminary investigation for the trial took two long weeks. The prisoners were brought, each in turn, to "the *Batavia* graveyard" from their respective place of detention, there to answer questions put to them by a court presided over by the *commandeur*, accompanied by four magistrates who included uppersteersman Claas Gerritsz, the only member of the court who had been one of the *Batavia*'s crew.

It is striking, in the minutes of this strange trial, to note how the judges swung between severity and clemency. There is no denying that Francisco Pelsaert was deeply concerned to be fair but even he, in keeping with the laws and customs of the time, did not hesitate to use torture of the most horrible kind. Cornelisz and those accused with him were indeed several times submitted to "trial by water" in which liquid is introduced by force into the stomach by means of a long funnel and the victim chokes while his stomach swells out of all proportion until it is distended like a goatskin bottle[3]. One often has the impression in

3 Some authors claim that the head of the victim was "partially" submerged in a bucket of water, which meant that he was obliged to drink great mouthfuls in order to reduce the level of the water and thus be able to breathe, the operation being repeated as many times as necessary... Obviously this method gave rise to insurmountable "technical" difficulties. In point of fact, it is clear from Dutch archives of the period that it was the well-known funnel system or less often the "bib" that was used. The latter obliged the victim

reading the record that, far more important than mere men, it is God who is conducting the proceedings, the court appearing to be no more than the instrument of his supreme will, for the references to his omnipotence and his mercy are constant.

Jeronimus Cornelisz, as the reader knows, was not especially endowed with physical courage. The court did not at all appreciate his first form of defence which was to blame his assistants, making out that he himself was a victim, and for this he was made to drink water, a lot of water : he soon confessed to many more sins, probably, than he had actually committed. At the same time, his accomplices were not spared and accordingly supplied so many details of their former spiritual director's sadism that he had no possibility of claiming the least mitigating circumstance.

The verdict was returned, case by case, on 28th September, and a very long verdict it was for Cornelisz. Indicted on no fewer than sixteen counts, the former supercargo was given the maximum sentence ; that

*A variation of the same torture, after a Dutch engraving dated 1626. The refinement here is that no direct violence is exerted on the person who it is intended should confess his "crimes". It is he himself who must, in order not to be asphyxiated, drink the water poured into a sort of rigid "bib".*

whose hands and feet were firmly tied, to drink the water in the more or less rigid collar or "bib" encircling his neck as soon as it reached the level of his nostrils to avoid being asphyxiated. This was the method used on the unfortunate English officers accused of commercial spying and conspiracy in the tragic "Ambon affair" in 1623. It is unlikely however that Pelsaert would have used this method on "the *Batavia* graveyard" for it required a minimum of equipment which he probably did not have.

is, all his goods and wages having been confiscated by the Company
both hands were to be amputated before he was hanged by the neck
until death ensued. Seven other mutineers received the extreme
penalty at the same time : Lenart Michielsz van Os, a cadet aged twenty-
one ; Mattys Beer, soldier, aged twenty-one ; Albert Jansz, gunner, aged

*Right :*
*Legend has it that this circle of*
*piled-up stones in the south-east*
*extremity of Beacon Island was*
*Cornelisz' prison. Legend only,*
*for in fact in the course of*
*meticulous excavations in 1967*
*various fragments of utilitarian*
*objects (a bowl, some bottles,*
*clay pipes, a mirror etc.) all*
*dating from the second half of*
*the 19th century were found,*
*both inside and outside the*
*enclosure. The most likely*
*explanation is that it was a*
*shelter built by the survivors of*
*the wreck of the three-masted*
*barque Hadda, who spent five*
*days on the island in 1877*
*before being rescued.*

*Above :*
*Seen from above, the so-called*
*"prison".*

twenty-four ; Jan Hendricx, soldier, twenty-four ; Andries Jonas van Luyck, soldier, aged forty ; Rutger Fredricx, locksmith, aged twenty-three and lastly Jan Pelgrom de By, a cabin-boy barely eighteen years old. The tyrant's henchmen were to have only the right hand amputated, save for the last three who would be spared this horrible preliminary torture.

The fate of the other prisoners seemed almost enviable in comparison. For them it was to be only a triple passage under the keel of the *Zaandam*, a standard punishment in the maritime world of that time, followed by a hundred lashes. But that might well not be all, for the dreaded courts of Batavia had always shown a tendency to increase punishments...

The sentences were read out in public in the evening of that day and

*Part of the west coast of Seals' Island. The exact spot where Cornelisz and his henchmen were hanged is not known. It may be supposed however that it would have been around here, the nearest point to Beacon Island. There would have been little reason for Pelsaert to render the carpenters' task more complicated by instructing them to take to one or other extremity of the island, which is a little longer than two kilometres, all the materials and tools necessary for building the gallows.*

the executions were to take place on Seals' Island the day after : the carpenters were already building the gallows. Cornelisz lost all his cockiness, turned deathly white and gave himself up to a crazy attempt to gain time at all costs. First, he recanted all he had said, claiming that confessions extracted under torture were nul and void. But Pelsaert would not allow the shadow of a doubt to remain regarding the former supercargo's culpability. Dutch law of that time was perfectly clear in this regard : no definitive sentence could be pronounced and still less could any punishment be meted out if the prisoner recanted his confession at the last moment. The *commandeur*'s logic seemed questionable though, for in order that the condemned man should declare that his earlier confessions had not been made under duress, he was forthwith submitted — yet again — to torture ! The prisoner thereupon confessed all they wanted to hear him confess and then implored the court to grant him his life at least until the *Zaandam* reached Batavia, so that he might one last time embrace his wife, who was waiting for him. Naturally this favour was refused. Changing tactics, he then declared that he wanted to receive the sacrament of baptism in order not to appear before his Maker with the soul of a sinner. This cunning request put Pelsaert in a very difficult position. How could he refuse baptism to one of the Lord's creatures ? Would he not be exposing himself to eternal damnation if he opposed the redemption of a sinner, however great his sins might have been ?

This problem of conscience was to Jeronimus' advantage and he was informed that the execution was postponed until a later date and that he would be baptised the following day. But the condemned man was not satisfied with the imprecision of the reply. Postponed for how many days ? As he insisted on knowing, the truth was finally divulged : the fatal date had been set for 1st October. His incredible response was : "Did I hear aright ? Barely three miserable little days ? How am I expected to wipe out a lifetime of sinning in such a short space of time ?" Quibbling right to the end, he tried everything possible to put off the fatal day. Thus, though locked into a specially-made prison, he yet managed, no one knows how, to obtain some poison which he took but which had no effect other than to give him severe stomach-

*2nd October 1629 : The time has finally come for Cornelisz and his principal accomplices to pay the penalty of their crimes. The flesh of their mutilated bodies will be left to birds of prey and their bones, buffeted by wind and waves, will imperceptibly return to dust.*

ache and vomiting which went on all through the night and left him very weak. However, he was given an antidote, which gradually brought back his strength and pugnacity, and his threats were renewed even more strongly, mingled with vain pleas for mercy.

On 1st October the weather was so thick that the departure for Seals' Island had to be postponed. The following day the sun appeared timidly through the clouds and the sea had become a little calmer, so the eight condemned men were taken across the strait. Pelsaert was present and agreed to the lesser felons' request that they see their chief pay for his crimes before them. His arms were therefore held down on the block and both hands were cut off. He barely had time before the rope tightened round his neck and put an end to his suffering[4], to cry out : "Revenge ! Revenge !" And his last sight of this world was the islet that he had transformed into a graveyard after experiencing there the ephemeral pleasure that limitless power procures. In a southerly direction, part of the superstructures of the *Batavia* could still be seen emerging from the sea, constantly battered by waves unfurling their long white sleave the length of Morning Reef.

*This was probably the last view of this world that the perpetrators of so many abominable deeds looked upon... "The Batavia graveyard" partly fills the horizon, while the waves breaking on Morning Reef paint a thin silver line from one end to the other of the tragic island.*

4 In this case there was no trap-door through which the prisoner's body would fall, breaking his neck. Here it was a terrible death by choking.

Instructions to Wouter Loos and Jan Pelgrom de By Van Bemel, both sentenced to the supreme punishment but who, for different reasons have instead been deposited here, on the great South Land. ————

With a sampan or a dinghy which you will maintain, with all its accessories, to enable you to move from one place to another, you will note that the south wind which is at present blowing along the coast will enable you to reach the latitude of 25° to 24° south, by dead reckoning, this point being situated about 50 miles from the place where we are at the present time. ————

It will be for you to decide, in view of the meteorological conditions and the suitability of the site, whether you should land there or elsewhere, in order to make contact with the people of this country by means of friendly signs. ————

It is for this reason that the undersigned commandeur has given you a number of Nuremberg toys and some knives, beads, little bells and small mirrors which you should distribute parsimoniously to the Blacks until you have won their confidence. ————

Once you have established relations with them, if they should appear to intend taking you to their villages to present you to their chiefs, you must have the courage to follow them of your own volition. Man may sometimes find good fortune in the strangest places.
If God watches over you, they will do you no harm and, indeed on the contrary, having never seen white men, they will offer you their friendship. ————

On such occasion, you must observe with the greatest diligence what raw materials, whether gold or silver, are to be found in their country and what value they place on such materials. Thus, having become very good friends with them, you will be able to ask them, either by signs or in language if you have learned to speak theirs, to watch for the passage of ships or of people coming from the sea, in order to obtain from them other goods for barter, such as iron, copper or Nuremberg toys of which you have various samples which, without doubt, will please them very much

The month of the year when ships are most frequently off the shores of this part of the continent are April, May, June and July. This means that you should be particularly vigilant at this time of the year and if you should see one, make signs with whatever means, smoke or other, that seem to you the most appriate appro appropriate.

Above all keep God always in your hearts, and never forget Him; this being so, there is no doubt that He will protect you and will, in the end, accord you a happy destiny. ————————————————

Done on board the *Zaandam*, on 16th November 1629.

*Francq Pelsart*

*Perhaps the steps of the first white residents of the Australian continent led them towards the enchanted setting of the nearby river, now called Murchinson. This was the territory of Aboriginal tribes who have unfortunately disappeared without leaving any trace of their oral tradition.*

These instructions are in contradiction with the fact that Pelsaert states in his journal that the two men were abandoned within sight of the estuary of a creek which, moreover, he took the precaution of having some of his men investigate. They reported to him that the water of the stream was salty at the mouth but became clear and perfectly drinkable a few dozen yards upstream. It may be supposed therefore that the *Commandeur*'s instructions were drafted before the *Zaandam* was within sight of the continent ; his subsequent attitude was dictated by the particular circumstances though slightly contradicting what he had written before.

Seven bodies were left hanging at a rope's end, a prey to the ravages of weather and time and, far from human sight, dust would return to dust. Francisco Pelsaert, for his part, was at peace with himself. Justice had been done. Furthermore, ten of the twelve chests had been recovered by the Indian divers assisted by two Dutchmen. The eleventh was found, but it was impossible to bring it to the surface for it was wedged under a piece of mast that had fallen across it. As for the twelfth, the reader knows what happened to that (act 6, p 119).

The last of the principal guilty parties, Wouter Loos, although his case had been tried with the others on "the *Batavia* graveyard", did not actually learn his fate until 13th November, on board the *Zaandam*. He was treated with surprising leniency in view of the role he had played in the rebellion. He was sentenced only to be abandoned on the continent, together with Jan Pelgrom de By who, although he had been transported to Seals' Island with the other men condemned to death, had aroused Pelsaert's pity at the last moment on account of his extreme youth[5], and thus his life was spared.

After they had refilled the water-casks with fresh water from the two high islands and put down some kegs of salted tammar-wallaby meat, and a last dive down to the wreck had been made, the *Zaandam* set sail. But the atmosphere on board was far from happy. Three days before, the captain, Jacob Jacobsz, accompanied by four men in the bigger of the ship's boats had gone to catch a drum of vinegar that had been seen drifting by. Pelsaert had asked them, while they were out with the boat, to go a little further to the small islands in the west[6] in order to see whether any floating objects freed from the *Batavia* had come ashore there. The sea had become steadily stronger after they left and the boat had not returned at the appointed time. Throughout the following two days all the islands around were searched, including North Island lying, as its name indicates, to the north of the archipelago, but to no avail. Pelsaert hoped all the same that they might have been swept towards the continent, but they were never found.

On the day after the *Zaandam* set forth, on 16th November, the two men whose death sentence had been commuted to abandonment on the continent, were left in a boat with a copious stock of small objects for barter, within sight of an estuary of clear water[7]. There was no show of emotion when it came to their departure. However the *commandeur*, aware of the solemnity of the moment, gave them a remarkable

*Right :*
*An aerial view of Whitecarra Gully where it is fairly certain that Wouter Loos and Jan Pelgrom de By were abandoned in the morning of 16th November 1629, having been given a small stock of cheap articles to facilitate their contact with the Aborigines of the region. There has been much speculation, some quite absurd, about what happened to them but in fact their fate will never be known.*

---

5  He was barely eighteen years old.

6  These were the unnamed islets within Noon Reef.

7  Glenys Mc Donald, a Northampton historian, is convinced that the place where the two men were abandoned was actually where Port Gregory is today and not at Wittecarra Gully, and her arguments have weight. In any event, the two places are so near each other that the story itself is not affected. The fact remains that total mystery surrounds the fate of the two men who, in our humble opinion, must have been quickly murdered by Aborigines. Nearly all the explorers who later set foot in this part of the coast of Western Australia noted the overt hostility of the Aborigines to "white ghosts".

letter of instructions, that suggested the eventuality of pardon by the Company at a later date.

The two men gradually disappeared in the mist... Would they die of hunger or of illness ? Would they be murdered by Aborigines in no time ? Despite several efforts made later to discover what had happened to them no one was ever able to find the least information and these first steps by white men on the Australian continent thus left no trace.

On 5th December, the *Zaandam* was within sight of the citadel of Batavia. But there Pelsaert was greeted by news of serious import : Governor Coen had died a few days earlier of dysentery. He was succeeded by Jacques Specx and already the mutineers in the ship's hold who had been given fairly light sentences dreaded the fate that awaited

them. The Councillors of the East Indies were gentlemen who did not make light of the Lord's commandments, still less of the higher interests of the Company. The next day, or the day after, their limbs would be broken before they were tied to the wheel or a noose put round their neck.

# act 12

## The strange history of a cameo and a vase

During his stay in the Indian city of Agra, where he frequently attended the Court of the Great Mogul Jahangir, Francisco Pelsaert observed that the English who had been there two years longer than he carried on a successful form of trading that they themselves nick-named the "toy business". The term was somewhat derisive, of course, since the "children" for whom the costly toys in question were destined were none other than His Highness the Great Mogul and the numerous princes and lords who gravitated to him. All these handsome and turbaned persons were immensely rich and could therefore satisfy their inveterate taste for the gaudy, acquiring "curios" that would be inaccessible to the majority of mortals on account of their cost, by the simple expedient of dipping into a copious supply of rupees minted from European coins that had been melted down locally.

As the prime purpose of the V.O.C. was to make a profit from any opportunity that presented itself, Pelsaert was not risking much when he introduced his distant compatriots to a type of commerce that the ill-informed "High and Mighty" had never dreamed of. They had received an initial report on the subject from our friend Francisco, but it was not until he returned home, in June 1628, that he was able to expound his theory in high circles, quoting examples which would inevitably whet the appetite of his listeners.

Jacques Specx and Hendrik Brouwer, two future Governors General of the East Indies, agreed with his proposal and the supreme assembly was all the more inclined to give him a free hand to pursue it in that his *Remonstrantie* had won him the reputation of being reliable, competent and well-informed. The next step was to find and assemble a quantity of articles that would appear desirable to the extraordinary customers. With this in view, Francisco Pelsaert, who was remarkably observant, had drawn up a list which included such varied articles as pearls and precious stones of exceptional quality and size, planispheres, *objets d'art* of particular rarity, paintings depicting battles, comic scenes, or nudes, and also utilitarian objects such as small boxes, hafts of fans or

*Detail of the fabulous antique cameo that travelled on the Batavia. This priceless gem had been entrusted to Francisco Pelsaert who undertook to sell it to the Great Mogul or to one of his well-to-do subjects. Peter Paul Rubens, attracted by the promise of exceptional profit, wanted nevertheless to remain anonymous in the transaction and therefore used the services of an Antwerp broker dealing in gems.*

fly-whisks, dishes, ewers, goblets and even chamber-pots, all in solid gold ! He added the pertinent comment : "The majority of these articles could well be sold at the Palace or in the camp, to enhance the profit, honour and reputation of the Company, by an agent knowing the language and customs of the country. (...) One often hears great lords here asking if there are precious stones in our country and whether we make quality articles that could be offered as gifts or regarded as collector's items, like those made in Venice, in England or in other European countries. It is therefore essential, both for the profit of our honourable Company and for the reputation of our country, that it be made clear that our small nation is not only on a par with England but indeed surpasses the whole world in talent and ingenuity."

The second act of this unusual story begins with the discreet appearance on the scene of Sir Peter Paul Rubens[1], the great Flemish painter, who, like Pelsaert, was a native of Antwerp. Rubens, who was perhaps the most cultured man of his century, spoke several languages fluently, including Latin and Italian, and it was said that he possessed the finest collection of antiques of his time. In 1628, the year when Pelsaert returned home, determined to remain there after spending nearly eight years in the trying climate of India, Rubens was 51 and his reputation as a collector of marvels had long since come to the ears of Nicholas-Claude Fabri de Peiresc, the most famous French antiquarian of the time. The latter had managed through friends in common to make contact with Rubens, and after pursuing an assiduous correspondence the two men eventually met and talked of old coins and agates. Given their learning and their similar tastes, they even thought of producing a book together on the subject of the most beautiful cameos of ancient times. Rubens was to draw them, so that the engraver might reproduce them in copper-plate engraving, while Peiresc would tell their history.

It was not by chance that they thought of telling the story of cameos. Rubens had a collection of which he was very jealous and kept carefully hidden. Even Peiresc was barely allowed to peep at it and to exclaim in ecstasy at a "most stupendious cameo", the exact description of which unfortunately we do not have. One may safely assume, though, that it was the Great Cameo, measuring 18 x 26.5 centimetres, the largest ever known in the world, of which Rubens did a superb drawing giving it, according to Peiresc, "even more life, width and depth", for the famous book which, unfortunately, never came into being.

What exactly did this gem represent ? Let us read the description provided by the "Royal Penningkabinet" at Leiden in the Netherlands, where this treasure is today housed, after a journey through history that we shall hear more of. Translated from the Dutch, the description reads :

"The scene shows a chariot drawn by centaurs, mythical creatures

*Right :*
*A painter of genius, a renowned antiquarian, scholar, businessman and diplomat, Sir Peter Paul Rubens had everything to make him immortal.*

*Nicholas-Claude Fabri de Peiresc is better remembered as an antiquarian than a politician. He shared Rubens' passion for collecting objets d'art.*

---

1 Rubens was knighted by King Charles I of England in 1629.

191

*Act 12*
*The strange history of a
cameo and a vase*

The Great Cameo is today the
chief attraction of the "Royal
Penningkabinet" (Numismatics
Museum) at Leiden in the
Netherlands. Unfortunately,
the precious stones that had
been set in a stellate frame in
Rubens' time were sold by a
subsequent owner and replaced
by glass. Likewise the present
frame of this authentic gem is
not gold but ordinary bronze,
painted gold. It is not known
how the Great Cameo was
presented in Roman times.

We know from contemporary
engravings what the star-shaped
setting of the Great Cameo
looked like. This setting was
probably made by Gaspar
Boudaen with a view to selling
the Cameo to the Great Mogul.
The four points of the star were
dismantled in the 18th century,
leaving only the frame. It was in
this state that King William I
acquired the gem at the
beginning of the 19th century.

Act 12
*The strange history of a
cameo and a vase*

with the body of a horse and the torso and head of a man. The talles[t]
person in the chariot, clothed in a tunic and a cloak, is clearly someone
important. He is wearing sandals and his left foot can be seen, some
what illogically, behind the wheel of the chariot. On his head is a laure[l]
wreath, the emblem *par excellence* of an emperor, and in his right han[d]
he is holding a fork of lightning (...) This symbol, peculiar to Jupiter
identifies him as the Supreme God of Roman mythology.

"The emperor is looking at a woman seated in front of and facing
him ; his left arm is resting on her shoulders. Doubtless this is th[e]
empress and she too wears a tunic and a mantle, and on her head [a]
veil. The diadem that adorns her head and the sheaf of corn set off by [a]
poppy bud that she is holding in one hand are an obvious allusion t[o]
Ceres, goddess of agriculture.

"In front of the emperor and
empress a small boy is standing,
dressed in military costume. He
is wearing armour and on his
head a helmet, and he holds a
sword in his left hand, while with
his right he is drawing an arrow
from the quiver on his back. He
is most probably the emperor's
eldest son, and the empress is
pointing to him, imitated by an
anonymous woman, certainly a
member of the family, perceived
to the left of the emperor and
pointing with her index finger at
the boy.

"Two galloping centaurs are
drawing the chariot. The details
of the harness of the chariot are
not visible. The first centaur carries a large shield on his back and
a trophy strapped to his shoulder
by means of a harness. He is
turning his head towards the
second centaur who is grasping
the aforementioned shield with
his left hand. Underneath the
chariot one can see a vase that
has been knocked over and, at
the feet of the first centaur, two
soldiers are being trampled on ;
the more visible one is dressed in
the manner of a Roman centurion
and carries a shield.

*Act 12*
*The strange history of a
cameo and a vase*

"Above the two centaurs hovers a Victory, her garment floating in the breeze. In her hands she holds a wreath that she is extending towards the emperor to whom she proposes to give it. What victory does it signify? It may have been won in a civil war, judging by the soldiers on the ground... or it may be simply an allegory on the theme of the eternal triumph of the emperor. No one can say with certainty.

"This cameo being unique in its kind, it is difficult to draw parallels and to date it precisely. The problem of dating is complicated by the fact that the artist who carved it has combined features of different styles. Although some people have suggested that it could be a scene from the first century A.D., in the reign of Emperor Claudius (41-54), the most widely held opinion is that this exceptional piece came into being towards the middle of the reign of Emperor Constantine, i.e. between

Act 12
*The strange history of a
cameo and a vase*

315 and 324. If that were so, the empress would be Fausta and the prince Crispus. The other woman might be Helena, mother of Constantine.

"However that may be, it is evident that such a gem must have been made to order, while the emperor was holding court. It was a rule that a Great Cameo should hang on the wall of Roman palaces. One or more artists worked in the imperial workshops for months or even years, cutting and polishing the stone. The fact that the emperor is in a central position and in a triumphant attitude confirms that the people with him were members of his immediate family or entourage. The allusion to the matrimonial stability of the imperial couple and the ostensible presentation of the elder son also reflects the context of the imperial court at this period. It is difficult to know to what degree the theme was imposed by the emperor but one may assume that it was not unknown to him and that he therefore played a large part in the creation of this unique work of art."

This was certainly a unique cameo, and superb also, that Rubens would undoubtedly have considered one of the purest gems of his collection. However, he was a collector for whom the intellectual appeal of the exercise was greater than his actual affection for the precious objects collected. Thus he was quite prepared, when the occasion warranted, to sell some of his treasures, provided he found a buyer able to satisfy his terms, for like many another, the great artist was no stranger to transitory financial difficulties. Indeed, we know for certain that his future father-in-law, Daniel Fourment, a dealer in tapestries and silks who had close business relations with the management of the V.O.C., was secretly charged by Rubens to arrange for a quantity of "agates" to be sold on his behalf in India (but no further details are known). Fourment even paid him an advance of 900 florins against the amount that would be procured by the transaction. This happened in 1626. Was the Great Cameo among these precious objects ? It is impossible to say with certainty. But if it was, could it be that Fourment, for the sake of discretion, asked the great jeweller Gaspar Boudaen to act as intermediary (for although he lived in Amsterdam he was a native of Antwerp

*Various details that emerge from comparison of the Great Cameo in the original and as "seen and adjusted" by Peter Paul Rubens.*

*Act 12*
*The strange history of a
cameo and a vase*

which would have recommended him to Rubens)? It is possible, even probable, for one may well imagine that Rubens, in view of his reputation, would scarcely have wished to be labelled publicly as trading in *objets d'art*. In point of fact this is just what he was doing, attracted as he was by the promise, prompted by Francisco Pelsaert's revelations, that he would be able to make a profit of between 60% and 70% (sic) if he were to sell his finest pieces in India!

The fact that Boudaen was a native of Antwerp supports the argument that the gem might well have been the very one that had thrilled Peiresc and that Rubens had drawn. Who could one count on better to sell the gem in India, and obtain a good price for it, than a "fellow countryman" well-versed in matters of antiquities and therefore more competent than anyone else to assess its value and fix the price?

Whether the cameo had been at one time the property of Rubens or not, the fact remains that Gaspar Boudaen appears on the scene at the beginning of the third Act, as the official owner of this gem and openly desirous of sending it to India. As for the means of doing so, he did not have much choice. He was obliged to turn to the V.O.C. A contract signed by the *Heeren XVII* at their ordinary meeting in Amsterdam on 18th December 1628 and the said Boudaen reveals that the cameo, considered so precious that even the "High and Mighty" themselves were not allowed to see more than a drawing of it, had been entrusted to Francisco Pelsaert, *commandeur* of the fleet that left Texel for Batavia in October that same year. Pelsaert was instructed to sell it in India, it being understood that the Company, for its pains, would keep 28% of the profit and that the balance, translated into foreign currency by the chief treasurer based at Batavia would be transferred, as soon as an opportunity arose, to the account of Gaspar Boudaen, who would receive a bonus of 8% on the current exchange rate.

The operation was thus carried out quite openly, even if the V.O.C. authorities did not know the identity of the true owner of the Great Cameo which was referred to simply as "Gaspar Boudaen's gem". Pelsaert, as the reader will learn later, was conducting his own personal

*In Pelsaert's view the Great Mogul, whose Court he had assiduously attended, was the perfect purchaser for the Great Cameo. But in that age all travelling and transport of goods took months or even years, and when the precious object eventually reached its destination, after transiting in the Abrolhos (!), Jahangir had died and his son Shah Jahan, who did not share his tastes, showed no interest in this priceless objet d'art.*

197

ANTONIO VAN DIMEN
GOUV'·GENER VAN INDIA.

commerce[2] in a small way, as so many other English and Dutch merchants habitually did, having for years found this a convenient way of adding, modestly, to the far too skimpy emoluments that they received from their respective employers. In any event, such trading was not yet formally frowned upon by the *Heeren XVII* who, paradoxically, only discovered these lucrative prospects when Pelsaert himself revealed them[3]. It was not until the end of 1628 that Governor General Coen was instructed to put an end to these practices, to search the vessels on their arrival and to punish those found dealing in such trade by confiscating their goods and by deducting penalties from their wages.

One may well imagine therefore that the fact of being very officially entrusted with the Great Cameo together with two dinner services in gold and silver might usefully obscure a parallel trade that the *commandeur* of the *Batavia* was carrying on without being troubled by his conscience and perhaps even without any personal profit, doing it simply to oblige certain friends.

However that might be, the Great Cameo was found, carefully wrapped and stored in one of the chests that had been shipped on the *Batavia*, together with other precious goods, on the tiny coral isle where the majority of the survivors landed after the catastrophe. Thus it must have fallen into the hands of Jeronimus Cornelisz who — as other survivors were to tell subsequently — liked to caress the treasures from time to time and allow his followers to admire them ; there is a certain piquancy in this when one remembers that the *Heeren XVII* themselves had not been allowed this privilege !

The fact that a wonderful antique *objet d'art* that, as the reader knows, had probably decorated the palace of the Emperor Constantine should have spent four months on this strip of dried-out land, adds an almost uncanny dimension to the *Batavia* tragedy and earns it a special place in the saga of maritime dramas.

Surely while Pelsaert was sailing towards the Abrolhos on the *Zaandam*, he must have been haunted as much by the fate of the gems that had been entrusted to him, officially or secretly, as by that of the

---

2  After Pelsaert's death in September 1630, Antonio van Diemen noted with indignation that amongst his personal effects were various small gems and, in particular, a very beautiful cameo in agate, which had been entrusted to him by Gaspar Boudaen himself and which bore the effigy of the late Great Mogul. The confiscation of all these articles had the effect of tarnishing the memory of the former *commandeur* of the *Batavia*.

3  The reader will remember that there was a furious altercation (see Act 2) between Pelsaert and Jacobsz regarding the latter's private trading which the *commandeur* probably considered far in excess of what was reasonable and therefore detrimental to the Company and its business.

people who had been voyaging with him. Had the Great Cameo been lost, or even only damaged, he would have had to answer for it personally to Gaspar Boudaen, for a subsidiary clause of the contract between the Company and Boudaen stipulated that the gem was shipped at its owner's exclusive risk and that in all events Pelsaert was responsible for it.

Most happily the Great Cameo was recovered intact on "the *Batavia* graveyard" and taken safely to Batavia, as Antonio van Diemen reported in the letter he wrote to Pieter de Carpentier on 10th December 1629, saying : "On the 5th of this month, the yacht *Sardam* (sic), returning from the South continent, anchored before the citadel of Batavia. (...) Gaspar Boudaen's large and costly gem has been saved". This was confirmed by Coen's successor as Governor General, Jacques Specx, in much the same terms.

But Pelsaert had not allowed for the fact that, all-powerful and immensely rich though he was, the Great Mogul Jahangir was nonethe-

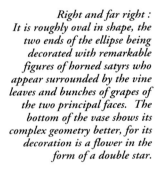

*Right and far right :*
*It is roughly oval in shape, the two ends of the ellipse being decorated with remarkable figures of horned satyrs who appear surrounded by the vine leaves and bunches of grapes of the two principal faces. The bottom of the vase shows its complex geometry better, for its decoration is a flower in the form of a double star.*

less mortal, and he must have been bitterly disappointed to learn, on the *Zaandam*'s reaching Batavia, that the Great Mogul had departed this world. With him had gone the principal and perhaps the only potential purchaser of the Great Cameo, for his son, Shah Jahan, the future builder of the renowned Taj Mahal, less frivolous and spendthrift than his late father, but certainly more cruel[4], was not very interested in these "trifles".

In fact, the Great Cameo was never to find a taker in India, despite the many efforts made, long after the death of Coen, Pelsaert and Boudaen, by successive Governors General and by the heirs of the official owner who travelled especially to India and to the Middle East in

4 He had his own brother's eyes put out so that he might be more certain of ascending the throne himself.

the hope of finding a purchaser for their priceless gem.

Thus it was that in 1656 it returned to
Holland where it arrived without further difficulty. Mrs Henrietta Drake-Brockman is doubtless right in suggesting that the subject of the
Great Cameo, borrowed from Roman mythology, would scarcely appeal to the taste of an
oriental prince. The frame might have been of
interest, encrusted as it was with splendid precious jewels, but not the essence of the gem,
that is the sculpted agate, although it was so
beautiful.

Later the Great Cameo was coveted by
Napoleon I for his personal collection and it
subsequently became the property of the Pabst
van Bingerden family until they parted with it
in 1823 for the colossal sum of 55,000 guilders
when they sold it to William I of the
Netherlands ; they had however first removed
the frame in order to obtain all the inlaid eme-
ralds, saphires and rubies. The king put it in
his "Penningkabinet" (Museum of Numismatics)
and thereafter it became possible for any and
everybody to admire its beauty at Leiden,
where the royal museum, formerly situated at
The Hague, was transferred in 1986.

The fantastic story of the cameo and its jour-
neyings is however surpassed by the yet more
extraordinary story of a vase, of even greater
value, that could have been on board the
*Batavia*. The conditional is certainly the mood
in which to relate this story, for numerous shad-
owy areas obscure the itinerary of this marvel-
ous *objet d'art*. What is certain is that once
again we find Rubens on the scene, for he
acquired it in 1619 at the Saint-Germain Fair in
Paris for the sum of 2,000 gold scudi[5]. It was a
vase of the Greco-Roman period, oval in section and carved out of a block of agate of a
light honey colour verging on milky white in
places. The stone, carved in relief, portrayed a
tracery of vine leaves, tendrils and bunches of
tiny grapes on each of the two main faces of
the vessel, while the sides were decorated with

Two thousand gold crowns.

*Act 12*
*The strange history of a
cameo and a vase*

horned and bearded satyrs resting on acanthus leaves. It was this truly marvellous treasure, of priceless worth, that Rubens was going to send to India, though by what means has never been established. It was an unfortunate decision that he made, for he was never again to hear of his treasure.

In a letter to Fabri de Peiresc, dated 18th December 1634, he refers bitterly to the disappearance of this gem : "(...) I still have the drawing and the model of a vase carved in agate that your honour has seen (and which I purchased for 2,000 gold scudi) but I did not keep the cast. It was no bigger than an ordinary decanter or any ordinary tankard. I remember measuring the capacity and finding that it was exactly the same as what we in our language so ineptly call a "pot". This gem was sent to the East Indies by ship and fell into the hands of the Dutch, but subsequently it perished at the hands of pirates, if I am not mistaken. Thus, despite the numerous approaches that I have made since then to the Company, I have never been able to learn anything of it whatsoever ".

Exactly how was it sent to the Indies ? Who were these mysterious pirates ? Henrietta Drake-Brockman once again builds up a fascinating intellectual structure from which she deduces that Rubens' beautiful vase had certainly been given secretly to Pelsaert and taken on board the *Batavia*. Her whole theory depends on the interpretation of a sentence in Latin : *"sed periit inter manus repientium, ni fallor"* which she translates as follows : "but it perished in the hands of those who appropriated it, if I

*Portrait
of William
Beckford as a
young man. Celebrated for
his writing as much as for his
marvellous collections of art, he
displayed magnificent liberality
in his early life.*

*After its mysterious overseas
travels followed by two
centuries' disappearance, the
famous vase came to light again
and for a while found its place
in the collection of rare objects
that William Beckford kept in
his huge Gothic extravagance,
Fonthill Abbey.*

am not mistaken". There is a subtle shade of meaning here which leads the late historical detective to conclude that the pirates in question were none other than the mutineers led by Cornelisz. It was therefore they who were accused (wrongly as we now know) of breaking it — unless the reference is really to those who acquired it from the Company which itself would have appropriated it, following Pelsaert's death, as part of the goods that he had carried illegally, not having requested permission to transport them.

In the latter case, it is difficult to see why Van Diemen would not have mentioned the vase in the list of things left by Pelsaert... It could mean therefore that Pelsaert (who was not Dutch but Flemish, which lends significance to the phrase "fell into the hands of the Dutch") had secretly agreed to sell this treasure clandestinely in India and that he had recovered it on the sly in the tent of Cornelisz the Dutchman, on the Abrolhos, and then hidden it hoping to find a purchaser[6]. The fact that Rubens did not learn of his death until much later would explain why so many years passed, in this strangely unclear business, before he reacted and turned to the V.O.C., the unwitting carrier of the article. The Company, however, not being directly involved, could only reply with a polite dismissal... which is just what it did.

Clearly the riddle will never be solved. But the famous vase, which is the main point of the story, had certainly not perished in anybody's hands. After disappearing for nearly two centuries, it came to light again in 1823 among the treasures that the celebrated English collector, writer and eccentric, William Beckford, kept in his fabulous country houses, first at Fonthill Abbey in Wiltshire and later at Lansdowne Tower, in Avon. From that time on, the vase is easy to trace until 1925 when the American Henry Walters purchased it, through a dealer in London. It is now one of the principal pieces in the famous Walters Art Gallery in Baltimore, U.S.A.

*The wealthy American collector, Henry Walters, and his wife Sadie Jones, late in life. Their collection of objets d'art was bequeathed to the museum which today bears their name, where the famous vase is one of its prized treasures.*

Although there is still a very slight doubt as to whether the Leiden Great Cameo did actually belong to Rubens, it is quite certain that the vase that he bought at the Saint-Germain Fair and the one exhibited in a New World museum are one and the same treasure. Even more impressive than the Great Cameo, this splendid piece of agate, so delicately carved, could therefore also have spent some time on Beacon Island ! An incredible fate that illustrates, if ever it were necessary, the frailty and vanity of all material wealth in this world.

---

6 In the period between his return to Batavia and his death, Pelsaert was to carry out several more missions in the East Indies for the Company.

# aCt 13

## *What became of the players and onlookers of this drama ?*

Francisco Pelsaert himself left us this incontrovertible record concerning the *Batavia*'s voyage that ended in such tragic circumstances ; it reads as follows :

*Note regarding the fate of the people embarked on board the Batavia : V.O.C. personnel and soldiers*

Men of little worth who deserted before departure by running away through the dunes [1]..................................................................................................6

Transferred to the *Galiasse* and the *Zaandam*, two consorts, on eve of departure..................................................................................................................3

Died from illness, especially scurvy, during voyage ............................10

Drowned during shipwreck, trying to swim ashore [2] ..........................40

Died on the island where the *Batavia* was wrecked, either from illness or from drinking sea-water [2] .........................................................................20

Reached the East Indies with the *Batavia* longboat...........................45

Murdered by Jeronimus Cornelisz by drowning, strangling, decapitation or butchery by axe.................................................................................96

Executed by Wiebbe Hayes after being captured in their attack against his positions on the "Cats' Island"........................................................ 4

Condemned to death and hanged on Seals' Island ...............................7

Condemned to death then reprieved and abandoned on the continent  2

Died accidentally on board the *Zaandam* during the return to Batavia [3] .....2

---

Very probably these were the dunes of Texel, or possibly Dunkirk where, in 1658, the famous Battle of the Dunes between French and Spanish troops occurred.  These six men's desertion could have been helped by the *Batavia*'s running aground in a place that was not specified but was probably very near to Dunkirk.

Certain authors do not scruple to state that, in his journal recounting the rescue operation with the *Zaandam*, Pelsaert, doubtless ashamed of his conduct in the hours following the accident, purposely said nothing about the death by drowning of 40 men as they tried to get out of the sinking ship or about the terrible pangs of death from lack of fresh water that were suffered by those who did reach land safely.  This Note shows that this is not true and that the unfortunate *commandeur* did not in any way seek to disguise the truth in order to clear himself of blame.

The description is inadequate, but it seems most likely that Pelsaert is referring here to Cornelis Pietersz and Adrien Theuwissen, two of the *Batavia*'s men, who were lost together with the captain of the *Zaandam*,

*Although their faces will forever be unknown, the temptation of getting a talented illustrator, who loves history and is well acquainted with the story of the Batavia, to do a drawing of each of the leading figures of this drama as he sees them, was irresistible -- hence we have the imagined portraits of Jeronimus Cornelisz (p 130), Francisco Pelsaert (left), Lucretia van den Mylen (p 213), Adriaen Jacobsz (p 214), Wiebbe Hayes (p 219, left), Gijsbert Bastiaensz (p 219, right).*

*Left :*
*If you were to ask a random sampling of Dutch people in the streets of Rotterdam, chances are not a single one of them would be able to tell you precisely who Francisco Pelsaert was. Indeed he remains one of the great forgotten figures of Dutch colonial history. Yet he was a fascinating man, and deserved better from posterity. The reason might be that his short but brilliant career was overshadowed by the accusations of cowardice that were later leveled against him for his behaviour following the shipwreck. He was also accused, without any proof to substantiate the claim, of illegally trading in objets d'art, a commercial practice to which he had actually introduced his employers.*

*Act 13*
*What became of the players*
*and onlookers of this drama ?*

It was on 20th September 1629 that Jan Pieterszoon Coen died of heart failure following the state of extreme weakness in which the "flux" (sic) had left him. The following excerpt from the minutes of the Council of the Indies gives a clear picture of the importance and solemnity of the founder of Batavia's funeral :

"At the head of the cortège walked the freemen, most of them in tears, formally grouped in 27 rows of four ;

"They were fo:lowed by a company of soldiers composed of picked men, then a company from outside the castle of Batavia, comprising 27 rows of five men.

"After them came the late Governor General's horse, very solemnly dressed in black velvet. It was led by the groom and his valet.

"Then came commissioner van der Lee, carrying the late Governor General's arms, followed by Job Christiaense Grij carrying his helmet with the black plume.

"After them walked upper merchant Nachtegael, carrying his stick, then upper merchant van der Burcht carrying his gauntlets and commandeur van den Broecke carrying his spurs.

"The paymaster general followed, carrying his sword.

"The coffin containing the mortal remains of the great Governor General was borne by four upper merchants, the captain of the burghers, three lieutenants and the captains of all the ships present."

Act 13
*What became of the players
and onlookers of this drama ?*

*Passengers of both sexes*
Died of illness or thirst on "*Batavia* graveyard"............9 children, 1 woman
Killed by the mutineers ........................................7 children, 12 women
Reached Batavia safe and sound on board
the *Zaandam* ........................................2 children, 7 women

Thus while 341 people were officially recorded in the ship's articles before her departure from Texel, 332 were physically present on board the *Batavia* when she set sail. Of this number, no fewer than 210 were to die before reaching their destination. What slaughter !

The reader will certainly be interested to learn what became of those survivors of whom we have heard most. Unfortunately the V.O.C archives on their subject are rather incomplete, but with bits and pieces of evidence gathered here and there it has nonetheless been possible to reconstitute, at least partially, the remainder of their passage through this world.

To render honour where it is due, let us see first what happened to Francisco Pelsaert. The new political and administrative scenario that evolved after the death of Jan Pieterszoon Coen was not to his advantage. Initially, the success of his rescue operation to save the *Batavia* survivors and recover the Company's goods was sufficient to stifle the criticisms with which certain people, intent on their own advancement and jealous of his over-rapid rise, were itching to attack him. What they criticized, regardless of his illness, was his having been unable to ensure strict discipline on board the *Batavia* during the voyage and the fact that he had abandoned to their unhappy fate the majority of his companions in misfortune, after selfishly appropriating the two ship's boats. On the other hand, his firm authority and scrupulousness throughout the trial on the Abrolhos, as well as the fairness of the sentences handed down by the court over which he had presided, were points in his favour. So he was actually granted a respite, being sent in April 1630 to be the right hand of Pieter Vlack, Councillor of the Indies[4], at Jambi on the island of Sumatra which the Portuguese were besieging : if they were to succeed, it would be a fatal blow to the flourishing trade in pepper exported from the sister island, Java, and which Portuguese activities had already endangered.

*His epistles full of bitter insinuations sent one after another to the high authorities of the V.O.C., following the return of the Zaandam to Batavia, make it quite clear that Antonio van Diemen, whose sour nature was perhaps the reflection of a particularly unfortunate physical appearance, had no love for the elegant Francisco Pelsaert.*

Jacob Jacobsz. It is quite logical that the captain and the two other men with him in the lost boat should not be included in the above list, for they had not been members of the *Batavia*'s crew.

4  A dignity to which, as the reader will remember, Pelsaert himself had been raised. Oddly, however, it would appear that he never sat on the Council. Probably Coen's successor, Jacques Specx, was afraid of causing a problem by making official the promotion of someone who had suddenly become almost *person non grata* and he thought it better to play for time, postponing his installation until he had himself received instructions. But letters and documents took half a year to travel to the other side of the world in those days and so Pelsaert was never able to sit on the Council and fulfil his high duties.

But the former *commandeur* of the *Batavia* was not taken in by the semblance of trust placed in him by sending him on an important mission. Sensitive as he was, he certainly suffered inwardly from the hostile attitude that some of the local hierarchy adopted towards him. He soon sank into a depression that was not helped by the insidious illness which continued to assail him, compounded by the terrible privations that he had recently endured. This being so it is understandable that, believing his days to be numbered, he decided to draw up a will as soon as he returned to Sumatra, on 14th June 1630 ; in it he made his mother sole legatee of all his worldly goods [5]. His last known letter, though written as soon as the *Zaandam* reached Batavia on 11th December 1629 (therefore long before his last mission to Sumatra) is surprisingly incoherent and reveals a physical and intellectual wreck of a man, whereas until then he had displayed not only great intellectual acuity but also an unusual analytical faculty and above all much skill in writing, and had an agile and concise style. But a few patches of light here and there reveal to what extent he was affected by the suspicion he felt growing all around him :

Portrait of Jacques Specx. Jan Pieterszoon Coen's death had been unexpected and therefore his election to the post of Governor General of the East Indies was intended to be provisional and in fact he was chosen only in consideration of his age. This provisional state of affairs was to last three years for it was not until 1632 that he was succeeded by Hendrik Brouwer, brother-in-law of the late Francisco Pelsaert. Specx's attitude to the former commandeur of the Batavia was always one of moderation for despite repeated attacks on Pelsaert by Antonio van Diemen, intent on his own advancement, he persisted in demonstrating his confidence in Pelsaert by appointing him second-in-command of a difficult military expedition to the island of Sumatra.

"I shall be able, God willing, to resume service with all the obedience that I have always endeavoured to tender to the Company. That has always been my policy, even when, already suffering from a poor general state of health I became a little weaker as the result of a serious illness that I contracted at the Cape of Good Hope and that had still not left me at the time of the shipwreck. On account of the latter, I was then forced to travel some twelve hundred miles in the longboat, in appalling conditions, plagued by hunger, thirst and other privations. (...) I have a perfectly clear conscience regarding my working relations with the Company.

He had never married.

I have committed no fault or error, nor any crime. I am sure of my good faith and can proclaim it before God and my employer."

The exact date of his death is not mentioned anywhere. It can only be said that it must have occurred at some time in the period between June and September 1630. A terse marginal note by Van Diemen on a Council of India minute, dated 13th September 1630, reports the death of Francisco Pelsaert [6]. Van Diemen, relentlessly pursuing his prosecution, adds that following Pelsaert's death jewels were found in his domicile showing that he had been carrying on illegal trading. He took care however not to accuse the deceased as yet of having attempted to procure personal gain, for he realized that there was always the possibility that Pelsaert's action might have been approved by the "High and Mighty" of the Amsterdam Chamber. Nevertheless, in 1632, when our unhappy hero's mother requested that her son's will be executed, this was refused by the V.O.C.'s superior governing body despite the fact that her request was supported by her son-in-law Hendrik Brouwer, outgoing Governor General of the East Indies. Indeed, a little later it was announced that all Francisco Pelsaert's assets would be confiscated and his arrears of wages stopped, which cast a posthumous slur on his memory for a very long time.

6 In a later letter to his superiors, Van Diemen stated that Pelsaert had "died after a long illness".

The former skipper of the *Batavia*, Adriaen Jacobsz, was even less fortunate in pleading his cause. The mutineers, under torture on the Abrolhos, accused him of being one of the principal instigators of an alleged plot to seize the ship. The author has already expressed his view about the veracity of such revelations extracted under torture. And indeed Jacobsz never admitted the crimes of which he was accused. Had he made such an avowal, it would of course have led him straight to the gallows. And if his intention had really been to lay hands on the *Batavia*, why on earth would he, of his own accord, have leapt into the lion's mouth by going to Batavia, when he knew that he would be blamed both for his fatal error of navigation and for the serious occurrences before then on board a ship of which he was captain? The fact that he chose such a risky course proves that he believed he had sufficiently strong arguments in his favour to convince those in high places of his innocence. Supposing, lastly, that he had really nourished the dark designs that some accused him of, would the shipwreck not have been the ideal occasion for him to get rid of the *commandeur* on the little "Traitors' Island" far from the eyes of too many embarrassing witnesses? Once that had been done, he would have had a free hand to seize the *Batavia*'s rich cargo and after sinking the dinghy to make away with the longboat to some welcoming Asian shore, accompanied by Cornelisz and the principal "conspirators". The remaining survivors would thus have been abandoned to certain death, and with

*Francisco Pelsaert's journal, carefully preserved in the National Archives at The Hague, is the source of our detailed knowledge of what happened in the period between 4th June and 7th July 1629, the date of the Zaandam's return to Batavia. It is a great pity that his earlier journals, covering the passage from Texel to The Cape and The Cape to the Abrolhos, were thrown overboard by drunkards immediately after the wreck, for had they not been lost, we should have known much more about the "demoniac atmosphere" that was supposed to have developed on board as the weeks went by, and also about what was said and done by the leading actors in a drama that was to become a tragedy. It is astounding that, despite the inhuman conditions in which he was living, the commandeur nevertheless found the time and the material means to draft this clear and exact document, in perfect handwriting, with no erasures, which reveals the strength of character and noble soul of a man whose memory was so unjustly tarnished.*

Act 13
*What became of the players
and onlookers of this drama ?*

them all possible witnesses of his crime would have disappeared...

The only charge that could be brought against Adriaen Jacobsz was in fact his notorious and scandalous liaison with Zwaantie Hendrix and his memorable binge at the Cape. Two very slender charges that today would have almost certainly resulted in acquittal, accompanied by warm congratulations on the masterly way in which he had safely conducted the overloaded longboat on a long and dangerous voyage thus making up for his earlier misdeeds. But the puritanism prevailing at the time was such that those sitting in judgment on him did not see things that way. A letter from Antonio van Diemen, as pitiless a critic as ever of other people's mistakes and weaknesses, gave him little hope of recovering his freedom in the near future. On 5th June 1631 he wrote

"We believe that Your Honours should again examine the case of the skipper of the *Batavia* and give orders concerning him. The accusations against him are serious and the fact that the ship and her occupants were so shamefully abandoned, thereby provoking the disaster of which we have learned, is inexcusable." Despite his repeated requests to be freed, Jacobsz was therefore left to languish and doubtless to die in the dungeons of the citadel of Batavia, unless he was subsequently condemned to death and executed. No statement regarding the fate that finally overcame him has been found in the Company's archives. As for Zwaantie Hendrix, the mistress from whom he could not bear to be separated, having played only a minor and passive role, she is not mentioned in the official documents. One may suppose though that she also had serious problems to contend with.

What is certain, on the other hand, is that Jan Evertsz the bo'sun, accused of the attack on Lucretia van den Mylen, did not have long to wait before learning his fate. He had barely arrived in Batavia with the other people on board the longboat when he was arrested, tried by a special court and sentenced to death. All his bones were broken and he was then put on the wheel. The charges against him had been confirmed by a detailed confession extracted from him and by certain witnesses.

The associates in the mutiny who, on account of Pelsaert's relative clemency had been sentenced only to corporal punishment, as we know, had to go before another court as soon as the *Zaandam* reached Batavia. The new judges did not have a modicum of pity amongst them and, on the contrary, were determined to make an example of the accused. Thus soldier (1st class) Jacob Pietersz was sentenced to "be

*Opposite right :
The beautiful Lucretia van den
Mylen. This is how Marten de
Vos or Frans Floris might have
painted her : dignified, serious,
glowing with the type of beauty
which was most admired at the
time in Dutch and Flemish
society.*

*Page 214 :
An outsdanding seaman, though
of an impulsive and lecherous
nature, Adriaen Jacobsz
can only be accused
of one single mistake :
he failed to keep
accurate track
of his ship's latitude.
He then proceeded to redeem
himself through a remarkable
feat of navigation when he
successfully managed to bring
the Batavia's long boat to safe
haven. His being brought to
trial on the strength of mere
rumours, and his lengthy
confinement in a dungeon
where he may very well have
spent the rest of his life, will
remain one of history's great
miscarriages of justice.*

213

214

*Act 13*
*What became of the players
and onlookers of this drama ?*

broken from head to foot and his body placed on the wheel until death ensued". It was the death sentence too for under merchant Salomon Deschamps, cadets Daniel Cornelisz, Hans Heijlweck and Lucas Gellisz who were all to be hanged and, in the case of Cornelisz only, the right hand to be amputated. Rogier Decker and Abraham Gerritsz, who were respectively cabin boy and ship's boy, were given a sentence that was as extraordinary as it was cruel, for their judges decided that only one of them would be sent to the gallows after drawing lots ! The survivor would simply receive a whipping, compounded by the dread ordeal of being made to wear a weighty halter on his neck. Six minor felons were sentenced to corporal punishments ranging from whipping to branding, and including the halter, before being put into irons in a dungeon for three years... These implacable verdicts were executed in public on Thursday, 1st February 1630, at the castle of Batavia. Right up to the last minute, the condemned men had to suffer the insults and

*The penalty of the wheel as administered in the first half of the 17th century and as it was very probably applied to Jacob Pietersz. First, the condemned man was laid out horizontally on a wooden horse, with wrists and ankles bound. Then the executioner began his task, breaking in turn each segment of the limbs and the backbone, by violent blows with a heavy iron bar. When an articulation had thus been made in the middle of the thighs, in particular, the sinister officiant could then bend the lower limbs of his victim until the heels met the back of his head. During this operation, the broken thigh-bones often perforated the bruised flesh and protruded. In this revolting position the tortured prisoner was then tied to a cart-wheel still fitted with the axle. This was then planted upright in the ground and the crowd was then allowed to come near to contemplate the sight at leisure and witness the agonizing and long drawn out death pangs of the condemned. Sometimes the executioner, having been instructed to be "merciful", cut short the victim's sufferings by strangling him. When this was not done, the death throes could last for hours or even, in the case of a particularly robust constitution, for days.*

# The citadel of Batavia

*This map of Batavia is dated 1627. Nothing had changed when Pelsaert and his small band of famished survivors reached Batavia safely on board the* Zaandam *in July 1629.*

*The citadel of Batavia was built according to a star-shaped design, traditional at that time and, strongly armed, it formed a fortress that was virtually impregnable. Indeed, all the native peoples of the island of Java who at first tried to resist the yoke that the Dutch colonizer was forcing on them, met with resounding defeat each time they courageously tried to storm the citadel's walls, however many and however determined they were. Within the walls were the guardhouse, the apartments and office of the Governor General, the council chamber of the East Indies Council, accommodations for the Councillors, the barracks and their outbuildings, the dungeons and the church. Guns, protected by a parapet, were arranged on either side of each point of the star.*
*In 1629, just two years after completion of the building works that had begun ten years earlier, the citadel was square and had four corner bastions that had been named "Diamond" and "Ruby", on the landward side, and "Pearl" and "Sapphire" on the side facing the sea.*

*On the right page engraving, the "Waterpoort" appears only as an opening cut in the ramparts of the citadel. The proud portico built of stone blocks that was to have been inserted here was at this time lying on the sea bed. Originally, all the buildings within the citadel were intended for military or administration purposes. Thus, having gone through the "Waterpoort", which looked onto the moat linked by a canal to the harbour where the Indiamen moored, one would have found the following : the guardhouse, the offices of the Company's senior management, the Governor General's apartments, the supplies store, the arsenal, tree-shaded courtyards, the armoury, the church.*

*There were five gates in all : one, as mentioned above, gave onto the sea, another onto a pool and the three others were in the side and back walls of the fortress. As from the end of the 17th century, various departments of the V.O.C. began to settle outside the walls of the citadel proper and gradually the soldiers themselves began to move to quarters outside. Meanwhile the management of the Company endeavoured to render the citadel more elegant by laying paved walks and gardens and constructing non-military buildings of fine appearance.*
*A similar portico replaced the one lost in such unfortunate circumstances. This was to be only temporary, however, for an incomparably grander entrance was built to form the new "Waterpoort".*

216

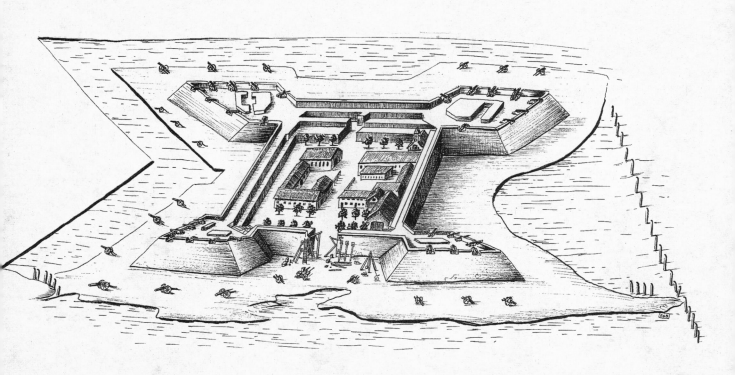

*Act 13*
*What became of the players
and onlookers of this drama ?*

gibes of a population who were horrified by the accounts of the carnage that had been perpetrated on the Abrolhos.

Now regarding the "good" ones in the story : it is known that Wiebbe Hayes, promoted to sergeant by Pelsaert, was again congratulated on his exemplary behaviour and the courage he had displayed, especially in the darkest hours of the attack by Cornelisz' troops. The Council of the Indies considered, moreover, that the decisive role he had played in taking prisoner the mutineers' leader and his principal accomplices deserved more than the 18 guilders monthly emoluments that the *commandeur* had awarded him. Although this was already a handsome figure, it was increased to 40 guilders a month and Hayes was promoted at the same time to the rank of standard-bearer with the promise of a future promotion in keeping with his merits. Thus provided for, the strategist of the "Isle of Cats" was to continue his career with the colonial troops. Perhaps he eventually died in battle in the Moluccas or elsewhere. Who can tell ? Perhaps he left behind him the risks of his profession and returned to the old world after his brief spell in the limelight. The fact remains that there is no trace of him after his return to Batavia.

*Standard battle dress for a soldier belonging to the V.O.C. in the 17th century. Apparel of this kind was not strictly regulated. For example, in some engravings of the period, one sees soldiers wearing helmets, while in others, such as this one, they wear a hat. During the long voyages of the Indiamen, soldiers would have been scarcely distinguishable from sailors, for both wore a loose-fitting jacket or tunic, baggy trousers, leggings or sometimes puttees, and a close-fitting cap or bonnet. So it was doubtless looking something like this, in rather colourless apparel, that Wiebbe Hayes and his brothers in arms so valiantly repelled the mutineers' attacks against their positions on the island of West Wallabi.*

The minister, Gijsbert Bastiaensz, tried to forget his sorrow in marriage with the widow of the bailiff of the city of Batavia, in 1631. But fate had decreed that he was not to enjoy conjugal happiness for long and he died of dysentery in the Banda Islands two years later. His daughter Judick, the Abrolhos "bride", was to suffer a sad fate. Her two successive marriages did not give her the material security for which she understandably longed and after the death of her last husband, at Ambon in 1634, she found herself "down and out". When this fact came to the ears of the *Heeren XVII*, in a moment of generosity unusual for them, they gave her a capital sum of 300 guilders as an outright grant, not a loan, "in consideration of her widowhood" and another, of the same sum, "to compensate for the affliction to which she had been submitted in the course of the *Batavia* tragedy."

To complete the list of principal actors in this drama there remains only Lucretia van den Mylen. After enduring so many ordeals and such distressing humiliation, she arrived in Batavia at the end of her terrible voyage only to find that

 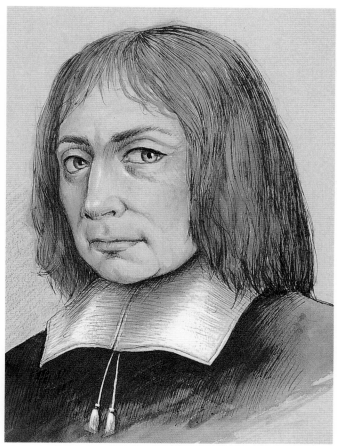

her husband had died shortly before. It seems that the single state was not much the fashion in Batavia, for she too soon started a new life with Jacob Cornelisz Cuick, a simple infantry sergeant, who happened to be the brother-in-law of her own half-sister. The couple, who had no children, managed to survive the thousand and one difficulties — largely problems of health — with which life in the colonies was fraught at that time, and returned to the Netherlands towards the end of the year 1635, where they settled at Leiden. We find one last mention of Lucretia in 1641, for her name appears in the baptism registry in a local parish, when she became godmother to one of her young nephews by marriage.

What a strange and chaotic destiny she had ! One imagines that her dreams must sometimes have been haunted by memories of the drama whose various acts were performed before her very eyes, and in which she had been forced to play a leading role, a drama so charged with emotion and with such incredible repercussions that it ranks among the greatest and most tragic of major adventures in the history of man.

*Right :*
*Gijsbert Bastiaensz certainly fails to show strength of character during the tragedy of the Batavia. The moral authority implied in his position should have given him the power to temper Jeronimus Cornelisz' cruelty. Yet he opted for a mostly passive attitude, taking refuge in prayer, showing but little outrage at the slaughter of his wife and children, failing even to stand up in defence of honour and virtue of his sole remaining relative, his daughter Judick. His attitude was at best am-biguous during the "Cats' Island" skirmishes, and the account he left us in his famous letter, dripping with self-pity, displays a remarkable lack of physical courage in the man.*

*Left :*
*The reader shouldn't wonder at seeing Wiebbe Hayes so magnifi-cently arrayed. The majority of non-commissioned soldiers of the time were younger sons of good families. The works of Rembrandt, Hals, Pourbus the Elder, de Vos and other Flemish old masters show that the wearing of the neck ruff was common practice among military personnel of all ranks.*

219

# act 14

## *The discovery of the wreck*

History, it is a well-known fact, often follows unusual paths. We might well still be searching for the wreck of the *Batavia* had the Second World War not given rise to a boom in, of all things, lobsters ! The story is certainly worth telling.

In the course of 1942 the Allied armed forces, especially the Americans, wishing to improve their men's daily fare introduced canned lobster which quickly, as was to be expected, became one of the favourite dishes in the mess. This sudden demand gave a fillip to an industry that had been in its infancy when war broke out. At that time, anyone who was fond of lobster, as yet not very widely known to the general public, could buy a dozen rock-lobsters for a few shillings ! This kind of price meant that catching crustaceans was no more than a marginal activity for commercial fishermen.

The sudden increase in demand, in such considerable proportions too, led a number of young West Australians, keen to succeed and also to benefit from new legislation that promised no less than exemption from national service to anyone who would take up this new type of fishing and undertake to sell 75% of his production to the cannery that had just opened at Geraldton, to turn their sights to the Abrolhos where it was known that there were sizeable reserves of the crustacean in question.

However, as the distance between the Abrolhos and the continent was on average some sixty kilometres and as the ocean was often very rough in these parts, there was obviously no question of going to sea every morning and coming home in the evening. So makeshift dwellings began to emerge on the Abrolhos, with no concern for their appearance, where our fishermen, encouraged by the prospect of good earnings, were prepared to spend a large part of their time [1].

*The monumental portico which had been designed to decorate the "waterpoort" of the citadel of Batavia consisted of 137 stones. The numbers engraved on these enabled the archaeologists of the Western Australian Maritime Museum to reconstitute the gigantic puzzle and to achieve this magnificent result.*

*Above :*
*Detail showing the way in which the squared stones are assembled. It will be noticed that some of them are finely decorated. Experts of our end-of-century period claim to be the past masters in the art of the pre-fabricated building system. If they see this structure perhaps they will be a little more modest in their claim.*

---

[1] This situation lasted until 1963 when the State Fisheries Department introduced strict regulations governing this form of fishing, authorizing it only in certain months of the year and limiting the number of boats

*It is probable that this mound of stones gave its name to Beacon Island, but it is unlikely that goes back to the time of the Batavia tragedy.*

It was in the course of this second protracted contact between man and the Abrolhos (the first having been for the extraction of guano in the last quarter of the 19th century) that some islets of the archipelago became inhabited, being selected in consideration of their accessibility by sea far more than for their attractiveness or their outlook. Some islands, at first glance more attractive than others, thus remained deserted, being too well protected by the reef encircling them or by reef flats on which there was insufficient depth of water, even at high tide.

Among the islands that for these reasons attracted the lobster fishermen's attention were Great and Little Pigeon Islands and also Beacon Island [2]. This island, lying very low in the water, an insignificant little

and also the number of pots carried by each boat.

2  At the northern extemity of this island there is a well-made cairn that can be climbed and which is made of limestone slabs piled up to a height of 1.75 metres, not counting the large wooden post that tops it, like a mast.  It has been established that this structure dates from 1897 and that it served as a triangulation point for a surveyor belonging to the colonial administration, A.J. Wells, who was instructed to carry out a surve

platform formed by the gradual accumulation of coral skeletons over thousands of years, was the island where Bevilacqua, Marten, Johnson, Gliddon and others established their quarters : on the north shore there was deep water where they could easily launch their boats, and there they built the cabins that were an essential part of their arduous but lucrative operation.

Having settled there for this purpose, they got to know, over the years, every little recess of the reefs around and especially all the nooks and crannies of Morning Reef, the edge of the "pedestal" that supported Beacon Island. And it was John Gliddon[3] who was historically the first, in 1957, to notice, lying on the bottom at a depth of a little less than ten metres, blocks of stone that were too perfectly squared to have been shaped naturally. However, not only was he not particularly communicative by nature and therefore didn't say a word about

*Johnny Gliddon, a seasonal resident on Beacon Island, was the first to spot the pieces of the stone portico lying on the bottom, along Morning Reef. But having no historical knowledge about the* Batavia *story he did not see any connection between them and the wreck of the* Batavia.

what he had seen, but also any connection there might be between these stones and the *Batavia*'s cargo, which was not obvious in any event, simply did not occur to him.

Three years later, in 1960, a Beacon Island fisherman known as "Pop" Marten discovered a skeleton when he was digging a hole to plant a wooden post, near his cabin. Not knowing much about anatomy, he left it to an acquaintance of his in Geraldton, to whom he had casually mentioned his somewhat unusual discovery, to complete the excavation and to establish formally that it was in fact a human skeleton. A police enquiry followed and the press gave some coverage to this strange find.

_____

f the various islets of the archipelago with a view to collecting guano from them. It is doubtless on account of this cairn, which is visible from fairly far at sea, that the islet became known as Beacon Island, instead of its former name of Goos Monument. Beacon Island became the official name in 1968, on the recommendation of Bill Newbold of the Geraldton Professional Fishermen's Association.

He had originally established his quarters on Great Pigeon Island but moved to Beacon Island in 1963.

This led to a controversy. Historians at that time were in general agreed that the *Batavia* had been wrecked in the southern group of the archipelago, named for this reason as we have seen, the "Pelsaert Group". Only Henrietta Drake-Brockman, a woman of 58 who had been conducting her own enquiry alone into the fate of the *Batavia* and had made it her life's passion, did not agree. Her arguments carried considerable weight, too. Having studied Francisco Pelsaert's journal, which she had taken the initiative of having translated from old Dutch, and a letter written by the minister, Gijsbert Bastiaensz, two of the leading figures in the tragedy, she maintained in spite of all opposition that the shipwreck could only have occurred in the northern group, for the simple reason that it was there alone that there were islands on which marsupials, in this case tammar-wallabies, were found, and also some water-holes including one which held water that was just drinkable. The discovery of a skeleton on Beacon Island, adding weight to her arguments as it did, although at that stage she did not believe much in the historic role of this islet, was therefore of the greatest interest to her, even though many pieces of the puzzle had yet to be fitted together. "Nonsense !" said the "conformists", "your famous skeleton may well be that of some sailor buried, like so many others anonymously..."

Nevertheless, in April of that same year 1960, a first small expedition, the result of a private initiative, went to the Abrolhos. Hugh Edwards, a journalist who was also an experienced professional diver who had always been fascinated by stories of wrecks, and Maur Hammond, a very talented underwater photographer plunged in and for two weeks worked tirelessly over the reef flats and reef slopes of the Wallabi group. Their meticulous searches led them to find the three-masted barque *Hadda*, sunk in 1877, and also a barge that had been carrying guano and sank in 1881. But no trace of the *Batavia*... So with some chagrin, they returned to the mainland.

The two companions had only just left when, by an extraordinary quirk of fate, Dave Johnson, one of the lobster fishermen living on Beacon Island, spotted an anchor and some cannon on the sea-floor while he was laying his lobster pots along Morning Reef. He was aware of the argument regarding the position of the *Batavia* wreck and immediately suspected that he was "onto something". But leaving aside the fact that being unable to swim, he could not dive down and look more closely at his find, he did not immediately realize the considerable *historical* importance of his discovery. He simply thought that one day some lucky fellow with the appropriate equipment would probably be able to bring to the surface this load of old iron and sell it for scrap metal, thus making a tidy profit. (The first Museum Act, by virtue of which any remains of the *Batavia* became Crown property, was not promulgated until 1964 [4]).

*A journalist by profession and a great diver in his spare time, Hugh Edwards was the first to carry out a systematic search in the Wallabi group for the purpose of locating the wreck of the Batavia. Although luck did not smile on him in this respect, he is certainly, on account of the active part he played subsequently in exploring the sunken ship as well as the important finds he made on land, one of those chiefly responsible for identifying the different islands and islets where important parts of the tragedy were played out. His perfect knowledge of the subject, together with his innate reporter's flair make his "Islands of Angry Ghosts" one of the great best-sellers of recent years.*

---

4 It was to be added to and strengthened by a second "Museum Act" (1969) and a "Maritime Archaeolo

In April 1963, following fruitful exploration of the site of the *Zeewyck* wreck in the "Pelsaert Group", the sixteen members of that expedition determined they would get together again to resume the search for the *Batavia*. But expeditions of this kind are always very expensive to mount and so when one of the members of the group, Max Cramer, a builder-cum-diver from Geraldton, offered to continue looking for the wreck, diving with his brother and friends who, like them, lived not far from the archipelago and who were prepared to lend a hand, the offer was accepted. It was with a little regret that the others did so, for the glory of being the one to make a discovery of this importance was understandably the dream of each of these adventurers.

In Max Cramer's own words :
"Mrs Henrietta Drake-Brockman's remarkable work had determined

*While it was Henrietta's deductions that led searchers to concentrate on the Wallabi group, it was Dave Johnson, the lobster fisherman, who had the glory of being the first to observe the wreck lying on the bottom and of having the intuition that it was the Batavia.*
*He subsequently played a leading role in the operations of raising the guns and other remains extracted from the wreck.*

he area within the archipelago where the wreck must be and I therefore decided to devote my leisure time to a systematic search on land, in the Wallabi group, where it was now almost certain that the wreck was situated. I thereupon set out to sift the debris scattered all over the sand of the various islets to see if I could find any fragments of pottery or remains of other utilitarian objects, even coins, etc. I began on Goss Island, for in the minister's account of the tragic events following

ct" (1973) and lastly, in 1976, the Commonwealth Government promulgated Federal legislation : the istoric Shipwreck Act. The object of these legal provisions is to protect wrecks of historic interest against ooting by covetous or ill-informed people.

the sinking of the *Batavia*, he refers to a small island with a white sand beach. Goss Island appeared to be the only one in the group answering to this description. Then one day after I had spent the week-end with my brother Graham and my friend Greg Allen, I happened to moor off Beacon Island where I had heard tell of a skeleton being found by Dave Johnson. I'd also been told that "Pop" Marten had found the base of a lamp. When we asked them about these finds, Dave Johnson kindly offered to take us to the most easily accessible of the sites of his discoveries, for in fact it turned out that he had made several[5].

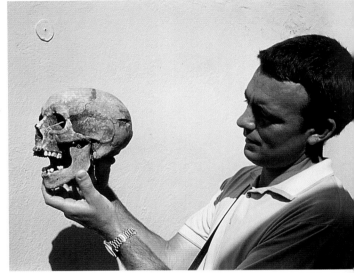

*Above left :*
*Uncovering the third skeleton, in August 1963. One of the members of the expedition, Dr. Naioom Haimson, is examining the traces of wounds that had been inflicted on the head and neck.*

*Above right :*
*In 1964 this time, Ron Taylor, photographer with the great expedition that had taken place two years previously, displays the skull of the fourth skeleton, the remainder of which is still under Dave Johnson's house. On the left temple one can see the trace of a fatal blow, doubtless made by a sword.*

"We dug in the place that our guide showed us (actually at the foot of a clothes hoist) and sure enough, there was a skeleton, about eighteen inches down in the sand. So far there seemed nothing especially indicative about our find, until suddenly we realized, on looking more closely at the skeleton, that not only was it, strangely, in a sitting position, but the cervical vertebrae were broken at the base of the skull and, in particular, there was lead musket shot in the ribs ! The historical significance of this skeleton, which was collected a little later on by researchers from the Western Australian Maritime Museum, was obvious. From that point on, things began to happen at top speed. For on Beacon Island there was a little sandy creek that could, at a pinch, be called a beach, and moreover on the island numerous fragments of very old household objects were found. It was clear that the survivors of the *Batavia* had been here. Then the weather got worse and we who had gone out for three days had to stay twelve days on

5 He had discovered other human bones while digging prior to laying the concrete floor of his fisherman cabin.

the island ! It was then that Dave Johnson, seeing us eagerly pursuing our search, naively asked me, on the morning of 4th June 1963 :

- Well, what are you actually looking for ?
- Why, the wreck of the *Batavia*, of course !

"Then, with a little knowing smile, he said :
- Come with me, I'll show you where it is...

"He took us in his boat to a point situated on the slope of Morning Reef and there we jumped into the water not really convinced we were going to see anything, for it seemed too good to be true. When the air-bubbles had cleared, my heart began to beat wildly as I saw the first remains of what I immediately realized must be the *Batavia*, on account of the guns lying on the bottom. Those must be the guns, I thought, that had been thrown overboard in a vain attempt to lighten the vessel so as to release her from her coral prison. The following day we returned to the same spot, and began an epic adventure in which, using four steel drums of forty-four gallons each, linked by means of a flexible 3-inch tube to the exhaust-pipe of Dave Johnson's boat, we applied the famous Archimedes principle and were thus able

*One of the many iron guns scattered around the wreck, caked with coral concretions.*

to lift from the bottom a composite[6] cannon, on which was the seal o the V.O.C. plus the letter "A", standing for the Amsterdam Chamber o Commerce.

"Obviously, there could no longer be the slightest doubt Everything fitted perfectly : thus Beacon Island was the infamou *"Batavia graveyard"* of the story, and the eastern most of the tiny islet bordering Morning Reef was Traitors' Island. Incidentally I might ad that as a builder, I estimated roughly that the blocks of stone lying or the bottom near the guns, which had been intended for the construc tion of a great portico, must weigh about thirty tons. Later, thes stones were raised and assembled (today one can admire the reconstit uted portico at the Western Australian Maritime Museum) and in a they weighed thirty-one tons !"

*Right :*
*The first gun recovered from the wreck, in June 1963, was of composite type and weighed 1.5 tons ! It is now exhibited at the Geraldton Yacht Club. The only other one like it, sawn through so that its complex composition can be better understood by the public, is to be seen at the Western Australian Maritime Museum.*

*Below :*
*One of the five bronze guns brought up in 1963. The seal of the Rotterdam Admiralty and the date of manufacture (1603) are engraved on the gun.*

When examination of the cannon that had beer brought to the surface formally confirmed its origin, the discovery by Max Cramer and his friends caused an enor mous sensation. A large-scale expedition was mountec without delay, with the army and the Royal Australiar navy placing at the disposal of the team two small boat equipped appropriately for this type of work and some o their best divers. As for the good companions of the expe dition to the wreck of the *Zeewyck*, they of course al joined in.

Their first dive onto the wreck of the *Batavia* tool place on 29th July 1963. It was to be followed by many

6 Cannon of this kind were made of a copper cylinder, outside which was a sheath of iron staves. Th whole was then iron-banded with hoops embedded in a soft solder. Copper was used again for the oute skin of the gun.

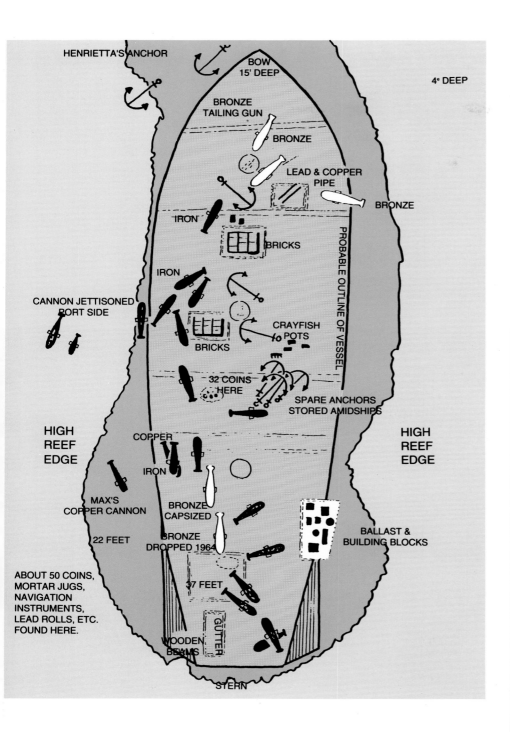

HENRIETTA'S ANCHOR

BOW
15' DEEP

4° DEEP

BRONZE
TAILING GUN

BRONZE

LEAD & COPPER
PIPE

BRONZE

IRON

BRICKS

PROBABLE OUTLINE OF VESSEL

IRON

CANNON JETTISONED
PORT SIDE

BRICKS

CRAYFISH
POTS

32 COINS
HERE

SPARE ANCHORS
STORED AMIDSHIPS

HIGH
REEF
EDGE

HIGH
REEF
EDGE

COPPER

IRON

MAX'S
COPPER CANNON

BRONZE
CAPSIZED

22 FEET

BRONZE
DROPPED 1964

BALLAST &
BUILDING BLOCKS

ABOUT 50 COINS,
MORTAR JUGS,
NAVIGATION
INSTRUMENTS,
LEAD ROLLS, ETC.
FOUND HERE.

37 FEET

GUTTER

WOODEN
BEAMS

STERN

*A plan of the wreck drawn after the underwater survey carried out in August 1963 by Lieutenant H. Donohue of the Royal Australian Navy, who was commanding GPV 958. The outline of the vessel was added later, and is approximate. This plan is not absolutely exact and the Western Australian Maritime Museum's archaeologists have since then drawn one that is much more precise. Nevertheless, this one tells us more, for many articles were removed in the period following the first plan and therefore inevitably do not appear on the second.*

others, interspersed by occasional days of forced inactivity due to the state of the sea. A varied harvest consisting largely of "bellarmines"[7], cannon balls, a gun-powder measure and an apothecary's mortar, was brought to the surface, and also four more superb bronze cannons that

---

[7] These small jars of varnished earthenware, holding approximately half a litre, usually contained "hollands" or "geneva" spirits, which is not the same as the gin drunk by the English, and is today as much appreciated as ever in Holland where it goes by the name of "borrl" or, in slang, "neut". The neck of the jar was decorated with a raised medallion portraying a bearded man, purposely made to look rather grotesque, whom the English disrespectfully likened to the Italian cardinal, Robert Bellarmin, a disciple of Saint Ignatius Loyola, future saint and doctor of the Catholic church. The Protestants of the United Provinces, and their German and English co-religionists, made him the butt of their jokes for with his penchant for controversy he deployed great zeal (often misplaced) in denouncing the "heresy" proposed by the reformed religion.

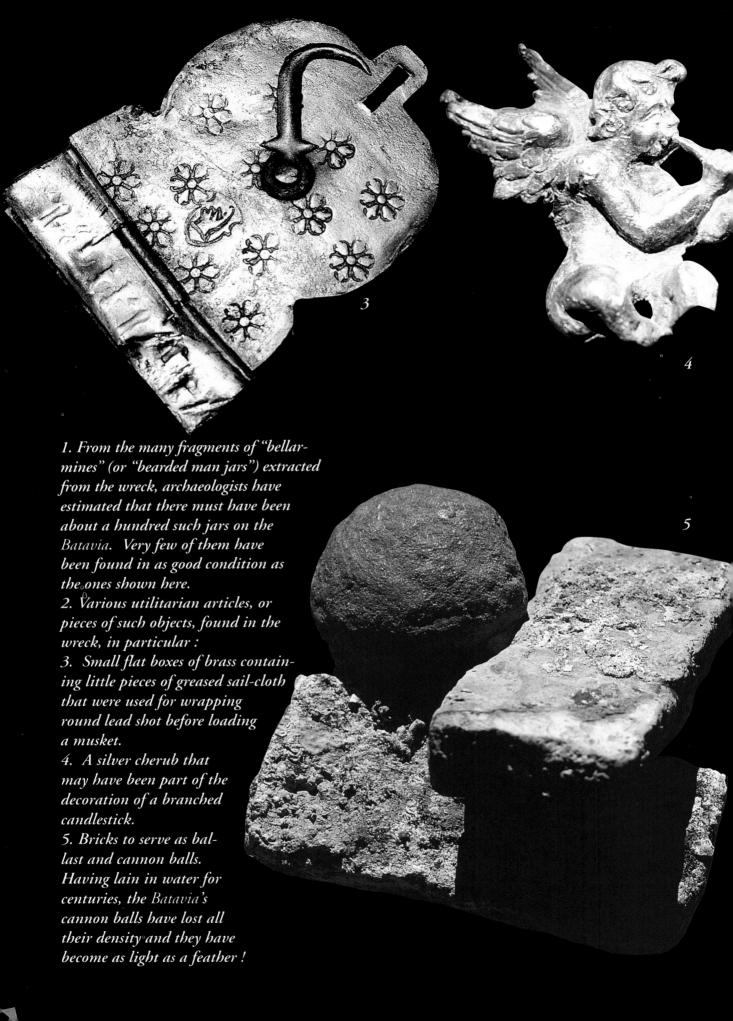

**1.** From the many fragments of "bellar-mines" (or "bearded man jars") extracted from the wreck, archaeologists have estimated that there must have been about a hundred such jars on the *Batavia*. Very few of them have been found in as good condition as the ones shown here.

**2.** Various utilitarian articles, or pieces of such objects, found in the wreck, in particular :

**3.** Small flat boxes of brass containing little pieces of greased sail-cloth that were used for wrapping round lead shot before loading a musket.

**4.** A silver cherub that may have been part of the decoration of a branched candlestick.

**5.** Bricks to serve as ballast and cannon balls. Having lain in water for centuries, the *Batavia*'s cannon balls have lost all their density and they have become as light as a feather !

6. Decorated dish and ewers of silver. The
ewers, finely engraved with designs chosen
to flatter the taste of the potential purchaser,
were obviously some of the famous "toys" that
were to be sold to the Great Mogul or to dignitaries of his Court. The *Batavia* was to inaug-
urate this new type of trade that Francisco
Pelsaert had advocated in his *Remonstrantie*.
7. Everyday spoons made of pewter.
8. Lacemaking bobbins, also pewter.

9

10

9 . - *This astrolabe was discovered in 1964, during another dive onto the wreck. It is exhibited at the Geraldton Region Museum.*

10 . - *The* Batavia's *bell, that marked the rhythm of life on board, primarily by sounding the change of watch, is admired by Jeremy Green (on the right) and Graeme Henderson (on the left) just after it has been recovered from the wreck. This evocative relic is now part of the collection exhibited at the Geraldton Region Museum.*

11 .- *Earthenware receptacles known as "Alborelli" and pots of similar kind, covered with a light-coloured tin glaze on which were painted polychrome designs. All these vessels would have been used for medicinal purposes and the fact that they were found grouped together suggests that they were in the ship's doctor's medicine chest.*

were hauled with great difficulty, given their enormous weight, to the nearest shore. But the most sought-after of all wealth to be found in a wreck is, understandably, the treasure in coin that it may contain, and at the conclusion of the first series of dives this had still not been found. After a long consultation, the participants finally decided, rather reluctantly, to use small amounts of explosive to release the part of the *Batavia*'s cargo that had become coral-encrusted.

This operation was in fact very successful, for it enabled them to recover, amongst other treasures, an astrolabe, various utilitarian articles, a large selection of silver coins — German thalers, Dutch rijksdollars, and others. Henrietta Drake-Brockman, despite her relatively advanced age and her lack of experience of diving, insisted on seeing for herself the object of so many years' dreams ; her youthful attitude and perfect physical condition astounded everyone at the Beacon

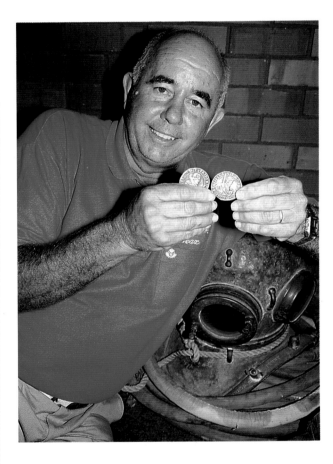

*Max Cramer shows the two gems of his small personal collection of articles found in the Batavia wreck : above, a silver thaler from the Holy Roman Germanic Empire, dated 1624 and bearing on the obverse the arms of the Duchy of Schleswig-Holstein-Gottorf and on the reverse the effigy of Frederick III (1616-1659), Grand Duke by the grace of God (Dei gratia), and right, a Rijksdaalder (also known as a Dutch thaler, or Rijksdollar) dated 1607, from the Province of Utrecht (one of the seven Protestant United Provinces).*

Island headquarters, and she was able, to view the wreck, to her satisfaction.

In August of the same year we find Hugh Edwards again : having decided to carry out some investigations on land, he went to the "high islands" of the archipelago where he noted that there were some rudimentary forts or emplacements built of dry stones. But it was the pupils of Aquinas school, Perth, who made two expeditions, in 196 and 1965, during which they carried out the first excavations that coul

*Henrietta Drake-Brockman's perspicacity cannot be too highly praised, for without her contribution, we should perhaps still be looking for the Batavia. She is seen here in August 1963 on Dave Johnson's fishing boat, registration number G 70, preparing to dive into the sea to view the wreck... and she will have the satisfaction of seeing the anchor that henceforth bears her name and remains on the reef. (next page,1)*

really be regarded as scientific, on the site of the "fort" that was nearer to the shore at the place known as Slaughter Point. In the course of these two trips, they found fragments of bellarmines, iron nails, small pieces of iron, a roughly fashioned ladle made of lead, and assorted bones (tammars, seals, birds) mixed with oyster shells, which proved undeniably that Wiebbe Hayes' people had certainly lived there and that they had built this structure, the first ever built by white men in Australia[8]. More skeletons[9] having been exhumed from the coral sand

*The Batavia's main anchor still lies on Morning Reef. Shown here is one of the eight that the ship carried ; it was recovered from the central part of the wreck in 1971, together with two other similar anchors, which suggests that they were not in use at the time of the tragedy, but had been stored amidships in the hold, near the foot of the main mast.*

---

8   The Houtman Abrolhos are too far from the continent ever to have been inhabited or, very probably, even visited by Aborigines who did not have boats of a kind that could have made the journey.

9   On Beacon Island five skeletons have been discovered to date, all by accident, for no large-scale excavation has been carried out on what was formerly "the *Batavia* graveyard". They were discovered as follows :
- 1960, March : First skeleton discovered by "Pop" Marten and Dr Maxwell D. Roilance, a few paces from William Bevilacqua's cabin (now John Gliddon's). These bones were given to the Netherlands, as part of the Ancods allocation ;
- 1963 : Second skeleton discovered in June, under the clothes hoist outside Dave Johnson's house. First of all, Max Cramer removed the skull and handed it over to the police. The musket shot that was found among the ribs can now be seen with other remains from the *Batavia* in the wheel-shaped window decorating the bar of the "Batavia Motor Inne" at Geraldton. In August of the same year during the large-scale expedition financed by the daily paper "The West Australian", excavation was carried through on the location of this skeleton. In the course of it, a cloth purse with a metal neck was found, containing two copper coins, which had probably belonged to the victim. Subsequently the police returned the skull, and with the other bones it was given to the West Australian medical authorities ;
- 1963 : In the same month, August, a third skeleton was discovered alongside Dave Jonhson's house, showing evidence of violence (a long gash on the skull, a wound on the right shoulder caused by a sword-blade, right foot missing). This skeleton is now a very remarkable exhibit in the Western Australian Maritime Museum (Fremantle) ;
- 1964 : In December a fourth skeleton was discovered by Ron Taylor, a television cameraman, and Hugh Edwards, journalist, while they were filming a reconstruction of the *Batavia* drama. It was Dave Johnson's revelations about the bones found while laying the foundations of his house that led to this discovery. The skeleton is only partially accessible, and the head alone has been recovered. There is a linear depression doubtless made by a sword) on the left temple. The cranium in question is at present in the Geraldton Region Museum ;
- 1990 : Fifth skeleton uncovered by John Gliddon, while digging a hole for a septic tank near his house.

1.- *Henrietta's anchor*

2.- *In the course of a dive in 1967, John Mikalinko is studying one of the* Batavia's *five bronze guns. This one was brought to the surface in 1972. Since then it has been in the Geraldton Region Museum. It was cast in 1616 by Arent van der Put for the Rotterdam admiralty.*

3 to 6 .- *The extensive manoeuvres of 1973 : equipped with powerful suction dredgers and compressed air chain saws, the Maritime Museum experts are at work on the site of the wreck. With this equipment they will be able to bring to the surface, as well as the carved stone blocks for the portico t the citadel of Batavia, some of the pieces of oak forming part of the structure and the hull of the vessel, in particular the sternpost (support for the rudder), the deckbeams and the hull planking (the external skin of the hull) from the rear port side.*

of Beacon Island meanwhile, the background of the tragedy of 1629 was gradually emerging, piece by piece, from the shadows. Virtually none of the pieces of the puzzle was missing now and it became clear that Pelsaert's account was very accurate.

The last part of the Act concerning the "discovery" was to be written in 1973 when experts from the Western Australian Maritime Museum which had opened barely four years earlier, decided to carry through excavation of the wreck and of Beacon Island in a truly scientific manner. This was to be an undertaking of greater scope, spread out over a much longer period of time and, in particular, operating with logistic and financial support of a different order altogether [10].

Accommodation, workshops and jetties were built for the purpose on "the *Batavia* graveyard" while a large vessel belonging to the

*Previous spread :*
*The "mirror" of the stern and an imposing portion of the Batavia's hull, reassembled from oak timbers from which the coral was removed and the timbers cut into pieces "in situ" before being brought to the surface, constitute the main attraction of the Western Australian Maritime Museum, together with the majestic stone portico that has been built exactly as it was to have been, from the great stones raised from the sea-bed.*

museum and christened Henrietta — a tribute to the instigator of the discovery of the *Batavia*, who had died shortly before — served as a base for the divers.

It was possible, with such extensive means at their disposal, to free from its sand and coral grave a large part of the oak ribs and hull of the *Batavia,* which they found astonishingly well-preserved. All the pieces were numbered and then cut into sections and brought to the surface, where they were chemically treated and assembled to form the magnificent reconstitution which, since then, has been much admired by visitors to the Western Australian Maritime Museum.

---

10  Millions of dollars (we were given a figure of 52 million) were spent on the whole operation covering the costs of the expedition proper, of conveying the relics to Fremantle, treating them, fitting together or reassembling (the portico) in order to give them the best possible public display. The generosity of the public authorities, who all too often are somewhat reserved when it comes to helping cultural enterprises, is particularly laudable ; this is, of course, an undertaking of national interest.

*July 1963. Having been brought to the surface one by one, the great stones that were to form the portico were first of all stacked on Beacon Island (left). Later, they were loaded onto the fishing boat Aquila and firmly secured (seen here in Geraldton harbour : above, left) ; Lewis Eves, Geraldton Region Museum's architect, is gazing with interest at this rather unusual cargo (above, right). It was subsequently taken by road to Fremantle, where archaeologists patiently applied their renowned skill to reconstituting the immense puzzle.*

Although the sea had inexorably worn away the part of the hull that had not been buried, it had fortunately had very little effect on the carved blocks of stone that were intended to form the great portico to the citadel of Batavia. Fate had decided however that the man who had persuaded the senior management of the V.O.C. to commission it, Jan Pieterszoon-the-Fearless, should never see the splendid portico in reality.

# act 15

# The renaissance of the Batavia

It is a marvellous story that began in the early 1980s when a 41-year old shipwright by the name of Willem Vos, a native of Broek in Waterland[1] who had his business in the eastern part of Friesland, took it into his head to build a 17th-century merchant ship, employing the techniques in use in the Netherlands in that far-off time.

The man in question, who in his youth had spent some years at sea, had since been living by his art, as a shipwright, spending the greater part of his time building "botters"[2], the little wooden sailing boats with a single mast for which Dutch week-end sailors have always shown particular affection. Occasionally, when business was slack, he occupied himself restoring old houses and churches or making models of ships for various museums throughout the country.

So here he was, with his sights fixed on a new task that some would describe as virtually superhuman. For there exist today no plans of the ships built in those days when ship-builders worked mainly by rule-of-thumb, trusting to their eye and to the knack that comes with experience. All we know, from various drawings and paintings, is their profile but nothing that could serve as a technical foundation for a re-building exercise. Regardless of this, Willem Vos, who had not yet chosen a particular vessel as his model, was nonetheless determined to go ahead with his project, all the more enthusiastic in that the advent of the plastics that he abhorred would inevitably be the death sooner or later of the craft that he had always carried on.

He soon realized what difficulties lay ahead. The fact that there was no vestige of a plan of the period was confirmed, but worse still, the estimated budget that he had just sketched out was enough to make one's head spin. It became immediately obvious that he must think out

*The replica of the Batavia nearing completion at Lelystad. Thanks to the enthusiastic interest of a public coming from everywhere to visit his extra-ordinary shipyard, Willem Vos is sure now of winning his slightly crazy bet : 1994 will be the year of the final resurrection of the fine Indiaman so full of symbolic meaning. One can imagine already the thunder od cheers and atmosphere of gaiety and emotion as she enters the Oostvaardersdiep, the very waters that her illustrious and unlucky predecessor sailed through, three hundred and sixty-five years earlier.*

---

1 A small township situated immediately north-east of Amsterdam, very near the well-known tourist centres of Marken and Volendam.

2 A typical Dutch term, which cannot be translated.

*Master shipwright Willem Vos,
who dreamed up the whole
project, and has been overseeing
it since.*

his project very carefully so that he could lay a sound and convincing proposal before corporate bodies and individuals whose patronage would be imperative if his dream were to become reality.

For five years, between 1980 and 1985, this determined man therefore searched museums and record offices, not only in Holland, but also in France, accumulating notes and sketches and working his way through all the specialized  books that he could lay hands on.  As the months went by he became one of the best-informed people regarding the "Vereenigde Oost-Indische Compagnie", the splendid V.O.C.,  and the opulent fleet that was the source of its glory.  Then friends of his who were impressed by his determination and also enthusiastic about his project put him in touch with the film director Paul Verhoeven who had just announced his intention of making a film about the dramatic story of the *Batavia*[3]. He liked the idea immediately, for the tragic fate of this "retourship" had always appealed to people's imagination — particularly to that of his compatriots, but also to that of people everywhere in the world who are enthralled by the great maritime epics and the drama that often surrounds them.

So the *Batavia* was chosen as model for the project. He now embarked on an intricate and laborious task. For there were no documents containing any practical information on the subject, apart from a resolution by the *Heeren XVII*, dated 17th March 1626, setting forth succinctly the main measurements of the vessel — draft, length, beam — and authorizing the construction. That was all, and very scanty it was. Most

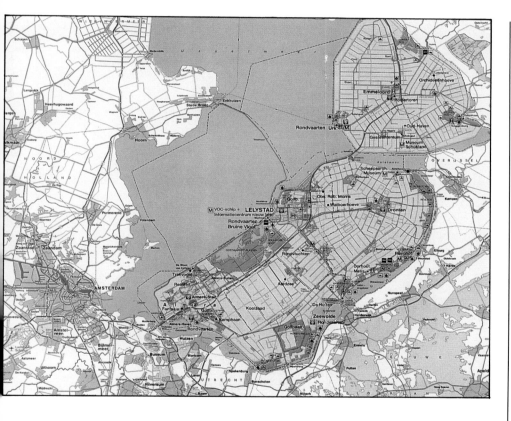

*A map of the Flevoland polder, which lies six metres below the level of the North Sea. The new town of Lelystad has been established on its north-west shore. Since 1985, large numbers of visitors have flocked to the shipyard where the Batavia is being built.*

*Next spread :
An aerial photograph of the shipyard on the shores of the Markermeer. The grey roofs belong to the building designed to receive the public, and also the various workshops. The impressive bulk of the Batavia dominates the whole site.*

fortunately, however, there were the drawings of a certain van de Velve which gave valuable information about ships of this generation. There were also, though dating from a slightly later period, the treatises — or rather, empirical tables of numbers for the use of shipwrights — drawn up by Nicolas Witsen and Cornelis van Yk, in 1671 and 1697 respectively. Although these tables were much later than the period of the building of the *Batavia*, they proved to be of great assistance to Willem Vos, since the building techniques employed in the V.O.C. shipyards, having

---

3 The two men met, and considered working together, but Paul Verhoeven eventually gave up his project and preferred to pursue his film-maker's career in the United States where he won international repute with his films "Total Recall" and "Basic Instinct".

been tried and proved, changed very little during the whole of the 17th century.

Little by little the project began to take shape. But to carry it through was made yet more difficult by the fact that its author had set his sights very high, declaring it imperative that maximum authenticity be the keyword of the *Batavia*'s reconstruction, with no recourse at all to modern technology, in the field of maritime engineering, that is to say.

By 1985, everything was finally ready. A foundation had been established, with the title "The Netherlands constructs a V.O.C. retourship". A big programme ! The Netherlands was given prominence in this way because Willem Vos was determined that his challenge should have a national dimension. He himself would simply be the catalyst and technical director, assisted by a team that would include a marine archaeologist, an architect and the curators of three museums, not to mention all the skilled experts, of course, each of whom was a specialist in a specific area of ship-building.

*Although it has never been ascertained exactly what caused a sudden shift of equilibrium (incorrect placing of ballast, exceptional overloading with guns ?), the superb Vasa sank in 1628 in 32 metres of water at the entrance to Stockholm harbour, barely a quarter of an hour after hoisting sail for the very first time ! However, the Vasa was to provide Willem Vos and his team with a mine of valuable information, especially regarding decoration. She is in fact the only 17th century ship to have reached us nearly intact. She was raised from the harbour bottom in April 1961 and since then the number of visitors coming to admire her has grown year by year. In view of this success a new museum was built recently to house the Vasa and was opened in 1990.*

One of the stated aims of the foundation was to take advantage of this unusual undertaking to provide unemployed young people with a maximum amount of work and hands-on experience and in view of this, the Netherlands Government gave very effective assistance subsequently, by underwriting the wages of all these young people, as a form of vocational training. Concurrently with this indirect assistance, several big national companies, too many to mention by name, joined in, one after another, granting subsidies to the foundation.

But we have not yet reached that stage in our story. Money, and indeed a lot of money, was going to be needed. Willem Vos, who did not know exactly what lay ahead, was, however, sufficiently experienced and realistic to know that the implementation of his rather crazy project was going to cost at the very least 8 million guilders ! And the initial capital at his disposal was no more than a symbolic sum.

On 4th October 1985, the project was officially launched by the Mayor of Lelystad, a township built on the Flevoland polder which, between 1950 and 1957, had been reclaimed from the Ijsselmeer, and was six metres lower than the level of the North Sea. This place was not selected by chance. The spot is in fact highly symbolic, for it was right here, in the area formerly known as "Oostvaardersdiep" (the passage for navigators going to the

East) that the first *Batavia* would have passed under sail from the port of Amsterdam, making for the Friesland island of Texel, where her cargo and her passengers were awaiting her.

In making a large site on the shore of the Markermeer available to the foundation, free of charge, the Mayor of the new township was looking far ahead, for the shipyard that was opening there promised to become in the long run a major tourist attraction provided of course that the project could be successfully carried through...

So on 4th October 1985, the enormous keel made of four pieces of oak fitted together and measuring no less than 37 metres in length, was ceremoniously laid. At that time the building team comprised only six men, pitifully few, but they were all fired by the faith that moves mountains.

In his speech on this occasion, Willem Vos expounded some of the fundamental ideas that were his guiding

principles. The new *Batavia* was certainly not to be an exact replica of the former, about which, after all, they possessed only very few details. Instead it was to be a reconstruction in which inevitably a large place would be left if not to improvisation at least to the imagination, in respect of a number of details. On the other hand, there was to be no deviation at all from the techniques of construction employed in former times. In this respect the *Vasa*, a man o' war built for the Swedish navy by Dutch shipwrights in the same year as the *Batavia*, provided a wealth of information. When the *Vasa*, which had sunk in Stockholm harbour at the start of her first voyage, was raised in 1961 from her bed of mud and brought to the surface, it was found, to the pleased surprise of all concerned, that she was virtually intact and in particular, was still embellished with all the splendid carving of the stern-castle. On the other hand, the original *Batavia*, whose hull — what little remained of it — had been so cleverly reassembled by the archaeologists of the Western Australian Maritime Museum in Fremantle, paradoxically furnished less information than the *Vasa*, for the part that had been spared the sea's rough treatment provided insufficient indication of the ship's original lines.

Nonetheless, the die was cast, for Willem Vos had finalized the specifications of his future masterpiece as shown below :

length overall : ............................................................56.60 metres
length between perpendiculars : ...................................45.00 metres

| keel length : | 37.00 metres |
| maximum beam : | 10.50 metres |
| height from keel to main truck : | 53.00 metres |
| height from keel to top of stern-castle : | 19.00 metres |
| draft, forward : | 4.25 metres |
| draft, aft : | 5.10 metres |
| tons of burthen : | +/-  600 tons |
| displacement : | +/- 1 300 tons |
| number of sails : | 10 |
| sail area : | 1,180 sq.m. |
| armament : | 6 bronze cannons, 24 iron cannons and 2 of a composite type |
| combined weight of the guns : | 30 tons |

*This view of the ship's underbody shows the bulkiness of the shape. To the right is the keel. The first strake of planking of the hull is called the "garboard". The planks nearer half-way up constitute the "turn of the bilge", sometimes known as the "chine". The planks right at the top, where they join the deck, are usually referred to as the "topsides". The gap between the planks was caulked with oakum soaked in tallow, and the seam sealed with pitch.*

The next task was to procure the appropriate materials, chief amongst which was of course the timber. The designer had calculated that he would need between 1,700 and 1,900 cubic metres of undressed oak, this noble timber being for the vitals of the vessel, while the three spars — fore, main and mizzen — and atop the same number of crows' nests, would be made of pine from the Russian Taiga and the German Black Forest. The 19-metre long bowsprit was to be carved from a single Danish larch, and would weigh a mere 4.3 tons !

Willem Vos went walking through the oak forests of the kingdom of

*The* Batavia *was armed with a total of 32 guns, 24 of which were made of cast iron, 6 of bronze and 2 were of the composite type. These guns varied in design and size. Eight different models, all in cast iron, have been produced at Lelystad for the reconstruction project. Six anchors only have been made for the new ship (the 1629 original would have carried more). The bower anchor is the biggest (4 metres) and heaviest (1,500 kg). The new* Batavia *also carries an anchor of more recent design and four kedging anchors.*

Hamlet, marking the standing timber whose natural shape corresponded most closely to the different parts of a structure that none knew better than he. The Harlingen firm Almenun was then engaged to do the rough dressing and squaring of each log, respecting scrupulously the numbering corresponding to their future use, before delivering them to the Lelystad shipyard.

The keel, the stem and the sternpost were all that could be seen by the public, not very numerous as yet, who visited the site, curious to see what was happening there. For in fact, in these early days, funds were sorely lacking and would continue so for several months, causing

*The bowsprit is fastened to the
stemhead by mortices and
secured with "gammon"
lashings. The bowsprit itself is
fashioned from the trunk of a
single larch, 19 metres long.*

*Miles of hempen cordage have
been spun in this workshop for
the ship's running rigging.*

Willem Vos to break out into a cold sweat at times, until the day when the substantial Dutch shipping firm Nedlloyd offered its powerful backing, thus paving the way for various other sponsors to follow.

At the beginning of 1986, the main elements of the backbone were assembled and the pre-fabricated stern structure, an edifice 19 metres high and weighing 9 tons, could be fastened in place. It was to be an-

other two years before
the skeleton of the
ship, with all of its 72
great oak frames, was
complete and ready for
the work of planking
and decking to begin.

His concern to res-
pect 17th century build-
ing methods to the last
detail did not however
mean that Willem Vos

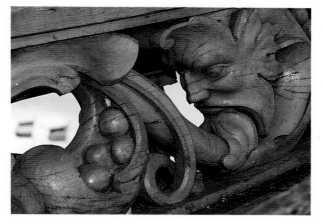

and his team were to forgo modern means of hoisting and modern tools
and instruments, such as chain saws, thickness planers, jointers and
electric drills. If they had obstinately used only the archaic methods of
3 centuries ago, not only would this have considerably slowed the work
of the shipyard, thus increasing the over-all cost of construction, but it
would also have had a negative effect on the training of young appren-
tices, for one of the primary aims of the project was to facilitate their
access to employment on the contemporary job market.

However, the man who was the soul of the project continued the
efforts he had always made, with considerable success, to marry the
techniques of past and present. The planking of the hull, for instance,

*Without the addition, forward
of the actual stem, of the curved
cutwater characteristic of most
17th century vessels, the
Batavia's rounded stem would
give her the clumsy appearance
of a massive barge. Soaring
over the prow is the bowsprit,
really the fourth mast of the
ship, set at a slant.*

*Left :
The scrollboards, covering part
of the cutwater, are a delicate
tracery of carving in oak.*

was shaped in the old manner. The ten centimetre thick oak strakes affixed on either side of the frames forming a sandwich half a metre thick, were bent on a frame mould to the appropriate curvature by applying heat to one face, while keeping the other face constantly wet.

The sails provide another magnificent example of returning to the ways and customs of old. Each of the ten sails — the main one alone measures 240 sq.m. — has been made of Scottish flax, woven on a loom belonging to the last cottage industry in the world capable of meeting such an order. The woven panels, each 61 cm wide and 1.2mm. thick, have been sewn together by hand, using a stitch known as the "Dutch double round stitch".

And the carving workshop has produced some veritable master-pieces, beginning with the figurehead, portraying a lion, the traditional

*Several views of the proud red and gold "Lion of Holland" figurehead, a faithful copy of the one that decorated the bow of the original Batavia.*

symbol of the Dutch merchant fleets of old. The coat-of-arms decorating the stern is embellished by oaken sculptures in the nordic renaissance style, all markedly symbolic. Above the mascarons (those grotesque figures intended to protect the ship by surveying the sea all around through their bulging eyes), the twelve Batavian warriors led by their legendary chiefs, Claudius Civilis and his lieutenant Brinio, who raised the flag of rebellion against the Roman oppressor, have already taken shape in the workshop and will occupy the port side of the transom. Facing them on the starboard side will be William of Orange and his son Maurits, heros of the war of liberation against the Spanish. Thus the ship's decoration will be in consonance with the cry of national pride that her name proclaims : Batavia !

The first impression that strikes a visitor towards the end of 1993, less than 18 months from the announced date for launching the *Batavia*, is

*Above and right :*
*This carving, known as a*
*"watchful eye", was typical of*
*ships of the period, and was the*
*real "guardian angel" of the*
*helmsman. It was situated in a*
*curious position, the arm*
*extended towards the helmsman,*
*its back and the lower part of*
*the body literally projecting over*
*the void.*

*Far right :*
*These grotesque figures, called*
*mascarons, with their menacing*
*faces, were supposed to survey*
*the sea around the ship and*
*ward off evil spirits. They were*
*traditionally placed on the*
*transom, just below the rail.*
*Those selected for the Batavia*
*are copies of ones that adorned*
*buildings in Holland*
*constructed between 1550 and*
*1650, in particular the*
*"Kanselerij" at Leeuwarden*
*and the St Jans Gasthuis*
*almshouse at Hoorn.*

*These statues of the leaders of the Batavian rebellion against the Roman legions, Claudius Civilis and his lieutenant Brinio, and those of the heroes of the Dutch war of independence, William of Orange and his son Maurits, are to grace the ship's coat-of-arms. They have been carved in the northern renaissance style.*

*At present supported by a veritable forest of timber braces and surrounded by scaffolding, the* Batavia *will be moved to the nearby water's edge on rollers placed on either side of the ship, with several cranes helping to take some of the load as well as guiding her progress, until she is placed on an enormous floating pontoon. Then the pontoon will simply be "sunk" and the re-born* Batavia *will at last be in her true element. Note the pronounced sheer (longitudinal curvature) of the vessel. This shape was characteristic of ships of the period and was intended to help prevent the vessel from sagging when working through heavy seas. It also helped lead any water shipped on deck to the midship scuppers.*

hat he has entered a human beehive. The frenzied activity in the different workshops and the incessant to and fro of tourists, welcomed and
conducted round the site by the 180 volunteers of the "Promotie Team",
create an atmosphere of exhilaration.

The *Batavia* already looks impressive despite her somewhat clumsy
air on account of the sheer (that is, the fore-and-aft curvature from bow
to stern of the deck), reminiscent of a Chinese junk, and the curve of
the massive stem, which would make her look a little like a snub-nosed
barge were it not for the great sweep of the cutwater and the magnificent curve of the scrollboards which perfectly restore the harmony of
the ship's lines.

No one doubts today that the challenge taken up by Willem Vos will
be won, even though expenditures have already reached the 14 million
guilders mark, and recently the definitive budget had to be modified

*Right :*
*The upper deck capstan, shown*
*here with its hand-spokes, is*
*located on the centreline of the*
*ship and, by the use of leading*
*blocks, can be made to work to*
*port as well as to starboard.*

*Opposite, above right :*
*The lower end of the shrouds,*
*with their seizings soaked in*
*tallow to prevent the*
*penetration of moisture. Each*
*ends in a dead-eye.*

*Opposite, above left :*
*Close-up of a "dead-eye",*
*showing its tarred lashings.*

*Opposite, bottom :*
*The gun-deck capstan. Unlike*
*the one we saw earlier, located*
*on the upper deck and in the*
*open, this capstan cannot be*
*used to tighten the standing*
*rigging. It was used only for*
*general handling and docking*
*manoeuvres.*

*Above :*
*This gun, mounted on its carriage, welcomes visitors to the gun-deck.*

*Right :*
*Hands-pumps of this kind were commonly used to pump out the water which gradually seeped into the hold of ships of the period, however carefully the caulking was done at the time of construction.*

*Left :*
The helmsman's "whipstaff". It
is pivoted through the deck and
its lower end (shown here) is
fastened to the end of the tiller
on which it acts as a lever.
About the middle of the 17th
century, this system was
replaced by the ship's wheel.

*Above :*
The *commandeur*, the officers
and passengers of distinction
had the use of two lavatories of
this type, located at the stern of
the ship. Ordinary seamen had
to content themselves with two
timber planks cantilevered over
the bow and known as the
"heads".

upward one last time, to the astounding figure of 22 million guilders ! But the size of the figure becomes insignificant if one takes into account the fact that nearly a million visitors have crossed the threshold of the shipyard since it opened and their entry fees, in addition to donations received from 38,000 recorded donors, have enabled the foundation to reach its break-even point and accordingly to view the future with serenity.

What will become of the *Batavia*, 1994 version ?  The use to which she will be put is  still the subject of debate.  The idea of having her follow the route of her unfortunate predecessor has not been altogether rejected, although it would scarcely correspond to the foundation's need to ensure a reasonable rate of return on the project. Who, after all, would be willing to pay a large sum of money for the privilege of enduring a long voyage in a ship with not a modicum of comfort, tantamount

*A row of "dead-eyes", used to tighten the shrouds and all standing rigging. The sailors went aloft using these horizontal rope steps fastened to the shrouds at regular intervals and known as "ratlines".*

to a floating prison where, in many places, it would be impossible even to stand upright ?

It has been suggested that at least part of the *Batavia*'s long voyage might be accompanied by modern cruise ships, whose passengers would simply admire and photograph the *Batavia* from a distance... but the idea does not arouse much enthusiasm.  Another has also been mooted, which would obviate her making the interminable outward journey by her own means by the simple expedient of loading her as deck cargo on a barge-carrier, one of those giant vessels capable of carrying the heaviest loads. But the cost of such an operation would amount to some 5 million guilders, which makes one think twice...

*Next spread :*
*A view of the poop or stern-castle. Built up over the aftermost portion of the upper deck, it extends from the transom to the mizzen mast. It housed the accommodation for the* commandeur, *the officers and passengers of distinction. The carvings on the foreground are called "servants". Their neck was used for attaching ropes.*

Whatever is decided, though, there is no doubt that in the not so distant future the *Batavia* will be sailing along the coast of the former Eendracht's land. She might even venture into the neighbourhood of the Abrolhos before sailing to Djakarta, the sprawling capital of a country that today has a population of 183 million. It will be a moving moment when she drops anchor in the port of the former Batavia, thus symbolically completing one of the most tragic voyages of all time.

# Foreword

The following is the original translation of the first account in Dutch, published in Amsterdam in 1647 by Jan Jansz, editor, under the title *"The disastrous voyage for the East Indies under the command of Françoys Pelsaert, shipwrecked on Frederik Houtman's Abrolhos, 28° 1/3 south of the equinoctial line ."*

The text, written in ancient Dutch, was translated in 1897 by Mr. William Sibenhaar, a Dutchman living in Perth, and was published for the first time the same year in Christmas edition of the weekly *"Western Mail"*.

The illustrations, all originals, have been taken not only from the above mentioned edition but also from the subsequent one, namely those by:

- *Joost Hartgers - Amsterdam, 1648*
- *Lucas de Vries - Utrecht, 1649*
- *Gillis Joosten Saeghman - Amsterdam, 1665*

# The Disastrous Voyage

## OF THE SHIP

# BATAVIA,

### headed for the

# EAST INDIES

under the command of Françoys Pelsaert,
shipwrecked on Frederik Houtman's Abrolhos,
28°1/3 south of equinoctial line.

# Journal and Historical Account of the Disastrous Voyage made to the East Indies

by the worthy Françoys Pelsaert of Antwerp, Captain on the Ship Batavia, which Sailed from Texel on the 28th of October 1628.

The fact that in June, 1628, General Pieter Carpentier came home safely from the East Indies with five richly-laden merchant-men, and that the Government succeded in releasing three of their ships from the embargo under which they had been placed by the English the year before, when returning from Surat under the command of Jan Karsbensz, of Emden, tended not a little to encourage enterprise and to occasion fresh equipment. In consequence of this the said Government resolved to send another fleet of 11 ships hither, with which General Jacob Specks was to sail. On these ships embarked also a man with wide experience, the mathematician Johan Walbeck, who was anxious to study closely the nature and condition of eastern countries. The Senate of Amsterdam, having in good time two ships and a yacht ready to sail, sent those to Texel in order to lose no time. The name of these vessels were Batavia, under the command of the worthy Françoys Pelsaert, of Antwerp; Dordrecht, having for her merchant-captain the collector of revenue, Isaac van Swaenswyck of Leyden; and the yacht Assendelft, under the command of the second merchant-captain, Cornelis Vlack, of Amsterdam. These being ready to sail, and the wind having become favourable, left Texel for the open sea on the 28th of October.

How they continued their journey, how they were separated by storm or other incidents, how nothing but the ordinary events of daily nautical routine took place, which it is unneccessary to mention and publish in print, since so many similar printed accounts of voyages have repeated this ad nauseam for every reader - all this we pass, in order to emphasize only that which is memorable.

The ship Batavia continued on her course alone, and her voyage had now lasted to June 4, 1629, being Whit Monday. She had reached the southern latitude of 28 - 28 1/2 degrees, about nine miles from the *Southland. There they got among the perilous banks of the Abrolhos, called by the Dutch the "Frederick Houtman's Cliffs". The *commander Françoys Pelsaert was unwell and kept to his cabin, as it was clear moonlight and fine weather, two hours before sunrise, and the skipper's watch. Suddenly he felt the ship shaking terribly, the rudder touching ground and the keel running against the cliffs, so that he tumbled out of his berth. Running on deck immediately he found all sails hoisted, the course north-east by north, a south-westerly wind having blown all night. The ship was surrounded by thick foam, but no great breakers. This, however, changed soon, since all at once they heard the sea breaking upon them amain. Then the Commodore spoke very sharply to the Skipper, and accused him of having brought them into this danger of life by his reckless negligence. The Skipper answered that it was not his negligence, that he had not slept, but that he had been awake and carefully watched everything. Seeing the surf in the distance, he had asked Hans de Bosschieter, who was on the watch with him, what "that white" could be. The latter had answered that it was the reflection of the moon, and with this they had contented themselves. The Commodore then asked what could be done and whereabouts they were. *God only knows*, said the Skipper; *this is an unknown dry bank, which must be a good distance from the mainland. I think we are on a shallow and perhaps it is low tide. Let us drop an anchor astern; possibly we may get off yet.*

---

• Australia

* Commodore

When the Commodore asked what depth of water they were in, the reply was that they did not know. So he sent for the lead line, which was in the steerman's charge, and found that there were but 17ft or 18ft of water astern and far less forward. Therefore, they had to accept the Skipper's surmise that they had got on an unknown shallow in the sea, and they consequently resolved to lighten the vessel by throwing the heavy guns overboard, and to put out to sea with the boats, in hopes that the ship might float again. Meanwhile they had sounded round the ship and found seven fathoms of water astern for a distance of

foothold on the deck. It was evident that they had run on these shallows during the high tide. They resolved to bring down the mainmast, trusting that the other mast would not cause so much danger every time the ship struck on the rocks. When they had done this, they found that they had made a great mistake, for they could not get rid of it overboard, and it caused them a great deal of trouble when they tried to bring the boat on board, on account of the violent breakers. Nowhere could they see any land that did not look as if the high tide was sure to cover it, except one island about three miles away from the ship. The

about a bow shot; but forward it was all shallow, so that they prepared a small anchor to be thrown out astern. Meanwhile rain set in, with a strong wind, so that the boat was washed overboard with a heavy sea. She drifted away, and they were obliged to send the sloop after her to be able to row her back. Before they were on board again it was day. They then found themselves surrounded by cliffs and shallows. The rapid fall of the water caused the ship to bump violently and to lurch, so that they could no longer retain

Skipper was, therefore, sent off to two little islets not far from the ship to see whether it would be possible to deposit there safely the people and some of the goods. Coming back about 9 o'clock, he reported that apparently those would not be flooded, but that the rocks and cliffs made them difficult and dangerous of approach, since on one side the sloop could not land on account of the shallows, while on the other side there were several fathoms of water.

Nevertheless, it was resolved, because of the wailing and weeping of the women, the sick and the children, and because of the dejected state of the less courageous ones, to land the people there first, and, meanwhile, to bring on deck the money and the most precious goods. To this end the chief officers tried their utmost; but the wrath of the Lord seemed to be upon their heads, for, in spite of all the efforts and endeavours to cant the vessel to leeward, the uneven and steep cliffs on which she rested would make her lean over to the other side, so that the people could only be got off very slowly. At 10 o'clock the ship burst asunder, and they had to bring up some bread from the storeroom in great haste. They had great hopes of getting water on the shore; but everything - heaven and earth themselves - seemed to be against them. Their zeal was made useless by the godless, lawless, gang of soldiers and sailors, who could not be kept out of the hold on account of the drink, so that they could not succeed in bringing anything up in safety, and the entire hold became flooded. They scarcely filled one cask and a half, which lay ready on the deck, with buckets and jugs. The whole day passed in this manner, and they had only made three trips with the people, in which 180 souls, 80 casks containing bread, and a few barrels of water had been saved.

When the Skipper had taken ashore some people and a casket of jewels, and had returned on board with the sloop after sunset, he declared to the Commodore that it was no use their taking water and bread on shore, since it was all devoured in the most lawless and ravenous manner, and everyone drank as much as he liked; his own orders had no force or effect, unless more stringent measures were taken. Thereupon the Commodore himself jumped into the sloop and went ashore, intending to return as soon as possible, having decided to bring the money ashore in the next journey. The great number of people and the scarcity of the water made it necessary to fix rations, for there was no appearance of the possibility of getting more water soon, and they would be obliged to make it stretch as long as possible if they wished to save their lives. No sooner, however, had he left the ship than a strong wind began

to blow, so that it was out of the question to get to the ship again; in fact they found it hard enough to get ashore, being in great danger of being swamped by the sea or carried away by the current. So that against their will they were compelled to stay on the land that night.

On the 5th they put some of the people, with some bread and water, ashore on the largest island, so that till further orders they were divided into two parties. The Commodore with the sloop and the Skipper with the boat returned to the ship, and with much labour, difficulty and hard rowing the sloop reached her only in the afternoon; but those in the boat were less fortunate, for the high seas prevented their completing the journey by rowing, and still more when they hoisted a sail to tack, principally through the want of sweeps, and they were compelled to return to the island.

Though the Commodore was close to the ship yet the breakers prevented their boarding her, in spite of all their trouble and the dangers they faced, for the seas ran even over the poop, so for a long time they beat about, hoping that a favourable opportunity would at last be offered. But everything was in vain. At last a carpenter of Amsterdam, named Jan Egbertsz, was bold enough to swim through the surf from the ship to the sloop. He begged that they should come to the rescue of the supercargo captain, Jerome Cornelisz (who was in the ship with seventy men) in order to save them, since their lives were no longer safe in the ship. It may be easily inferred from this of what mind they were in, both parties, on one side with the wish to help, on the other with the anxious desire to be rescued. As it seemed impossible to effect this, the Commodore asked for five or six planks from the ship, if it was possible to throw them overboard, so that they might fish them up and make sweeps for the boat out of them. Further he advised them to make a couple of rafts to take refuge on in case of need. Finally he sent word to the effect that he, the Commodore, would certainly take the first opportunity of reaching the ship with the sloop and the boat, in order to get the money and bring it safely ashore. With these messages the said carpenter, Jan Egbertsz, swam to the ship again. When he had arrived there safely they immediately threw out six planks, which were secured by those in the sloop. The latter were then obliged, to their sorrow and regret, to return to the island. When they reached the land, they found the carpenter busy making a sweep out of a piece of a boom that had floated ashore. In the afternoon it began to blow and storm very hard from the north-west, so that the ship was so entirely buried by waves that they could often not see her and that it seemed more than a miracle that she kept together. Those on the shore calculated in the evening how much more there was of the fresh water that they had saved in small casks, and found that on the smallest island, where with the boat and the sloop they counted 40 people, there were 80 cans of water, and on the larger island for 180 people there were still less. Therefore it was an anxious prospect, and those of the crew began to mutter, asking why they should not go and look for fresh water on the islands or thereabouts, since they could not remain without very long or they would die of thirst together. The Skipper mentioned this to the Commodore, also that unless an order of this kind was given, there was a danger of mutiny and of the mutineers leaving with the boat. The Commodore, however, did not yet see his way clear to consent to this, and he proposed that they should await the event of the weather and what would become of the ship, for they would have to answer before God, the authorities, and the Government in Batavia for leaving all those people and the rich possessions of the company thus lightly without any further attempt to save them. Many protested against this decision, and those who were willing to search for water on the islands or on the southern mainland, promised that as soon as they should find fresh water anywhere, they would return, in order to provide the others with as much water as should be found necessary. Finally, after having weighed and discussed everything, the Commodore was persuaded after much begging and praying to resolve (as will be seen from the resolution hereafter) that they should steer with the boat for the islands or the mainland to look for water, so that they might not perish of thirst; that if they found none, they should continue their voyage by the grace of God, till they reached Batavia, in order to inform the General of their sad and unheard-of calamities, and at the same time to ask for help to rescue the remaining people. One consideration was that there was no hope of getting more water out of the ship unless she should burst open and the cask should float ashore and be secured. It was true it might rain for many days, and much water might thus be collected for their use, but all this was very uncertain, and not to be depended upon.

Before carrying out the resolution just made, the Commodore asked the Skipper to order some of the crew to go with him in the sloop to the other islet, in order to acquaint the people there with the preceding resolution. He was dissuaded from doing this, because they feared that they might keep the Commodore there, and he might have occasion to regret it, and also because none of the men were very much inclined to start out with him. But he persisted in his intention, stating that if they would not consent to his going to the other island, he would tell the people of their intentions not to go out and find fresh water for the whole number. He was ready to die with the people honourably, and not to leave the company's ship and goods. Then they consented. He obtained a boatswain's mate and six men at his service, who were ready to take him in the sloop to the island, though on condition that if he should be detained there they should be allowed to leave with the sloop and go on. This being agreed they started, the Commodore taking with him a cask of water for those on the other island; but when they came near the shore the boatswain and his men refused to land, saying: *"They will keep you and us there; we don't wish to go nearer; if you have anything to say to them you can call out; we are not going to run any risk for your sake."* The Commodore was very indignant at this slight, and wanted to jump overboard in order to swim ashore. But the boatswain pulled him back and held him, telling his crew to row back. Those on the island saw all this with great regret.

The Commodore thus being hindered in carrying out his kind intentions recommended his unfortunate brethren to God's care, and, much against his wish, returned in the evening.

In this sad state of affairs, the Commodore at last resolved to go and look for fresh water on the islands. Therefore, on the 6th of June, in the morning, he wrote on a leaf of a book of tablets:-

"That he and the others thereby named were going out with the boat to find fresh water on the neighbouring islands or the mainland in the south, promising to make haste and return to their friends as soon as possible."

This document he placed under one of the bread barrels, which they left on the shore. Then he sailed with the boat, and for three days searched two islands for fresh water. On the cliffs of the larger one they

they would not find any fresh water on the islands; they had already dug a good many holes in vain, so that they would be obliged to seek the mainland to the south, which they durst not try in a boat that was not well founded, fearing that they would not be able to withstand the sea. Against the evening they saw the sloop rowing towards them, which they had left about the ship. Gillis Fransz, second mate, was in her with ten men, gone out to find fresh water also. Seeing that their efforts in this direction were vain, and that those in the boat were inclined to sail for the mainland, south, they asked to be allowed to go thither also in the sloop. This was accorded, partly because their number would increase the chance of finding water, and also because, if the weather was rough, they would thus get the water more easily across the

found some in the small hollows, left by the rain; but the washing ashore of the sea had spoilt most of it, making it salt, so that it was not good to drink and therefore, useless.

On the 7th they stopped with the boat at the largest island in order to get her into better repair, for it was plain that

breakers, for they were disinclined to let the sloop return to the people on the islands and on the wreck.

The 8th, when the boat was in good trim and everything ready in order to sail in the morning from the islands to the mainland, the Commodore read out to his crew the following resolution, drawn up beforehand, to which all consented with a solemn oath:

"Since, on all the islands and cliffs round about our foundered ship 'Batavia', there is no fresh water to be found, in order to feed and keep the people who are saved, therefore the Commodore has earnestly requested and proposed that an expedition should be made to the main Southland to see whether it is God's gracious will that fresh water shall be found of which so much may be taken to the people that they shall be certain of having enough provision for a considerable time; that then, meanwhile, someone shall be told off to go to Batavia, in order to let the Lord-General, and his councillors know of our disaster and to ask him for early assistance. To which we the undersigned have all voluntarily consented, since necessity forces us thereto, and since, if we acted otherwise, we could not answer for our conduct before God and the high authorities. Therefore, we have unanimously agreed and resolved to try our utmost and do our duty and to assist our poor brethren in their great need. In certain knowledge of the truth we have signed this with our own hand and have all of us sworn to it on the 8th of June, 1629!"

was signed~

FRANÇOYS PELSAERT
CLAES GERRITSZ
JACOB JANSZ HOLOOGH
CLAES JANSZ DOR
ADRIAEN JACOBSZ
HANS JACOBSZ BINDER
JAN EVERTSZ
CLAES WILLEMSZ GRAHFT
MICHIEL CLARSZ

Thereupon they commenced their voyage in the name of the Lord, and sailed into the open sea. In the afternoon they were in latitude 28 deg. 13 min., and shortly afterwards sighted the mainland, probably about six miles north by west of their foundered ship, the wind blowing from the west. They were there in about 28 or 30 fathoms of water, wherefore in the evening they turned away from the land, but went near it again about midnight.

On the morning of the 9th they were still about three miles from the shore, the wind, with some rain, being mostly north-west. They guessed that during these 24 hours they had made from four to five miles in a north-westerly direction. The shore in these parts stretches mostly north-west and south-east; a bare and rocky coast, without trees, about as high as at Dover, in England. They saw an inlet and some low sandy dunes, which they thought they could approach; but, coming close, they found that near the beach the breakers were very rough and that the sea rolled high on the land, so that they could not very well risk the landing; since the wind rose more and more.

On the 10th they had to move about for a period of 24 hours on account of the strong wind and storm, which blew harder and harder from the nor-west, so that they were obliged to let go the sloop, which they had taken with them, and even to throw overboard some of their bread and other things that were in the way, as they could not otherwise bale out the water. In the night they were still in greater danger of sinking on account of the strong wind and the high seas. They had no means of keeping off the shore. They could carry no sail. They were at the mercy of the sea. That night a steady rain poured down, and they hoped that the people on the islands might also have some of it, and provide themselves with water.

On the 11th, it became calmer, and the wind turned to the west-south-west. They therefore turned northward, but the sea was just as rough and high.

On the 12th, at noon, the weather steadied down and cleared up. They were then at latitude 27 deg. They kept close to the shore, the wind being south-east, but they had no opportunity of nearing the land with the boat, for the breakers were too strong and the coast too steep and jagged, without any foreland or inlet, as is usually found on other coasts, so that it seemed to them a bare and cursed country, devoid of green or grass.

On the 13th, at noon, they were at latitude 25 deg. 40 min. They found then that they had drifted north a good deal, and had doubled the cape, keeping mostly northward during these 24 hours, as the coast now stretched north-north-east and south-south-west. The rocks were of

redstone, a good deal battered and broken. There was no foreland. These rocks were all along of very much the same height, and made landing impossible on account of the breakers and high seas.

On the 14th, in the morning, there was a gentle breeze, but during the day a calm set in. At noon they were in latitude 24 deg., keeping north with an east wind. The current still took them every day much around the north, greatly against their wish, for with but little sail they were close to the shore.

In the afternoon, seeing inland some smoke, they rowed thither, hoping to find an opportunity of landing. They were quite rejoiced, for they imagined that where there were people there would also be fresh water. Having reached the shore, they found the ground to be a steep and rough incline; stony and rocky, against which the breakers beat violently, so that they saw no means of landing. It made them very dejected, for they feared that they would have to depart without landing. At last six men, trusting themselves to their swimming powers jumped overboard, and reached the shore with great difficulty and peril, while the boat remained at anchor outside the breakers in 25 fathoms of water. The swimmers having reached the shore, looked the whole day for fresh water everywhere, till in the evening they became convinced that their search was vain.

They then happened upon four people, who were creeping towards them on their hands and feet. When our men, coming out of a hollow upon a height, suddenly approached them, they leaped to their feet and fled full speed, which was distinctly observed by those in the boat. They were black savages, quite naked, leaving themselves uncovered like animals.

As those on the shore had spent the whole day without finding water, they swam aboard again towards evening being all a good deal hurt and bruised, since the breakers had dashed them roughly against the rocks. Then getting ready and lifting the grappling iron they started in search of a better opportunity, sailing along the coast all night with but little sail, and keeping outside the breakers.

On the morning of the 15th, they came to a point where a large reef extended at about a mile from the coast, and, so it seemed, another reef along the shore, so that they tried their best to steer between the two, for the water there appeared to be calm and smooth. But they did not find an entrance until the afternoon, when they saw an opening where there were no breakers. But it was very dangerous, very stony, and often not holding two feet of water. The shore here had a foreland of dunes about a mile broad, before the higher land was reached.

When they had gone ashore they commenced to dig holes in the said foreland, but found nothing except salt water. Some of them therefore went higher up and fortunately found some small hollows in a cliff, full of fresh water that the rain had left there. They quenched their great thirst greedily, for they had almost succumbed. Since they had left the ship they had been without wine or other drink, except a daily allowance of one or two cups of water. They also collected a fair provision, about 80 cans of water, remaining there the whole night. It seemed that the blacks had been there just before, for they found the bones of crabs and the ashes of the fire.

On the 16th, as soon as it was light, they resolved to go further inland, hoping to find more such hollows with fresh water in the mountains. But their search was vain, for they found that there had not been any rain in the mountains for a long time; nor was there any appearance of running water, for behind the mountain chain the country was flat again; bearing neither trees nor vegetation, nor grass, and being everywhere covered with high anthills built of earth, which in the distance were not unlike Indian huts. There were also such multitudes of flies that one could not keep them out of one's mouth and eyes. They next saw eight black people, each carrying a stick in his hand. These approached them to a musket-shot's distance, but when they saw our people coming towards them they took to their heels, and would neither speak nor stop.

Seeing that there was no chance of obtaining more water they resolved toward noon to leave and, setting sail, they passed through another opening of the aforesaid reef, a little more to the north. They were in latitude 22 degrees 17 minutes, and imagined they were approaching the river of Jacob Remmessensz, but the wind ran to the north-east and they could not keep to the shore. They were obliged to resolve on trying to continue their voyage to Batavia as soon as possible, with God's help, in order to inform the worthy Governor and his councillors of their disaster, and to ask them for immediate assistance to rescue those who were left behind. For already they had sailed away from their ship and people more than 100 miles, without finding enough water to assist the others, and just obtaining sufficient to keep themselves on a ration of about two cupfuls daily.

On the 17th the sky was clouded, so that they could not take their bearing at noon; but with a north-west by north topsail breeze and dry weather they ran safely north-east for about 15 miles.

On the 18th they could again not take their bearings at noon, but guessed that during those 24 hours they sailed about 10 miles with a west-north-west wind, having rough weather with rain and wind, the latter running to the north-east slightly north at noon. They then steered west. This rough, rainy weather continued on the 19th, and again they could not take their bearings. But they guessed that with a north-west by west wind they had come about seven miles north-north-east.

On the 20th, at noon, they found themselves in latitude 19 deg. 22 min. and calculated that during the last 24 hours they had made about 22 miles north, the wind being west-south-west, with a shaky topsail breeze and sometimes rain.

On the 21st they were once more unable to take their bearing at noon; they guessed that they had made about 23 miles north, while the wind changed from the south-west to the south-east; the breeze subsided now and then into a calm.

On the 22nd at noon they were in latitude 15 deg. 10 min., at which they were not a little astonished, as they could not make out how they had gained so much latitude; but it appeared that the storm had driven them rapidly north. During these 24 hours they sailed north about a distance of 24 miles, the wind being mostly south-east with a shaky topsail breeze.

On the 23rd they were unable to take bearings. They guessed that they had sailed north-west about 16 miles. That day the wind ran to and fro from east to west, the weather being variable and rainy and frequently calm. In the evening the wind became south-south-east with a breeze.

On the 24th the weather was dry, a topsail breeze blowing from the south-east by south. At noon they were in latitude 13 deg. 36 min., and had during those 24 hours made 25 miles north by west.

On the 25th they had a south-east wind, dry weather and a topsail breeze. At noon they were in latitude 11 deg. 30 min. and had made 31 miles north by west. That day they saw floating on the water much rockweed.

On the 26th, they had reached 9 deg. 36 min., having sailed about 24 miles north by west, with a south-easterly wind and dry weather.

On the 27th the wind was south-east, a topsail breeze and rainy weather, so that they could take no bearings. In the afternoon they sighted the coast of Java, being then as they guessed in latitude 8 deg., and four to five miles away from the shore. They, therefore, took their course west-north-west along the coast, till in the evening they saw a cape in front of them, off which lay an islet covered with trees. They sailed past this cape in the dark, finding that a reef extended away from it, and that behind it there was a deep inlet. Into this inlet they sailed north-north-west, and dropped anchor in eight fathoms of water on a hard ground. There they remained all that night.

Having weighed the anchor on the morning of the 28th, they rowed ashore to find fresh water, as they were very much exhausted by thirst. On the shore they found to their great delight a running streamlet, and thanking God for His mercy, they quenched their great thirst. Having filled their casks with water, they sailed again at noon, continuing their journey to Batavia.

On the 29th, at midnight, in the second quarter of the moon, they saw an island ahead, which they passed on the starboard side. At daybreak they had reached the western inlet; thence the course lies west-north-west, though one loses sight of the shore on account of the curve, for before one reaches the Troubens Islands one meets the coast again. At noon they were in latitude 6 deg. 48 min. That day they had made about 30 miles, mostly west-north-west. About the middle of the afternoon they sailed between the two Troubens Islands, on the most westerly of which there are a good many coconut palms. In the evening they were still a mile away from the southern corner of Java, and at the third hour-glass of the second watch they began to approach the Straits which separate Java from the Prince's Islands.

On the morning of the 30th, being close to the aforesaid Prince's Islands, they were becalmed and that day they only made two miles, but towards evening a slight breeze came up from the land.

On the 1st of July the weather was calm in the morning, and at noon they were still about three miles from the Island of Dwars-inde-wegh (Right-in-the-way). The wind was changeable, and towards evening it began to blow more from the north-west, so that they could pass the said Island Dwars-inde-wegh. In the evening it was quite calm again and the whole night through they had to row.

On the 2nd, arriving in the morning at the island called "Toppers-hat", they had to drop the anchor till eleven o'clock on account of the calm, waiting for the sea breeze. But no wind came, and that whole day they had to row again, making only two miles before that evening.

In the setting sun they saw, about the island Dwars-inde-wegh, a sail astern, wherefore they ran under the shore dropping the anchor in order to wait for her.

Having weighed anchor before daybreak on the morning of the 3rd, they made for the strange ship in order to ask for some guns to use in their defence, as they did not know whether it was war or peace between the Dutch and the Javanese; but when they came nearer they saw three ships, the nearest being the yacht Sardam, which took the Commodore Françoys Pelsaert on board. From the merchant-captain, Van Dommelen, he learnt that the largest vessel was named Frederick Hendrick, and had on board the member of the Privy Council for India, Mr. Raemburgh. He sailed thither, and coming on board gave this dignitary, with a sad heart, the account of their great calamity. He was treated with the greatest kindness, and advised to remain on the ship till she reached Batavia. The other vessels were the Brombershaven and the Wesop under the command of Captain Grijp, who had sailed from Surat in the company of the worthy Pieter Van den Broeck, but had been parted from the others when at sea.

On the 4th the vessel Bommel, coming from Surat sailed up to them, bringing word that some more vessels had been sighted by her crew outside the straits, but that they could not tell whether they were English or Dutch.

On the 5th, at the fall of darkness, they arrived in the harbour of Batavia, not knowing how they might sufficiently thank God the Lord for His mercy.

# To the Reader.

I have not yet at present a daily account of the events that took place about the ship and among the people who reached the islands while the Commodore had left for Batavia to seek assistance. The following meagre narrative and account of judicial proceedings and confessions are all that has come to hand so far. They contain, however, the principal horrors and murders that occurred and also the justice done to the perpetrators. Still the want of a continuous record has prevented my polishing this story in such good order as I had wished. I would, therefore, request anyone who should be in possession of further information or notes to place them in the hands of the printer, so that they may be added to a second edition.

For the same reason I trust that the deficiencies of this my work will be excused. With this I bid the reader farewell, recommending him to read all with judgment and discrimination.

having been on the island for about a month after the ship had run aground, and seeing the ship reduced to fragments, began to realise that his first intention of seizing the vessel had to be abandoned. Therefore, he considered that his next alternative, being at the head of affairs during the absence of the Commodore, was to murder all the people except 40 men, and then with the scoundrels that remained under his command to seize the yacht that was expected to arrive from Batavia to rescue them, and to go pirating with her, or to run into port at Dunkirk or somewhere in Spain.

Daily meditating this scheme of his, he selected the following miscreants for his

The supercargo, Jerome (Jeronymus) Cornelisz, a chemist of Haarlem, together with some of his men, as David van Sevangh, an assistant, Gysbert van Welderen, Conraedt van Huyssen, and other accomplices, had formed the intention to float the ship off if she had not come to grief. This supercargo and some of the crew remained on the wreck ten days after the ship had been reduced to this condition, until at last she was almost entirely broken to pieces. He did not know how to get ashore. For another two days he found refuge on the bow-sprit. Then he succeeded at last in floating ashore on a spar. Together with him there floated ashore a cask of fresh water, a cask of wine, and a cask of vinegar.

Meanwhile Webbye Hays, who had been sent with some men to a long island to look for fresh water, found some after a 20 days' search.

The supercargo, Jerome Cornelisz,

counsellors and helpers: - David van Seevangh, Gysbert van Welderen, Conraedt van Huyssen, Cornelisz Pietersz, of Utrecht; Jan Hendricksz, of Bremen; Rutgert Frederiksz, of Groningen; Hans Jacob Heylwerck, of Basel, and others, making them sign the following contract and swear to it:-

"We, the undersigned, in order to take away all distrust that exists or might arise amongst us, bind ourselves herewith, on the salvation of our souls and on the solemn oath that God shall truly help us, to be true to each other in everything, and to love each other as brothers; also promising not to do each other any injury whatsoever in person or possession without first declaring verbally to each other the breach of the peace, in knowledge whereof we have signed this contract on the 12th of July, 1629, on the island Batavia's Kerckhof."

Webbye Hays and his men, who were still away looking for fresh water, and who, as has already been related, were successful after twenty days' search, made three fires as a signal. But this signal was taken no notice of, for that day was the day of the general murder. Some that escaped the carnage and came to his island on wooden rafts brought him the terribly sad tidings of what had happened. He therefore having with him now forty-five men, resolved to defend himself and his men, and to be ready for resistance if they came to fight him, making for his purpose weapons out of hoops and nails, which they tied to sticks.

Now that the people, all except 30 men and four boys, were mostly massacred and put out of the way, these miscreants resolved to go to the high island with two flat-bottomed sloops, in order to attack Webbye Hays and his men by surprise, and to kill them, thinking that otherwise he might give warning to their intention to any yacht that should come to their rescue, and thus their design would be frustrated.

Another party of people being on another little island, David van Seevangh went thither towards the end of July with a well-manned sloop, attacked them by surprise, and massacred them all, except seven boys and some women.

These blood-thirsty tyrants were well-nigh intoxicated with murder, and were roused to such bold pride and arrogance, that they did not hesitate to lay hands on the company's precious materials that had been saved, making all sorts of new-fashioned clothes out of them, which they trimmed with as much gold lace as was possible.

Jerome Cornelisz set the example, and had his helpers, whom he trusted best, and who were most ready to take part in the massacre, dressed in red cloth, trimmed with two and three bands of gold lace. Giving a still freer course to their viciousness, they further divided among themselves as booty some of the remaining women, in the following manner: - Jerome Cornelisz took for his share Lucretia Jansz, the wife of Bondlwign van der Mylen; Conraedt van Huyssen took Judith Gysberts, the eldest daughter of their minister, Gysbert Sebastiaensz, who had to suffer this patiently if he would save his life; futhermore, Tryntje* and Susan

Fredericks, sisters, also Annie Bosschietsters, Annie Herders, and Mary Lowijssen were distributed among the remaining men. To this end various laws were prescribed to these women, to which they had to bind themselves, under oath, if they would save their lives, as will be seen from the following Act: -

"We, the undersigned, bind ourselves on our soul's salvation, and by the help of God, to be true to each other, and stand by each other according to our oath aforesaid, nor to have secretly or publicly any designs against each other, or to suffer such designs to exist, but in everything to consider the common weal first and foremost, and to content ourselves, according to the laws hereby framed with the following women, Lucretia Jansz, Judith Gysberts, Annie Herders, Tryntje and Susan Fredericks, Annie Bosschietsters and Mary Lowijssen, to keep them accordingly, and to do everything that is most conducive to the peace. In knowledge whereof we have signed this contract on the 16th of July, 1629, on the island Batavia's Kerckhof."

At last the arrogant boldness of this Jerome Cornelisz rose so high that the name of supercargo was too insignificant for him, since there was no trade to be done there. For this reason he assumed the title of Captain-General, making his people, numbering 36 men, recognise him as such on oath of fidelity and obedience, as may be seen from the following document: -

"We, the undersigned, all here present on this island, being councillors, soldiers, ship's mates and also our minister, nobody whomsoever excepted, accept as our chieftain, as captain-general, Jerome Cornelisz, to whom we swear severally and unanimously in the name of God to be faithful and obedient in whatever he shall command us; and whosoever shall do ought to the contrary shall be the Devil's own; herewith we cancel and retract all previous public and private promises and oaths, comprising all secret comradeships, tent-mateships, and other alliances of whatever name or nature they may be. We further desire that the ship's crew among us shall no longer be called ship's mates, but shall equally with the other soldiers be named and reckoned as belonging to one and the same company. Thus given and signed on the island, named Batavia's Kerckhof, on the 20th of August, 1629."

*Catherine

Signed as follows:-

Conraedt van Huyssen
Jacob Pietrsz Cosyn
Gysbert van Welderen
Reymier Heindricksz, *Butler*
Andries Jonas van Luyck, *Soldier*
Matthys Beur van Munsterburg, *Soldier*
Jaques Pilman van Pres, *Soldier*
Andries Liebent van Oldenburg, *Soldier*
Hans Hardens, of Ditmarsz, *Soldier*
Jenriaen Jansz van Bremen, *Ship's mate*
Jan Willemsz Selyns, *Cooper*
Cornelisz Pietersz van Utrecht, *Soldier*
Jelis Philipsen van Malmidier, *Ensign*
David van Seevangh
Wouter Loos van Mastricht
Gysbert Sebastiaensz, *Minister*
Jan Hendricksz van Bremen, *Soldier*
Rutgert Fredricksz, *Lockmaker*
Hans Fredricksz van Bremen, *Soldier*
Luycas Jelisz, *from the Hague, Ensign*
Abraham Jansz van Yperen, *Musketeer*
Olivier van Welderen, *Ensign*
Isbrant Isbrantsz van Purmerent, *Assistant*
Jan Egbertsz, *Carpenter*
Hendrick Jaspersz van Montfoort, *Soldier*
Johan Jacob Heylwerck van Basel
Albert Jansz Assendelft, *Musketeer*
Gerrit Willemsz van Enckuysen, *Mate*
Jan Pilegram de Bye van Bommel
Salomon de Scanis, *Second Merchant*
Tewis Jansz of Amsterdam, *Carpenter*
Claes Harmensz van Campen
Rogier Decke van Haerlem, *Boy*
Abraham Gerritz, *of the Sierra Leone*
Lenart Michielsz van Os, *Ensign.*

Seven or eight days after this they sat in council once more, and resolved to attack Webbye Hays and his men. If these were put out of the way they would have no one to fear.

Moreover, one Pieter Lambertsz, a boatswain's mate, had escaped with a little boat that had been roughly put together, and made his way to the other island. Him and the boat they wanted to bring back, intending to punish the deserter. Selecting twenty-two of the lustiest rascals, they went thither; but after a hard fight they were obliged to return unsuccessful. A few days after - it was July - they made another attempt. Three boats were manned with 37 men. Jerome Cornelisz went personally, trusting that his own presence would give them the upper hand. Coming close to the island they steered straight for the shore. But Webbye Hays and his men stuck to their post, defending themselves bravely, standing off the beach up to their knees in water. Then these cursed assassins, seeing that they could do nothing with violence, dropped the lion's skin and tried that of the fox. They asked their former companions to unite with them, making use of the minister to persuade them. The latter, after a good deal of going backwards and forwards, induced them to cease fighting for that day, under promise that the next day the agreement should be confirmed with oaths, and that they should give Webbye Hays and his men some pieces of cloth for clothing, in return for which they should once more enter into possession of the misappropriated boat. When the others heard that Jerome Cornelisz, through the intermediation of the minister, had made this agreement, they were by no means contented with it. Conraedt van Huyssen

declared in anger that he would fight the next day, in spite of those who wished otherwise.

David van Seevangh, who also regretted these peace negotiations, tried meanwhile to persuade to his side some French soldiers belonging to Webbye Hays' company, promising them each 6,000 guilders. They were to come over to them next day, while the settlement of peace was taking place, and then they would the more easily despatch all Webbye Hays' company. When the two companies had parted on the said conditions, David van Seevangh told Jerome Cornelisz of his action with regard to Webbye's soldiers. The latter was pleased with this piece of felony, and in order to offer a still stronger inducement to the soldiers, he secretly sent them the following letter by one Daniel Cornelisz, on the 23rd of July:-

"*Dear Brethren and Friends,* - Jean Hodgaer, Jean Renouw de Mirinbry, Thomas de Villier, Jean Bonniver, and Eduart Coe, *the more we consider your former faithful and fraternal friendship for us, the more we wonder that you, who left willingly at the request of me, your merchant captain, in order to take a survey of the high island, do not return to report on your mission, for we have always esteemed you and taken you for our best and truest brethren and friends, and have continued and still continue to seek your alliance and comradeship, which we hold in as much esteem as our own lives. But we think it strange that you seem to lend an ear to the inventions of a few miscreants who had here deserved death for mutiny, and were therefore sent to another island. They found their way into your midst without our knowledge. We sent Jean Coos de Sally to the island merely on account of Jean Thierson, who was sent because he had drunk out of the casks. For we feared that Jean Coos might help him. Afterwards we learnt that we had misjudged in this, for Jean Coos offered to stab Jean Thierson if he might only be allowed to die with us. Should he still be inclined to do this, it would be an act of friendship and a service most agreeable to us. Well then, beloved brethren and friends, return to us, together with Jean Coos, help us in the cause of justice and in the punishment of the criminals. In particular try to deliver unto us alive those who robbed us so treacherously the day before yesterday of our chief help, the boat, viz.: Lucas, the bottler's mate; Cornelis, the fat trumpeter; Cornelis, the assistant;* deaf Jan Michielsz Adriaen, *the musketeer;* squinting Heynorick, Thenmis Claesz, Cornelis Hellincks, *and other ship mates who are with you; for unknown to you they have a compass, with the help of which they intend to leave secretly, with the boat, for the mainland. The merchant has an especial liking for and confidence in Webbye Hays, and wishes that you shall secretly inform him of this. For further details we refer you to the report which the bearer, your comrade, Daniel Cornelisz, will give you verbally, if you will give him a safe-guard. Dated the 23rd July, 1629, on the island Batavia Kerckhof.*"

This letter having come into the hands of Webbye Hays and his men, they at once perceived that a trap was laid for them and were on their guard. When the scoundrels and their captain, Jerome Cornelisz, in all numbering six, came the next day with the promised stuffs in order to confirm the concluded peace, and went ashore without any suspicion that their treachery had come to light, they were immediately attacked by Webbye Hays' men. Four of them were killed, being David van Seevangh (the assistant), Conraedt van Huyssen, Gysbert van Welderen (ensign), and Cornelisz Pietersz, of Utrecht (soldier). Jerome Cornelisz, their self-made captain, was made prisoner, and Wouter Loos escaped.

Wouter Loos of Mastricht having escaped the danger and brought tidings of their unfortunate experience to his comrades, they unanimously proclaimed him provisional captain in Jerome's place. In order to carry out his new function well, he did not leave Webbye Hays in peace long, but attacked him again the next day with two well-manned boats, hoping at last to succeed in their blood-thirsty design, or to deliver Jerome Cornelisz from their hands.

But Webbye Hays was a prudent man, and being on the watch, he saw the two boats approaching. He immediately drew up his men on the beach, and they defended themselves so successfully that the rascals were compelled to go back. Four of Webbye's men were severely wounded.

These are the principal events that happened during the absence of Commodore Françoys Pelsaert among his unfortunate people. We shall relate of the sequel of their story what we have been able to learn.

# Continuation of the Voyage.

When the Commodore, François Pelsaert, had arrived, as we related before, in the harbour of Batavia, he waited but till the next day before he went ashore and made his appearance at the court. There he acquainted the Governor-General, Jan Pietersz Coen, and his councillors with his misfortune, asking for speedy help to rescue the ship-wrecked people, and to save as much as possible of the company's goods. A few days, however, lapsed before anything could be done. Then the ship Saerdam was assigned to him, which had to be manned with a sufficient crew, and provided with victuals. Ten days passed before everything was ready.

He was not able to sail until the 15th of July. A land breeze was blowing. In the afternoon they reached Man-eater's Island, where they met the ship Leyden. This vessel had left the home country on the 8th of May, 1628, sailing from Texel together with the ship The Arms of Enckhuysen. The latter ship had been blown up through an explosion of the powder magazine on the 12th of October of the previous year, about the Sierra Leone. The ship Leyden had only succeeded in rescuing 57 of her people, 170 having been killed. But the people on the Leyden were now in very fair condition, for they had spent a month at Sillebor, on the island of Sumatra, which had set them up again.

Towards evening they also saw the ship Beets or Wigge, from Hoorn, which had likewise sailed among the fleet of the worthy Jacob Specks.

On the 16th it was rather calm, and that day they did not make much headway with the sails, though the current carried them pretty fast out of the Straits, for by evening they saw the Prince's Islands. On the morning of the 17th, they had the Prince's Islands east-north-east of them, being becalmed the greater part of the night, but before sunrise the breeze started from the south and they steered south-south-east. About noon the wind changed slightly to the east so that they could only bear south by west. In the afternoon of the 18th,

they took their bearings at 8 deg. 25 min., southern latitude, the wind being south-east, their course south-south-west. They calculated that they made that day 25 miles south-west by south. In the afternoon of the 19th they were in latitude 9 deg. 5 min. steering south by west with a south wind and having made about 24 miles south-west by south. On the 20th, at noon, they were in latitude 11 deg. the wind being south-east by east, their course south by west; that day they had made 20 miles south-south-west. On the 21st the wind was changeable, and sometimes fell to a calm. In the morning they had rain, catching 30 or 40 cans of water. At noon they were in latitude 10 deg. 38 min., and calculated that they had sailed 11 miles south-west by south. On the 22nd the wind blew with a topsail breeze from the south-south-west. Taking their bearings at noon, they found themselves in latitude 12 deg. 41 min., so that they must have made 19 miles south-west by south. On the 23rd the wind was gusty with showers, and at noon they were in latitude 14 deg., having made about 22 miles. On the 24th the wind was south-east, their course south-south-west, bearing gradually more south; at noon they were 15 deg. 14 min., and had made about 22 miles. On the 25th, with an east-south-east wind, having made about 17 miles south-south-west, they were at noon in latitude 16 deg. 16 min. On the 26th the wind was east, their course south-south-east bearing south; at noon they were 17 deg. 52 min., having made 23 miles. On the 27th, at noon they were in latitude 18 deg. 55 min., having the wind east by south, with alternate calms; they had made about 15 1/2 miles south. On the 28th the wind ran to the south-south-east, with a fair breeze and a heavy shower; so they steered more east, the course being south; at noon they were 19 deg. 45 min. On the 29th the misty weather prevented their taking bearings, but they guessed that they had made about 20 miles south. On the 31st, the weather cleared up and at noon, they took their bearings, being 20 deg. 9 min., south latitude, and in longtitude 132 deg. 8 min: then the wind began to turn south and they steered more east, sailing south-east till night, when the wind became once more west-south-west. On the 1st of August, having sailed south-west by south with a south-east wind, they were at noon in latitude 21 deg. 13 min., their longitude being 133 deg. 35 min. In this manner they continued till the 5th, when at noon they were in latitude 24 deg. 45 min., and in longitude 130 deg. 45 min. till evening they sailed south-west with a south-south-easterly wind; then the wind became very changeable and they had repeatedly to alter their course. On the 6th at noon, they were in southern latitude 24 deg. 32 min.; there was a great swell from the south-west, and the wind was very variable, so that they had to steer now east, now south. On the 7th, they had reached latitude 24 deg. 49 min., sailing south-west with a south-south-easterly wind; but at night the wind changed to the east-south-east, and they steered south in a drizzling rain. On the 10th at noon they were in southern latitude 27 deg. 54 min. and sailed mostly east with a north-east wind, according to its variations, the weather being very rough. On the 11th, before noon, the wind blew west, so that they sailed west-north-west being in latitude 27 deg. 57 min.; at night it blew with a strong breeze from the south and south-south-west. On the 12th at noon having reached 27 deg. 2 min. they had the wind from the south by west and steered east, the weather being changeable in the afternoon, the wind ran to the south-east, so that they changed their course. On the 13th at noon, they were 23 deg. 5 min. The wind was south-east, the weather calm, so they sailed south-west and south-west by south; but afterwards the wind became changeable, and they had accordingly to change their course repeatedly. On the 14th the sky was overcast, and they could take no bearings, but they guessed that they were in the same latitude, the wind being south-west by south, and with a big swell from the south they sailed east-south-east. On the 15th they were in latitude 26 deg. 30 min.; they had a southerly wind with a strong breeze and showery weather, so that they sailed east-south-east. On the 16th at noon they were in latitude 26 deg. 16 min. south, the wind was south, but during the

night it ran south-east by south, wherefore they took their course seaward to the west. On the 17th at noon, they could take no bearings, but calculated that they had made two miles south, having had all night a stiff breeze from the south-south-west. In the morning the water became smooth, and the wind changed to the east. On the 18th again they were unable to take bearings, but guessed that they were in southern latitude 27 deg. 15 min.; it was fine, and the wind was east-south-east, so that all day they sailed due south. On the 19th, at noon, they were in latitude 28 deg. 29 min. and had a shaky breeze from the east-south-east, which during the morning changed to south-south-west, after which it became calm. On the 20th, at noon, they were in southern latitude 29 deg. 10 min., the wind was south, they took their course, east by south, during the night they had a shaky breeze and variable winds. On the 21st, they could take no bearings, but guessed their latitude as they had done before; they sailed with a south wind, bearing east; having a strong roll form the south-south-west, they next went east by south. On the 22nd at noon, they found themselves in southern latitude 29 deg. 19 min, the wind was south, their course north-east, then the steersmen guessed that they were about 15 leagues from the wreck of the ship. On the 23rd, having reached a latitude of 28 deg. 14 min. with the wind south-west, their course east, they guessed that they must be alongside the coast, and therefore, their course east, they guessed that they must be alongside the coast, and therefore, during the night, they drifted for two watches with the sail partly brailed.

Having proceeded till the morning of the 25th, they found themselves at noon at a southern latitude of 27 deg. 56 min. They found that, as usual, during those 24 hours the current had taken them northward; they saw a good many breakers, and imagined they also saw some islands and surf, but this appeared to be caused by the reflection of the sun; they had then the wind south and more or less by east. During the first watch of the night it ran south-south-east, wherefore they took their course westerly; it then became calm, but the sea ran terribly high from the south-south-west. On the 26th, at noon, their latitude was 28 deg., 5 min., the wind was south by west, the sea high and hollow; in the afternoon the wind changed to south-south-east, they then took their course westward; when they had run like this about nine or ten hour-glasses, the high seas compelled them once more to steer east. On the 27th it was calm during the greater part of the day, so that they steered boldly westward; at noon their latitude was 28 deg. 13 min; then the seas began to roll from the south; towards evening a cool breeze rose from the south-west, wherefore they sailed south-east, but during the night they were again repeatedly becalmed.

On the 28th, having reached latitude 28 deg. 35 min. they sailed east with a south-south-west wind; then they saw the first seaweeds floating, from which they guessed that they would soon see the land; for two watches of the night they progressed rapidly south, but during the day-watch they drifted with the sail partly brailed, for the morning the wind changed again to south-east by east.

On the 29th their latitude was 28 deg. 10 min., the wind was south-east by south; the weather was rough; the mainsails were lowered half-mast, so that again they lost latitude; in the evening they bore seaward, sailing all night south-west by west. On the 30th at noon, their latitude was 29 deg. 55 min; the wind was south-east by south, the seas rolled high from the south-south-west. On the 31st, before noon, it was very calm, they took their bearings and found that they were in latitude 29 deg. 19 min. After noon the wind rose from the west; they took their course north-east by east, not knowing how far they still were from the land. In the morning the wind ran round to the south-east and the east-north-east.

On the 1st September, with variable winds, they reached a latitude of 29 deg. 16 min; they found it impossible to get round to the east. On the morning of the 2nd the wind ran north with a topsail breeze; at noon their latitude was 30 deg. 16 min. they then found that they were driven rapidly south; in the evening the wind veered to the

north-west, wherefore they sailed north-east by north. On the morning of the 3rd, the wind was west. They saw much seaweed floating, and therefore took their course east.

At noon they sighted the southern continent stretching north-north-west and south-south-east, when they were still about 3 miles away from it, they saw it stetching, they guessed, for about four miles south, and then ending; it was a flat and barren country, with dunes here and there, as in the north. At 25 fathoms they had a splendid sandy bottom. They were then in latitude 29 deg. 16 min. They took their course north-west, with a west-south-west wind; but the rollers pressed them so close to the coast, that in the evening they had to keep a mile from the shore, since about the second hour-glass, or the first watch, the anchor broke into two pieces, so that they had to drop another in haste, not without some danger. On the morning of the 14th, the wind was south-west by south with a high roll; during the day the wind changed to south-south-west; they then weighed the anchor and were under sail before noon, bearing west-north-west seaward, to get off the lower shore. At noon they were in southern latitude 28 deg. 50 min.; here the land began slightly to run off north by west and south by east; in the afternoon the wind became south, wherefore they sailed north, about evening they noticed some dry land, straight ahead or west of them. When they were about a musket-shot away from it, they found at 25 fathoms the bottom like that of a fine beach, wherefore they turned, keeping away from it at about half a mile's distance east-south-east. At about five miles distance from the continent they cast the anchor in a depth of 27 fathoms on a clear bottom, the night was calm, the weather splendid, with a south by east wind.

On the 15th the wind was south-south-east, the weather lovely. At daybreak they weighed the anchor, and having sailed south-south-west for an hour they perceived ahead in their course some shallows and islets on which the breakers ran. The wind gradually veered round, and became east, so that they could sail more south, and even south-south-east. This reef or dry land stretched south-south-west and north-north-east; alongside they found at 27, 28, or 29 fathoms a sandy bottom. At 11 before noon, they lost sight of the mainland, being then in southern latitude 28 deg. 59 min., close to a point of the reef jutting out west-south-west of them. The bottom was dirty and sloping, at a depth of 50 or 60 fathoms of water. In the afternoon a calm set in, so that the current took them right west, and a good deal west, they left the breakers behind. They guessed that then they were about eight miles from the

north-west. In the evening such a stiff breeze arose that the whole night through they had to sail with a half-mast sail, and to take the wind variously. On the morning of the 7th the weather calmed down, so that they could once more hoist the sails. At noon they were in latitude 29 deg. 30 min. They then turned north to get sight of the mainland. Then, as the wind blew sharper, from the west-north-west, they were obliged to turn seaward. On the 8th at noon, being in latitude 29 deg. 7 min. they took their course north-east, so that in the evening they again sighted the breakers;

mainland. This calm lasted all night, and they drifted so close along the breakers that they could hear their roar the whole night. On the morning of the 6th the breakers were out of sight. About 11 the wind came from the west-north-west. They were again approaching the breakers being at noon in latitude 28 deg. 44 min. Then it began to blow very hard from the north-west, so that during that afternoon they tacked. Finding that the current took them a good deal north-west, in the evening they turned again seaward from the breakers, having a dirty rocky bottom at 40 fathoms. This dry land extended south-east and

they therefore bore west-south-west seaward all night, with a north-west wind. Then it began to blow so hard, that they had to take down the topsails. On the morning of the 9th, they once more turned to the land, being at noon in latitude 29 deg. and spending the rest of the day in turning to and fro; in the evening a severe storm blew from the north-west, and they found it difficult enough to keep going with the reefed sails. On the 10th the wind was west, with a topsail breeze, having hoisted the sails again they reached at noon the southern latitude of 29 deg. 30 min.
On the morning of the 11th it was calm,

but the sea was high, the wind blew from the west-south-west, so that they could not gain any distance north without approaching the breakers. At noon they reached the latitude of 28 deg, 48 min., with variable winds. All that night they sailed with a reefed sail. On the morning of the 12th they set sail again in an easterly direction, till at noon they found themselves at 28 deg. 13 min. Therfefore, they went somewhat south again, in order to approach the land exactly at 28 deg., 30 min. The wind was south-west and the sea high. In the afternoon, two hours before sunset, they sighted the breakers again, from which they guessed they were still two miles away. Then, dropping the lead-line, they found splendid sandy bottom at 100 fathoms; but having come half a mile nearer and sounded again, they touched a dirty stony bottom at 80 fathoms. Therefore, during the night, in the second watch, they turned seaward, and continued so till the day-watch, when they turned again landward, in order to approach the shore.

On the 13th, three hours after sunrise, they once more discovered the breakers, and having taken their bearings, they found that they had lost a mile to the north, as the wind had been south-south-east; as they had arrived at the most northerly point of the Abrolhos, and always seemed to get too high or too low, whereas it was dangerous to approach them from the outside, they resolved to bear through the rollers and the dirty depths, below the outer dry land; and then tacked again a little, with the wind south-south-east, their course east. Coming a little closer in, they immediately had a clear bottom at 30 to 35 fathoms of water; at noon they were in latitude 28 deg; shortly after they saw again the southern mainland. A stiff breeze began to blow, consequently they anchored at about two miles from the shore, in 30 fathoms of clear sandy bottom. On the 14th it blew hard from the south-south-east, so that they could not weigh the anchor, and had to lie still all day. On the 15th, the wind continued with equal force till noon, then it became calmer, so that they could lift the anchor on board and wind it up; having set sail, they reached at noon the latitude of 27 deg. 14

min. The wind was south-south-east, and they tacked all day in order to advance south; in the evening they found that they had made two miles. It was dark, and they anchored again in a clear sandy bottom at 30 fathoms depth. On the morning of the 16th, at daybreak, they weighed the anchor again, and took their course more or less south, with a west-south-west wind. In the afternoon the wind changed to west, then to north, so that they could sail west. Towards evening they saw the wreck of their ship Batavia, and the Commodore was seen from the high island, though the mates said it was not one of the islands. At two o'clock in the night they anchored in a clear, sandy bottom at 27 fathoms depth.

On the morning of the 17th they again weighed the anchor. The wind was north. They were still about two miles from the high island; they approached it in south-westerly direction. Before noon, having come about the island, they saw close to the wreck, on a long islet, some smoke, at which they were much rejoiced, hoping to find all or most of their people alive. Having cast the anchor, the Commodore, taking with him a cask of water, and bread and wine, went with the boat to the highest island, which was nearest by; but on arriving there he found no one, at which they were all very much astonished. Jumping ashore, they saw a little boat with four men rowing round the northern point. The one whose name was Webbye Hays jumped ashore, meeting the Commodore, welcoming him, but begging of him to return immediately to the ship, as there were a party of miscreants on the islands about the wreck, who intended to come in two boats and seize the yacht on its arrival.

He related how he had become a captain of forty-seven people, who, to save their lives, had kept all that time on a little island, since some of the people, who were left behind, had turned scoundrels and murdered some one hundred and twenty-five people, being men, women and children. About fourteen days ago the supercargo, Jerome Cornelisz, the chief of these scoundrels, had been captured by him. Four of his principal counsellors and accomplices, viz.: the assistant, David van Seevanck,

Conraedt van Huyssen, Gysbert van Welderen, and Cornelisz Pietersz of Utrecht, soldier, had been killed. These had repeatedly come across to fight him and his men, but every time they had been bravely kept off; then they had used traitorous and sinister means to conquer and murder them, offering them peace through the intermediation of their minister, Gysbert Sebastiaensz, whom they forced to go backward and forward. When they came to conclude the peace with solemn oaths, promising to forget and forgive all that had passed, David van Seevanck and Conraedt von Huyssen tried to bribe some soldiers to treason, offering them each six thousand guilders, if, when they returned next day after the conclusion of the peace, these men would side with them and help to kill the others. But Webbye's men had understood this, and, perceiving that it was aimed at their life, they killed these fellows, and captured their captain, as related above. He further described how that same morning, one rebel, named Wouter Loos, who had been proclaimed chief after the capture of the former captain, Jerome, had attacked them with two boats full of men, whom they had bravely resisted, and kept off, four of Webbye Hays' men having been severely wounded in the fray. When the Commodore had learnt all these tidings with deep regret, he immediately rowed aboard again, ordering Webbye Hays to row back to his people, and to bring the prisoner, Jerome Cornelisz, to the ship, which was done as ordered. But before the Commodore could get to his ship he saw a rowing boat with people approaching round the southern point of the high land, wherefore he prepared for defence, with the intention, if possible, to overpower and capture the scoundrels. Meanwhile he continued his course to the ship.

On reaching her, he found that the rebels were boldly coming on in the same direction. When they were close enough he could distinguish their red cloth dresses, trimmed all over with gold lace. The Commodore asked them why they came on board armed. They answered that they would tell him when they were on board. After this insolent reply he ordered them to throw their weapons into the sea, and to come across or he would know how to force them to obedience.

Seeing that they had no escape, they obeyed, and coming on board, they were at once put in irons.

Their examinations commenced at once. The first one to be examined was Jan Hendricksz, of Bremen, soldier, who immediately let out and confessed to have killed and helped to kill 17 or 20 people, but everything at the express orders of Jerome Cornelisz, their captain, who had forced them to it. Having further been questioned as to the causes and circumstances of all this, and as to what had led them to such inhuman cruelty, he stated his willingness to reveal everything, also how all had happened in the beginning, viz.: that the Skipper, Adriaen Jacobsz, Jerome Cornelisz, and the first boatswain had made a compact with the others to seize the vessel Batavia, before it was wrecked, to kill the Commodore and all the crew and passengers, except about 120 who were in the plot, and to throw the dead overboard into the sea; then to go pirating and free-booting with the vessel. Wherefore Jerome Cornelisz and his men on the island had made sure that the Skipper would have killed the Commodore on the way, or have thrown him overboard into the sea, and having been on the island for a month, he thought he could do nothing better than kill all the people but forty, with whom he would seize the yacht on its arrival. He felt, however, that this could not be done unless Webbye Hays and his men, who had been sent to the long island for water twenty days before, were put out of the way. They had started upon this fiendish expedition, and made some attacks already but had not succeeded.

Towards evening Webbye Hays brought Jerome Cornelisz to the Commodore on board ship as a prisoner. The Commodore looked at him with deep sorrow, not being able to conceive what had induced him to forget himself so far that he had become the cause of such inhuman murders. Being examined in the presence of the Council, the Commodore asked him why he had allowed the devil to lead him so far astray from all

human feeling, and had done that which had never been so cruelly perpetrated among Christians, without any real need of hunger or thirst, solely out of cold bloodthirstiness, and to attain his wicked ends. To which he replied, that they should not blame him for what had happened, putting it all on David van Seevanck, Conraedt von Huyssen and others, who had been killed in the last encounter with Webbye Hays' men. He said they had forced him to it, threatening otherwise to take his life. One had often to do a great deal to save oneself. He denied ever having had the intention to help to seize the vessel Batavia, and as to the project of seizing any yacht that should come to their rescue he said Seevanck had proposed this, and he had only consented, but without meaning it seriously, since he supposed that they would never be delivered from these unfortunate islands. For he had heard one, Ryck Wontersz, say that Skipper Adriaen had intended to seize the vessel, if it had not been wrecked, and to throw the Commodore overboard, which made him think that they could never have reached Batavia, but that the Skipper must have gone to Malacca; or should it have happened that the Commodore had reached Batavia,

and that a yacht were sent to their rescue, he would have tried to give warning. In this manner, he tried to excuse himself with his glib tongue, telling the most palpable lies, and making out that he had been altogether innocent and ignorant of everything, often appealing to the mates, as if they could have known his inner thoughts, saying that they would give a similar testimony. At this the matter was left that day and he was again incarcerated.

On the 18th September before daylight, the Commodore and the Skipper went with the two boats to the long island, where Webbye Hays was with his men. He took the soldiers from thence, arming each with a good musket. With those he proceeded to the island named "Batavia's Churchyard", which was close to the wreck; his intention was to catch the remaining scoundrels, who were still there, and make them prisoners. When they saw the Commodore approaching with his two well-manned boats, their hearts immediately failed them, and their courage sank before they had made any resistance. They said to each other, *"Now we are all dead men"*, thinking that they were going to be killed in hot haste. But in this they were mistaken. When the Commodore had landed, he caused all the rebels to be bound hand and foot, and to be secured as prisoners; then his first work was to seek the jewels that lay scattered here and there. Those were all found except a gold chain and ring, though the ring came to light after all.

Going to the wreck in the evening, they found the ship lying in many pieces, a part of the keel, showing the flat of the hold, from which everything was washed away from front to back, except some of the planking, which still rose above the water. It was almost exactly in the same spot where it had been first. A piece of the front of the vessel broken off at the curvature was rocked on the dry places. In it were two pieces of cannon (one of metal and one of iron) fallen from the ramparts, without anything more. Thereabouts lay further to one side of the stern, part of the vessel, broken off at the crossing of the sternboard. Then there were several fragments of a smaller size, drifted apart to various places. Altogether it did not look promising and there was little hope of saving much of the money and the goods.

The Commodore was somewhat comforted by the butler, Reymier Heindricksz, who informed him that about a month ago, on a calm and fine day (almost the first since their arrival there), he had gone fishing about the wreck, because the fish seemed to be plentiful there; that with a spear he had hit on a money chest, and hoped it would not have been washed away since. Upon which the Commodore asked him further how the wreck had fared since his departure, and how long the vessel had remained together. He answered that for a week she had held together, then the prow and the higher parts began to be washed away, not being able to resist the daily violent storms and the strength of the breakers; at last the port-side was broken to pieces. He had been astonished to see so strong a vessel so easily broken asunder and demolished. Then at different times floated ashore and were saved several barrels of water, a barrel of French wine, and four and a half barrels of Spanish wine, also one barrel of vinegar. All this stood them in good stead. But before this the Lord had sent them during the night of the 9th and 10th July a steady rain (the same rain the Commodore had had about the mainland when he and his boat were in great danger of sinking) which furnished them with a good deal of water; so that with this and with that which they had fished out of the sea, all the people might have kept themselves from thirst for a long time, everyone receiving daily three cups of water and two cups of wine; if only the Devil, their chief, had not tempted them to such horrible murder.

In the evening the principal scoundrels and their helpers, that had been captured and put in irons that day, were taken to the Seals Island, to remain there till they would be sent for, to be once more examined. It was thought that they would be better secured there.

On the morning of the 19th the Skipper was sent to bring ashore the following miscreants, who were imprisoned in the ship, with a view to examining them as to the wicked life they had led: Jerome Cornelisz, the supercargo; Jacob Pietersz, of Amsterdam, a subordinate officer, who had been their lieutenant and one of the council of mutineers; Ian Hendricksz, of Bremen, a soldier, one of the chief murderers; Rutgert Fredericksz of Cromigen, a locksmith; Hans Jacob Heywerck, of Basel, ensign; Luycas Jelisz, of the Hague, ensign; Hans Fredericksz, of Bremen, soldier; Ian Willemsz Selyns of Amsterdam, chief cooper; Hendrick Jaspersz of Montfoort, soldier; Hans Hardens, of Ditmarsz, soldier; Jacques Pilman, from near Verdun, soldier; and Gerri Haes, of Santlu, boatswain's mate. From cross questionings and free confessions of all these it became evident that day what a wicked life these out and out miscreants had led on the island, not refraining from shamefully misusing the company's goods, cloths and materials, gold trimmings, and other wares, which they had fished up. With these they had clothed themselves, trimming them with so much gold lace that the material was hardly visible, as might be observed from Jerome Cornelisz' clothes, who, it appeared, set the example in all this. Neither had they refrained from appropriating to themselves the rescued goods and clothes that were private property, and from distributing these for use as if they had been left to them by bequest. Jerome Cornelisz had gone so far in his satanic pride, that he had not scrupled to wear different clothes every day, and to deck himself out in silk stockings and garters with gold trimmings. He had clothed those of his adherents whom he trusted most in the work of assassination with red cloth, trimmed with two or more bands of gold lace. He had invented fresh patterns of cassocks for every day. Clearly he had been convinced and had persuaded the others, that this vain and wicked revelry would last forever.

When most of the murdering was done, he distributed the following remaining women among his followers as a booty, in this manner:- Lucretia Jansz, the wife of Boudewijn Vanner Mylen, he kept for himself; Judigh Gysbert, the eldest daughter of the minister, he gave to Conraedt van Huyssen. The remaining women, the sister Catherin and Susan Fredericks, Annie Bosschietsters, and Mary Lowijssen, were allotted to the other men. To prevent all disastrous dissension, he made a code of regulations, which everyone signed under oath, as is given in the preceding pages. The women also, if they wished to save their lives, had to swear allegiance to those regulations.

On the 20th of September, before noon, the boat was sent to the vessel to bring ashore some necessaries, and the long boat to the island on which Webbye Hays and his people were to find some fresh water. They had, after having been on that island 20 days, miraculously found two wells of fresh water, which, nevertheless, rose and fell with the high and low tide, so that at first they had imagined that it must be salt water.

On the 21st the breeze blew fresh from the east-south-east. They then noticed that the water remained very low there, and the longboat could not come back from the island that day on account of the strong wind, they therefore spent that day examining the prisoners.

This strong wind continued on the 22nd, and the longboat did not come yet. Towards noon the Commodore and the Skipper and three men went in a boat to the wreck to survey its exact position, but when they reached it the breakers were so terrible that the divers durst not undertake to swim across, so in the evening they returned to the vessel without having done anything.

On the 23rd the wind was still as before. That morning the prisoners who had been sent to the Seals Island were sent for to be examined, which occupied the whole day. Meanwhile the Skipper was again sent to the wreck to see whether any of the goods could be secured; but they returned stating that it was still impossible on account of the terrible breakers.

On the 24th September, nothing particular happened except that the Skipper went aboard with the boat in order to bring some necessaries on shore, as it was not yet possible to work at the wreck.

On the evening of the 25th, the weather being still, the Skipper and the boatswain were again sent to the wreck to see whether it was possible to set to work. When they had arrived there, it was noticed from the shore that they were busy getting something out of the water. The Commodore, therefore, sent the other boat to their assistance, well manned, he himself following in the smallest boat, with a man and two boys, in order to join them. When he arrived there he found them busy with a bundle of tinsel and a chest of money, which they had fished up there. They brought them on the dry land at some distance from the wreck. The Commodore passed into the other boat, where they were fishing and just bringing up another chest of money; the divers from Gugerat declared that they had found six more money-chests and that it would be quite feasible to bring them up. Meanwhile the second chest that had been brought to the surface was propped and moved to the dry land, so now they had already obtained and secured four chests; the divers prepared for the return of the Skipper. Then, however, the wind rose with such force and the sea ran against the wreck so violently that they were obliged to leave. Therefore they fetched the secured chests from the dry places, and took them to the island Batavia's Churchyard. The remainder of the day they spent in examining the prisoners.

On the 26th a strong wind blew from the south-west, so that they could not work at the wreck, wherefore the boat was sent to another island to bring them a capstan and some empty oil casks that were there. Before noon another boat went out to get water. Meanwhile the Commodore sent for Cornelisz Jansz, of Amsterdam, assistant, and Aris Cornelisz, of Hoorne, barber, in order to question them on that which had happened while they tried to escape from being killed. In the afternoon the weather became calm and the water smooth, so that the Skipper immediately went to the wreck with a well-manned boat, in order to bring up and secure the money chests they had discovered on the previous day. When he returned late in the afternoon he brought three of them. One of them he had as yet been obliged to leave, as it could not be got until a piece of cannon and an anchor, which were lying crossways on top of it, had been removed with great labour and trouble.

On the 27th there blew a stiff breeze from the south, and that day they were unable to work at the wreck. Before noon the longboat returned from the high island, bringing the two above-named persons, Cornelisz Jansz and Aris Pietersz, whose testimony was to be heard against the other assassins and miscreants. That day, therefore, was devoted to the examination.

On the 28th the same stiff south wind continued, and it was still impossible to work at the wreck, so that they proceeded with the examination, and pretty nigh finished it. The intentions of the principal miscreants and murderers became sufficiently evident from their own confessions, from various testimonies, and, alas! from the dire results of their actions. This will be seen from the following written testimonies. The Commodore, therefore, resolved to call together the Council, and to discuss and consider maturely the proposition, whether these murderers and miscreants, the blood of whose victims was calling loudly for revenge, should be put in irons and taken to Batavia before the Lord Governor, or whether they should be here

sentenced and put to death according to their desserts as an example to others; for the danger existed that the ship and all her cargo might be lost, if they went to sea with so many half and wholly corrupted people. It was their duty to prevent this catastrophe, which undoubtedly threatened the vessel through the presence of such miscreants as Jerome Cornelisz and his accomplices, especially as already some, or perhaps all the remaining mates, might have imbibed the poison of their ill-intentioned seduction. Being still contaminated with the recollections of the wicked life of brigandage, they might, when at sea, break out and be corrupted and tempted by the great riches of the wreck, belonging to their Masters. Upon this consideration the following resolution was passed.

On this day, the 28th of September, 1629, the Commodore, Françoys Pelsaert, and his ship's counsellors of the yacht Sardam, on the island Batavia's Churchyard, situated near the wreck of the vessel Batavia, in latitude 28 deg. south, about nine miles from the mainland have resolved as follows:-

"Having, after many hardships and dangers (for which God be praised), arrived on the 17th September of this year, 1629, with our yacht Sardam, about the high island, two miles from the wreck of our unfortunate ship Batavia, the Commodore, who went with bread, water and wine to the people on the land (whom we knew to be there on account of the rising smoke), in order to feed and refresh them, was met by a little boat with four men, who cautioned him to return on board directly, since on one of the islands near the wreck there were a party of miscreants who intended to seize the yacht that had come to their rescue. The supercargo, Jerome Cornelisz, the chief of these miscreants, who had had the intention of surprising and murdering those who were now warning the Commodore, had been captured by the latter. The Commodore immediately sent for this man and had him brought on board as a prisoner. He returned to his ship, in order to communicate to his people the sad tidings he had so unexpectedly received and to make them prepare for defence. But already, while on this journey, eleven of these miscreants came rowing towards him in a flat-bottomed boat. He went on board the vessel, ordering the rebels to surrender. They submitted, and were imprisoned on board. All these, and also Jerome Cornelisz, who was brought on board in the meantime were examined. Again it became sadly evident what horrible, abominable murders these men had perpetrated, viz.: the said Jerome, further David van Seevangh, the assistant, and Conraedt von Huyssen, ensign, both of whom had been killed on the high island a fortnight ago, at the time when Jerome Cornelisz had been captured; also Jacob Pietersz, a subaltern, who had escaped on that occasion. The intention had been to kill all the people except 40 or less, and next they had planned to conquer and kill a certain number, about 47 men, who had fled from the murder to the high island. They had made repeated assaults on these, but had been driven back every time. According to their own confession, they had wished to seize upon the first yacht that should come to their rescue, and sail to Spain, Barbary, or some similar place, living as pirates."

"They had further, according to their own confession and testimony, murdered more than 120 people, men, women, and children – drawing many, and killing others in all sorts of cruel ways, the principal assassins still being alive: – Lenart Michielsz von Os, soldier; Matthys Beur, of Munsterburg, ensign: Jan Hendricksz, of Bremen, soldier: Albert Jansz, of Assendelft, musketeer: Rutgert Fredricksz, of Groningen, locksmith: Jan Pilegram de Bye, of Bommell, steward: and Andries Jonas, of Luyck, soldier: besides their accomplices. Having therefore inquired and examined daily from the 17th of this month of September until this day in order to find the truth of all this, we have obtained knowledge of the following facts, from our examination as well as from voluntary confessions:– Jerome Cornelisz, supercargo of the vessel Batavia, after sailing from the Capo de Bonna Esperansa (Cape of Good Hope), entered into a conspiracy with the Skipper, Adriaen Jacobsz, intending to seize the vessel, and to assassinate all the people except one hundred and twenty; further, to sail as pirates and, finally, to run into port in Spain or some other place. This scheme they were unable to carry out, on account of their shipwreck. He, himself, confessed that it was by his orders, and with the approval of his Council, that so many people were murdered in order to reduce the company to a small number. He had further planned with David van Seevangh, Conraedt van Huyssen, and Jacob Pietersz, to seize the first yacht that should arrive, but meanwhile they intended to try and conquer the people on the large island or bring them to submission. If then a yacht had come they would have induced the crew to come ashore with a boat, and made them drunk; after which it would have been easy to put them out of the way, and to surreptitiously seize the vessel by night.

They thought this plot could not very well fail, for they calculated that such a yacht would not carry more than 20 or 30 men. Having after a long cross-examination of all the remaining people, with God's help, obtained an exact and true knowledge of these terrible deeds, the Commodore has proposed a choice between two courses. Either these reprobate miscreants, tainted with every crime and divested of all human pity, are to be put in irons on the vessel and taken to Batavia, to the Lord General to be punished according to their desserts by especial order of the authorities, our Lords and Masters; or they are to be punished at the very place where their crimes were committed, in order to expose the ship and the crew to no further danger. This question has been ripely considered and during its discussion attention has been also paid to the fact that Jerome Cornelisz is not only tainted with abominable crimes, but has moreover adopted a most abominable creed, maintaining that there is neither devil nor hell, and trying to inculcate this belief on his comrades, thereby corrupting them all. It has, therefore, been unanimously approved and resolved, as best serving the interest of the Company, and in order to secure from further danger both the vessel and the precious cargo just retrieved from the waters, to sentence and condemn Jerome Cornelisz, aforesaid, and his most willing fellow assassins, those that have made a profession of murder. As they are hereby sentenced and condemned as follows:— First:

Jerome Cornelisz, of Haerlam, chemist, having been supercargo on the vessel Batavia, shall, after having been baptised according to his request, on Monday, the 1st October of this year 1629, be taken to Seals' Island, there to the place where justice will be done. There, first both his hands shall be cut off, and he shall next be punished with the cord at the gallows there erected, and so done to death. His goods, money, gold, silver, monthly wages, and other pretensions that he might have to make in India will be confiscated on behalf of our master, the General East India Company.

Jan Hendricksz, of Bremen, soldier, about 24 years old, who, according to his confession, borne out more fully by subsequent examination, has murdered, or helped to murder 17 or 18 people, and has also had the intention to help to seize the first yacht arriving, shall likewise be taken to Seals' Island, to the place where justice will be done, and first have his right hand cut off, and then be punished with the cord at the gallows until he is dead. All his clothes, monthly pay, and whatever he might have to claim against our Lords and Masters will be confiscated.

Lenart Michielsz van Os, ensign, about twenty-one years old, having, according to his confession, murdered, or helped to murder, twelve people, misbehaved with married women, and kept Annie Bosschietsters, the wife of Jan Castersz, of Tonninghen, as his concubine, shall likewise be taken to Seals' Island, to the place of Justice, and have his right hand cut off; and be punished with the cord at the gallows until he is dead, and all his clothes, monthly pay, and what further claims he may have, will be confiscated on behalf of our Lords and Masters.

Matthys Beur of Munsterburg, about twenty-one years old, having, according to his free confession, murdered, and helped to murder nine people and having kept Susan Fredericks, a married woman, as his concubine, shall be brought to justice on Seals' Island, first his right hand will be cut off, and then he will be punished with the cord at the gallows until he is dead. His clothes, monthly pay, and goods, are forfeited to the company, our Lords and Masters.

Albert Jansz, of Assendelft, musketeer, about 24 years old, having confessed of his own free will that, being persuaded by Jerome Cornelisz, he had promised to assist in seizing the vessel Batavia. Further that he had cut the throat of Andries de Bruyr, of Haerlan, a cabin boy; that he had helped to kill Jan Pinten, an Englishman; that he had tried one

night to kill Aris Jansz, of Hoorn, barber's assistant, but that the bluntness of his sword had frustrated his design, though he had given him a cut on the shoulders which did not penetrate, so that his victim escaped in the water through the darkness of the night, that he had further committed all sorts of wanton acts after the wreck of the vessel; shall for these reasons be taken to Seals' Island, and according to his sentence first have his right hand cut off, and then be punished with the cord at the gallows until he is dead. His clothes and monthly pay will be confiscated on behalf of the Company.

Jan Pilegram de Bye of Bommel, late steward on board the wrecked vessel Batavia, about eighteen years old, having according to his own confession, led a very Godless and bestial life, in words as well as in deeds, murdered a boy on Seals'Island and helped to Kill Janneken Gijssen, the wife of Jan Hendricksz of The Hague, musketeer, also Andries Jansz; having further insisted on the sixteenth of August last of being allowed to cut off the head of Cornelisz Aldersz of Ilpendam, a labourer, and, when this was refused, cried very much because the favour had been granted to Matthys Beur; having misbehaved himself with the sisters Susan and Catherine Fredericks and Annie Bosschieters, all of them married women, shall be taken to Seals' Island and be punished with the cord at the gallows, until he is dead, his clothes, monthly pay, and whatever claims he may have against the authorities, our Lords and Masters, will be confiscated.

Andries Jonas of Luyck, soldier, about 40 years old, having confessed voluntarily that when Paulus Barentsz was killed in the water he had thrust a pike through his throat and caused him to die; that he had cut the throat of May Soets on Seals' Island she being at the time pregnant; also that he had helped to kill Jannie Gist and Jan van Hummel; finally that he had lent assistance on every wicked expedition; shall therefore also be taken to Seals' Island and be punished with the cord at the gallows until he is dead. All his clothes, monthly pay and whatever he might have to claim against our Lords and Masters, the Company, will be confiscated.

assistance. Moreover, Jerome Cornelisz affirms that the said Rutgert like Matthys Beur, has allowed himself to be made use of willingly in everything, so that he has no excuse whatever to bring forward. Therefore, he shall be taken to Seals' Island, and punished at the gallows until he is dead. All his clothes, monthly pay, and whatever he has to claim will be confiscated on behalf of the Company our Masters.

We have further resolved as to the following miscreants who are still in custody, and whose misdeeds have not yet been fully inquired into and confirmed, so that the proofs must still be doubted and considered, leaving it uncertain whether they deserve death, or whether their lives may be spared

Rutgert Fredericksz of Groningen, locksmith, about 23 years old, confessed voluntarily that he had tied the hands and feet of Jacob Groenewal, the first trumpeter, who was going to be drowned, when Seevangh and De Vries carried Groenewal into the sea; also, that when the Prevost, Pieter Jansz, and fourteen of his men were thrown into the sea from the rafts, and Paulus Barentsz and Bessel Jansz, both of Herderwijok, and Nicolaes Winckelhaeck and Claes Harmansz, of Magdeburg, escaped swimming, finding refuge on this island, he had been ordered by Jerome Cornelisz to kill them; that he Rutgert Fredericksz then gave Paulus Barentsz two cuts with his sword, and from him fell upon Claes Harmansz, killing him only. When the assistant, Andries de Vries, was also to be killed, he and Jan Hendricksz and Lenart Michielsz were all called into Jerome Cornelisz's tent, who gave them each a sword to put Andries de Vries out of the way with; to which end he willingly gave his services. But De Vries, seeing that he was in danger, fled into the water, where Lenart Michielsz pursued him and killed him with two blows of his sword, thus preventing Rutgert Fredericksz from giving any

without incurring the disgrace of our Lord General, that they shall remain in irons till further charges shall be proved against them, either to be taken to Batavia, or eventually to be committed to sentence on the voyage, namely:

Wouter Loos, of Mastricht, soldier, who was made captain of the rebels after the capture of Jerome Cornelisz.

Jacob Pietersz, of Amsterdam, corporal, who has been a counsellor of Jerome Cornelisz, David van Seevanck and Conraedt van Huyssen.

Hans Jacobsz, of Basel, Ensign.
Daniel Cornelisz, of Dordrecht, Ensign.
Andries Liebent, of Oldenburgh, Ensign.
Hans Fredericksz, of Bremen, soldier.
Cornelisz Jansz, of Haerlam, boatswain's mate.
Jan Willemsz Selyns, of Amsterdam, cooper.
Roger Decker, of Haerlam, formerly boy to Jerome Cornelisz.

Further, having found from various testimonies and from incontrovertible evidence that Webbye Hays, of Winnhooten, soldier, when he was on the high island with forty-seven souls, protected them faithfully and preserved them bravely from the murderous party that intended to put them all together out of the way, attacking them for this purpose three times, we have found good, since there are no officers over the soldiers to appoint the said *Webbye Hays* a sergeant, with a pay of eighteen guilders a month. Also we make *Otter Smit*, of *Halberstadt*, and *Albert Jansz*, of *Elsen*, both ensigns, for their faithful help to *Webbye Hays*, corporals on a pay of fifteen guilders a month.

Given under our hand on the island "Batavia's Grave" at the above date and signed.

*Françoys Pelsaert*
*Claes Gerritsz*
*Symen Jobsz*
*Jacob Horstenman*
*Jacob Jansz*
*Jan Willemsz.*

Here follows, to throw still further light on the occurrences among these wicked murderers on the island, the verbal examination and free confession of Jerome Cornelisz in its daily progress since his imprisonment, until the sentence of death had been pronounced on him and his accomplices.:

To-day, the 17th September, 1629, in the afternoon, the Commodore, Françoys Pelsaert, and his ship's council have resolved to examine, and if necessary to put to the torture, Jerome Cornelisz, chemist, of Haarlem, late supercargo on the shipwrecked vessel Batavia, now imprisoned on board on account of the horrible misdeeds committed by him.

Jerome Cornelisz, having been led in, was asked why he had allowed the Devil to divest him of all human feeling and to tempt him till he had become worse than a tiger, why he had shed so much innocent human blood, and had nourished the intention of shedding ours also. To which he replied that it was not all his fault. It was David van Seevanck, Gysbert van Welderen, and Conraedt van Huyssen who had done most of it, and forced him to it, threatening to kill him. He begged to receive a hearing to be able to prove his innocence, having been charged to give truthful account of all that had happened from the beginning.

He said that ten days after the wreck he had still been on board the vessel, though it was mostly broken to pieces by that time. For two days he had been on the bowsprit mast, and finally floated ashore on a portion of the bowsprit, together with three casks of water, wine and vinegar, having

been on the island about a month. David van Seevanck, Conraedt van Huyssen, ensign, and twelve others had armed themselves in their tent, and coming in to him one evening between 10 and 11 o'clock, they had said, *"There are too many people and there is too little food; we intend to surprise the people in their tents, and to reduce the number to 40."* Jerome Cornelisz had then begged of them not to do this, and suggested that they should send the people to the high island to look for the 20 who had been sent out for fresh water; but they would hardly listen to it. Still at his earnest intercession they were moved to send some of them there. Seventeen days after this David van Seevanck had gone with a longboat full of them to an island, where some of those people were by themselves. He had surprised them with his mates and killed them all except seven boys and some women. On his return he had told Jerome Cornelisz what he had done, adding that he wished those on the high island were disposed of also, so that they might not have to fear any danger on that side. Seven or eight days later they had again come to Jerome, telling him that they wished to go across to fight the remaining people on the high island, the more as Pieter Lambertsz, a boatswain's mate, had saved himself thither in a just built little boat. They wished to bring this boat back, and, if possible, to kill all the people. For this project they had seized twenty-two men. Jerome had said that this plan did not please him. He had begged of them, so he related, to prepare a boat or a shallop to sail to the mainland, and then to India. This they had considered impossible, and, carrying out their own resolution, they had gone across with the twenty-two men. On their return, he (Jerome Cornelisz) had once more begged of them to rig out a vessel, but all in vain. They had again started, this time with three boats and thirty-seven men. On this occasion Jerome had joined them himself, as he said, in order to prevent the fighting as much as possible by his presence. They had gone straight to the island, but the others had defended their shore well, standing up to their knees in water. Meanwhile Jerome had tried to speak to those on the island in

order to come to an agreement if possible. In consequence of this, through the intermediation of the parson, who went backward and forward between the two parties, the fighting had been discontinued for that day. Jerome and his side had promised to bring across some of the material the next day, so that those on the high island might clothe themselves properly; on the other hand, they would be re-possessed of the little boat. Jerome's people had by no means been pleased with the treaty, and in their anger they had desired to continue the fight. Conraedt van Huyssen had declared that he would lead his men to battle in spite of anyone. But Jerome, according to the agreement, had gone across with the promised material, with some others, in all six people, namely, David van Seevanck, Conraedt van Huyssen, Gysbert van Welderen, Wouter Loos, and Cornelis Pietersz, of Utrecht, four of whom had been killed in an ensuing fray, whilst Wouter Loos had escaped and he, Jerome Cornelisz, had remained a prisoner.

The Commodore proposed to put Jerome Cornelisz to the torture, in order to obtain the real truth from him, since he was trying to exculpate himself before the council with plausible stories, putting all his own guilt on people who are dead, and therefore cannot answer for themselves.

Jerome Cornelisz being bound and pulled up, and feeling the pain, prayed for a surcease, being willing to confess whatever he knew of that which they would ask him. His request was conceded, and the examination resumed. The Commodore then asked him why and in what manner he had intended to seize the yacht. He related that at the time when the 22 men were at the high island fighting, and he had gone to bring them back, David van Seevanck, with him in the longboat, had told him a dream of the ensign Lucas Gillisz, to the effect that a yacht had come which they found it necessary to seize in order to sail therein to Spain or some other place, and they had resolved to do so.

He was further asked in what manner he had intended to carry out this intention. He answered that if a yacht had come, they would have induced the crew to come ashore in a boat and made them drunk, in order to kill them the more easily; thus they would undoubtedly have captured the yacht. He said that when this plot had been made the others had wished to see the company's jewels; in order to value what would be everyone's share, he had opened the case and shown them these.

On the previous day, the 18th of September, while Jerome Cornelisz and the soldier, Jan Hendricksz, were locked up together in the hold of the yacht Sardam,

this statement, confessed it to be correct.

Jerome Cornelisz, being bound to be put to the torture, begged for a surcease, promising to speak the truth about all that he knew. The Commodore then asked him why he had tried to persuade Skipper Adriaen Jacobsz, to seize the ship Batavia. He denied having done this protesting that he had not even known of such a plot; he seemed anxious however to relate at length the origin of his unruly life.

When he had set sail from Sierra

and the boatswain, Jan Willemsz, of Dort (Dortrecht) was lying just above them, the latter had overheard Jerome Cornelisz asking Jan Hendricksz why on the morning of the 17th, when they were about to fight those of the yacht, he had not captured the Commodore's boat, and why their muskets had not fired; had their powder been wet? Whereupon Jan Hendricksz had answered, *"If we could have fired a musket, we should have captured the boat for a certainty; but the powder burnt away in the touchhole three or four times."* Jerome then had said, *"If you had used cunning you would easily have conquered while on the water, and then we should have been all right."* Jerome and Jan Hendricksz being confronted with

Leone, he had noticed that the Skipper had become very familiar with Lucretia. He had reproved him for this, and asked him what his intentions were with the woman. The Skipper had answered that her skin was beautiful and fair, and that he wished to make her comply with his desires, and that he intended to tempt her with gold or other means. A short time after this he, the aforesaid Jerome, had again spoken to the Skipper, asking him why he was not so familiar with Lucretia now, but seemed to have taken a fancy again to Swaantje*.

_____

*Swanny

The Skipper had answered that the cook's wife had said the woman was a loose woman, and moreover Swaantje liked him to talk to her and while away the time with her. When they reached the Cape, and the Commodore had gone ashore Jerome Cornelisz had entered the cabin and unexpectedly opening the door in the passage he had found the Skipper and Swaantje together, wherefore, going away, he had closed the door. Two days after, the Commodore went ashore again in order to get cattle inland. Thereupon the Skipper had likewise started for the land, taking Jerome and Swaantje with him. They had enjoyed themselves till the evening, when they went to the yacht Assendelft, where the Skipper behaved in a very reckless manner. In the night they had gone to the ship Buren, where he became worse, and at midnight they had returned on board. The next day the Commodore had called him into the gangway, and reprimanded him on the score of his reckless behaviour, especially in the act of taking Jerome and Swaantje ashore without consent. His chief had told him, among several other kind exhortations, that if he did not refrain from his improper proceedings measures would have to be taken to check him. When the Skipper had come upstairs again he had said to Jerome, "By God, if the other ships were not close by I'd give him such a hiding that he would not be able to leave his bunk for a fortnight; but I swear that as soon as we sail I'll get away from the ships and then I'll be my own master." To which Jerome had asked, "How would you manage that? The mates will be on the watch also". To which he replied, "That's nothing. I'll manage it during my own watch, for I haven't much faith in the first steersman, and less still in my brother-in-law. I don't think I could come to an understanding with them."

The Commodore asked him further when he and his counsellors had resolved to seize the vessel, but he protested absolute ignorance on this point. He was, therefore, once more put to the torture and some water already poured into his mouth, when he promised to obey, and to tell what he knew. He had heard for the first time of a plot to seize the vessel Batavia on the day of the shipwreck; and this publicly from the lips of one Rijckert Woutersz, at the time when the Commodore and the Skipper went to the mainland in the longboat. If the ship had not remained a wreck, they would soon have seized her and thrown the Commodore and all the people except one hundred and twenty overboard. They were only waiting for a good opportunity, which they thought would occur when the Commodore would be occupied putting those in irons who had interfered with Lucretia. They would then first of all set sail to Madagascar or Saint Helena. He had also, he said, heard all this from Conraedt van Huyssen, and moreover that the latter, when the aforesaid person would be punished or put in irons, would be the first to rush into the cabin with a sword, and to throw the Commodore overboard.

He was again asked whether he had no knowledge of this before the ship had foundered, and answered in the negative. But when orders were once more given to continue with the torture, he prayed again to be confronted with some of his accusers, which was granted.

Jans Hendricks, soldier, was called, and asked whether he was also one of the conspirators, who had planned to seize the vessel. He answered that he knew nothing of the conspiracy, neither had he known of it on board, but after the ship had foundered he had heard from divers people, now dead, that such a plot existed between the Skipper, Jerome, the boatswain, Rijckert Woutersz, Albert Jansz, of Assendelft, Cornelisz Jansz, of Haarlem, surnamed *Boontjen, Gysbert van Welderen, Conraedt van Huyssen, and ten or twelve others. The idea had been first to nail down the trap door of the soldiers' berths, and then to get the mastery of the ship. Albert Jansz, of Assendelft, was undoubtedly one of the accomplices.

Albert Jansz, of Assendelft, was called and freely examined as to the manner in which they had intended to seize the vessel and who it was that had induced them to it. He answered that he knew nothing of this, but that he had heard Jerome say, when ashore, that they were inclined to do it and that some of the men had their swords ready in their bunks. He would confess nothing further. Then being put to the torture, he still maintained that he had not known of the plot.

When the torture had commenced he begged to be let free, and he would confess the truth. He said that Jerome had come to him on board persuading him to take part in the seizure of the vessel, but he had neither answered yes nor no. When a little more water had been poured into his mouth, he confessed that the boatswain, Jacob Pietersz Steenhouwer, and he, and several others had swords in their bunks for this purpose. Being further threatened, he confessed that the Skipper had been the chief, that they had numbered ten or twelve, and that the mutiny was to have taken place during the night. The idea had been to nail down the trap door, and in this manner to carry out their design the more easily.

Jerome Cornelisz was then again led into the tent and bound to be tortured, as it seemed difficult to obtain the real truth from his lips. He then was asked whether he had not tried to induce Albert Jansz, of Assendelft, to join them. He confessed that this was true, but the Skipper had ordered him, and tempted him to it. He was further asked why the Skipper had been so embittered against the Commodore. He said he did not know, and that he had wondered why the Commodore liked the Skipper, and put up with so much from him. The Skipper, however, had told him that he began to hate the Commodore in Surat, when they were on the voyage home. One evening he had been insubordinate in language, and Capt. Grijp, and the second merchant Wolebrant Geleynsz had reproved him, saying that this was not the right way to return homeward in peace; he should not treat the Commodore like this, or should at least dissemble a little for their sake. Jerome, when he had heard this, had asked the Skipper if it was only hatred that prompted him, whether he had not better throw the Commodore overboard secretly, they would then not have caused such loss to their Lords and Masters, nor killed so many innocent people. But the Skipper had answered that it was not only out of hatred of the Commodore, but also for their common advantage; the mates could not gain much profit in India, and with the vessel he thought he could do quite a deal. When Jerome had furthermore asked him whether he saw no risk in the enterprise, and

*Little Bean

whether he thought he could carry it out, the Skipper had answered, "Let me have my way. I'll manage it. I am pretty sure of my cousin from the Schie*, but I have little faith in my brother-in-law, the second mate, or in the first mate either."

Jerome being still further examined, was asked when they had intended to carry out the plot. His answer was, as soon as the Commodore would have put the men in irons on account of the occurrence with Lucretia. When he was asked whether the Company and the Commodore had deserved this from him, he said, "No." On the contrary, he had been treated with more honour and kindness than he merited; but the Skipper had tempted him to it, speaking to him of the riches they would gain, and saying, "I shall go to the devil anyhow. If I reach India I shall get into trouble whether or no."

After a further examination, he was again asked why he had set it about among the people that the Commodore in leaving the vessel had ordered him to try and reduce the number of those who were rescued to forty. He denied having received this order from the Commodore, but David van Seevanck had thought it necessary to make the people believe this.

He also confessed that he, David van Seevanck, and Lucas Gillisz, had resolved among themselves to seize the first yacht that would come to their rescue, and sail to Spain or thereabouts, for none of them doubted that the Skipper would have thrown the Commodore overboard into the sea and gone with the boat to Malacca, where he would obtain a yacht in order to save the people and the money; or if he dared go to Batavia, they did not doubt that the Lord General would give him a yacht wherewith to find the ship and the people, and in that case they would be ready.

Being asked why he had ordered Mr. Frans Janz of Hoorn, the chief barber, to be killed a short time ago, he answered because he had stood in the way of David van Seevanck, and had not wished to dance to all their tunes, so that they had not much confidence in him.

Being asked who had been the most innocent and least culpable among them, he said, Jacques Pelman, Jeuriaen Jansz, of Bremen, both boatswain's mates; Reynert Hendricksz, of Barckloft, butler; Abraham Jansz, of Amsterdam, and Jan Willemsz Selyns, of Amsterdam, cooper. He also

*The river on which Schiedam is situated.

declared that the council had consisted of the following four men: – He (Jerome Cornelisz), Conraedt van Huyssen, David van Seevanck, and Jacob Pietersz Steenhouwer; and whenever it had been resolved among them to kill anyone it was immediately carried out. Further, that in order to take away all mistrust among themselves they had taken the oath of fidelity. Whoever had been comprised in this pact and signed it had been spared.

This document may be read in the preceding pages.

Huyssen, had taken Andries de Vries and led him to the huts of all the sick people, eleven in number, ordering him to cut their throats, which the latter had done.

Also, when Cornelisz Pietersz, of Utrecht, had cut the throat of the carpenter's assistant, Hendrick Claesz, this had been in the presence of Jerome.

He was further accused in the presence of Albert Jansz of Assendelft, that when he had ordered the latter to cut the throat of Andries de Bruyn, the cabin-boy, he had first sent the lad to catch some birds, and

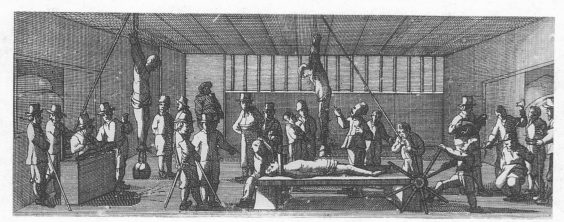

Jerome Cornelisz, being again led in, was asked whether he had consented to the seizure of the vessel, and whether the Skipper had persuaded him to it. He said he had given no advice on the matter, but the Skipper had persuaded him to it. Being also asked whether, if a yacht had come, and it had been in their power they would really have seized it, he confessed that they would decidedly have done so if they could have overpowered the other people on the island, which they were daily trying to do, apprehending that the others would give warning to any yacht that came. He further confessed, in the presence of Jan Hendricksz, that when Nicolaes Winkelhaeck, Paulus Barensz, Bessel Jansz, of Harderwijck, and Claes Harmansz, of Madeburgh had fled from the water where they thought to kill them, to the tent of Jerome, he had ordered Jan Hendricksz, saying: *'Go and kill them'*, which the latter had done.

He had also said, when the minister's people were killed, *'The parson won't live long either.'* Further, when the sick people were killed, he, Jerome Cornelisz, together with Gysbert van Welderen and Conraedt van

then Assendelft to follow him, in which manner the deed had been done.

When the whole account of these examinations and confessions had been read to Jerome Cornelisz he was asked whether it was in accordance with the truth. He then declared freely and without torture that everything had happened as related.

Lenart Michielsz, ensign, being examined in the presence of Jerome Cornelisz, confessed freely and without torture, that he had been sent on a raft by Jerome Cornelisz, together with David van Seevanck and Matthys Beur, to the island of the traitors, in order to go and drown there Andries Liebent, Hendrick Jansz, of Oldenburg (alias Masken), Thomas Weichel, of Copenhagen, a boatswain's mate, and Jan Corenlisz Amesvoort. This had been carried out, except that Lenart Michielsz had obtained pardon for Andries Liebent. Jerome confessed this to be true.

He also confessed that he had sent the aforesaid Lenart Michielsz, together with Cornelis Pietersz, of Utrecht, to call Hans Jacobsz, Jan Hendricksz, and Mr. Francis, the barber, out of their tents, ordering them to go with David van Seevanck, and

Conraedt van Huyssen in the little boat to Seal's Island in order to kill all the people there, which they did, except 17 persons who were let off.

Further, he, Jerome, had called Lenart Michielsz, Jan Hendricksz and Rutgert Fredericksz into his tent, giving them swords to kill the assistant, Andries de Vries, which they did.

Moreover, he confessed that when he had decided to kill the minister's family he had handed some food to Conraedt van Huyssen, telling him to invite the minister, his daughter, and himself, Jerome, to take a meal with him; that in the afternoon he had sent for Lenart Michielsz, Jacob Pietersz, Jan Hendricksz, Wouter Loos, Andries Jonas, and Andries Liebent, telling them that in the evening he would be dining in Conraedt van Huyssen's tent, and during that time he wanted them to kill the minister's family; all this had been thus carried out.

He also confessed that on the night of the 12th July he had caused the aforesaid Lenart Michielsz, together with Lucas Jelisz and Jan Hendricksz, to be called out of their tents, ordering them to go and cut the throats of Passchier van den Enden, musketeer, Jacob Heynoricksz, carpenter, and a sick boy. This order they had carried out.

On the morning of the 6th August he had been in the tent of David van Seevanck, and called to him Jan Hendricksz, giving him the dagger which he carried about him all day, saying, *"Go and cut out the heart of Stoffel Stoffelsz, that lazy lout, who stands there working as if his back was broken."* This Jan Hendricksz had done.

He confessed that on the 16th of August he had given his sword to Jan van Bommel, saying, *"Go and try whether it is sharp enough; cut off the head of Coen Aldertsz, of Ilpendam (hooplooper), with it."* But as Jan van Bommel was not quite strong enough for this, Matthys Beur cut off Aldertsz's head in Jerome's presence.

Finally he confessed that though he was a married man, he had nevertheless taken Lucretia Jansz, the wife of Boudewijn van der Mylen, into his tent, keeping her two months against her will.

On the 24th September Jerome Cornelisz, being present at the examination of Rogier Decker, of Haarlem, formerly cabin waiter on the shipwrecked vessel Batavia, confessed that he had called the said Rogier Decker into his tent on the 25th July, giving him a cup of wine, and at the same time handing his dagger to him with the words, *"Go outside and stab Hendrick Jansz, of Purmerant, to the heart."* This order the said Rogier had carried out.

On the 28th September, since Lucas Jelisz, of the Hague, ensign, according to the above confessions of Jerome Cornelisz, had also been concerned in the murder of Passchier van den Enden, he was likewise questioned on this point. He confessed in the presence of Jerome that by Jerome's order David van Seevanck had commanded him together with Lenart Michielsz and Jan Hendricksz, to kill Passchier van den Enden, musketeer, and Jacob Heyndricksz, carpenter. Coming at the tent, Jan Hendricksz had rushed inside, and cut Passchier's throat, but Jacob Heyndricksz they had only ordered to remain in his tent. Then David van Seevanck had gone to Jerome, saying, *"Jacob Heyndricksz is a good carpenter; let him live."* But Jerome had answered, *"He is nothing but a turncoat and quite unreliable. He will only tell on us some day; he must be put out of the way."* To prove the truth of this, Lenart Michielsz and Jan Hendricksz (who were called in for the purpose) affirmed the statement on the salvation of their souls, saying that they would die if it were not so. But Jerome denied it, calling it a lie. He recalled at the same time all that he had so far confessed, saying that it had been wrung from him by the threat of torture.

On account of his unreliableness and contradictory confessions, trying all the resources of his subtle mind to give the lie to those who accused and convicted him in his presence, he was again, and now for the last time, threatend with torture and asked why he mocked us in this manner. Had he not, on different previous occasions without torture confessed everything - the origin and the circumstances of the plot to seize the vessel Batavia, as well as the horrors that had afterwards occurred? Thereupon he declared again that all he had confessed was the real truth; but that he had constantly retracted his words in order to gain delay, hoping that they would take him to Batavia, as he longed to see his wife once more. He knew well enough, he said, that he had done much wrong, and he craved no mercy for it. Jan Hendricksz and

Albert Jansz, of Assendelft, volunteered the information that one evening Jerome Cornelisz had asked them to dinner, and told them, among other things, that if the ship had not been wrecked they would have seized it a few days after. The chief persons in the plot had been the Skipper, Jerome Cornelisz, the boatswain, Conraedt van Huyssen and others. They would have nailed down the trapdoor of the soldiers' berths. Jerome having been confronted with this statement, confirmed its truth.

On the afternoon of that same day the Commodore read out the whole account of the examination and confession publicly before all the people on the island, in the presence of Jerome Cornelisz, and asked him whether it was in accordance with the truth. He answered that there were certain statements in it by Albert Jansz, of Assendelft, Jan Hendricksz, and others which contained unfounded accusations against him. Then the Commodore once more protested before God to the prisoners there present, that if they were to aggravate Jerome Cornelisz's guilt in the least degree, they would have to answer for it on the day of judgement before the throne of the Almighty. The prisoners thereupon spoke out unanimously, and exclaimed that they had not aggravated his guilt in any way whatsoever. If they had, they were willing to burden their own salvation with it: they would die for it and answer for it on the day of judgement before the throne of the Almighty. Wherefore the Commodore addressed Jerome for the last time, asking him why he mocked the council with his unpardonable vacillations, speaking the truth one moment and denying it the next. He then finally replied that he had only done this to lengthen his life; but he had done enough wrong, and could not escape his punishment.

There follows, another confession in aggravation of the charges against Jerome Cornelisz aforesaid:

We, the undersigned, Webbye Hayes, of Winschoten, sergeant; Claes Jansz Hooft of Ditmarssen, trumpeter; Albert Jansz, corporal; and Jan Kastensen, of Tonninge, musketeer, attest and testify on our manly truthfulness, that we have seen with our eyes and heard with our sober ears, today, the 2nd October, 1629, that Lucretia Jansz, the widow of Boudewijn van der Mylen, one hour before Jerome Cornelisz was to be executed for his great misdeeds, bitterly lamented to the said Jerome over the sins he had committed with her against her will, and forcing her thereto. To which Jerome replied, *"It is true, you are not to blame for it; for you were in my tent for twelve days before I could succeed."* He continued further relating how in the end he had complained to David van Seevanck that he could not accomplish his ends either with kindness or anger. Seevanck had answered, *"And don't you know how to manage that? I'll soon make her do it."* He had then gone into the tent and said to Lucretia, *"I hear complaints about you." "On what account?"* she asked, *"Because you do not comply with the Captain's wishes in kindness; now, however, you will have to make up your mind, either you will go the same way as Wybrecht Claes, or else you must do that for which we have kept the women."* Through this threat Lucretia had to consent that day, and thus he had her as his concubine for the term of two months. In sign of the truth we have heard everyone of the above words from the lips of Jerome Cornelisz and in the presence of several witnesses, we have put our ordinary signature to this. And we shall be at all times prepared, if it should be required, to confirm it with our solemn oath. Actum on the island, "Batavia's Churchyard", near the wreck of the foundered vessel Batavia.

# Copy of an original letter by the predikant

# Gijsbert Bastiaensz

## Written in his own hand in Batavia and addressed to his brethren, concerning his dangerous and ill-fated voyage to the Indies in the year of our Lord 1628[1].

### May God be with us, Amen.

I send my warmest greetings and best wishes to my brother Jan Bastiaensz, my brother-in-law Hugo, sister Anneta, sister Sara, treasurer Pandelaer, my cousin Schepens and all his family, all the predikants, Willem Reyersz Swanenburg, Janneken Maertens, and in a word to everyone to whom greeting is due. The following brief account is meant to appraise you of what transpired during my voyage - but it grieves me greatly to tell the tale and I take pen in hand with the gravest misgivings. However, much time has passed since the events that I am about to relate, and I have since learned to trust in the Lord's mercy, and to remember that he tries his creatures but for their greater good. Furthermore, by the Lord's grace, I have recovered much of my strength and vigour - for I was long so weakened that I could scarcely stand. Here, then, is the story of my adventures - bought at the cost of what suffering! - during the course of this long and distressing voyage.

As you already know, we set sail from the port of Texel on the 27th of October 1628, and this very day the ship ran aground and we thought we would all perish there with our vessel. But by the mercy of God's Providence, we were able to free ourselves from the shoals and to continue our journey, first along the shores of England, then of Sierra Leone, and on to the Cape of Good Hope. The doings of this part of the voyage - of no particular import - will be known at Amsterdam, God willing, through the ship's log[2] which is in the hands of the High and Mighty Lords. After rounding the Cape, this is what happened: a dispute had broken out between our captain and the commandeur, brought about by two women, one of which had been ill-treated on board the ship; this was to have

---

[1] The original, in Old Dutch, appears in *Ongeluckige Voyagie van't schip Batavia*, Lucas de Vries edition. Utrecht 1649.

[2] The *predikant* does not seem to be aware that the ship's log was thrown overboard by the mutineers.

disastrous consequences for our vessel. For this reason we had distanced ourselves from the fleet, which is how we came to strike fast on some shallows near the great Southland. This took place on the 4th of June 1629, second day of Pentecost, and this same day, together with certain others among which were my wife and children, I was put ashore by the longboat on an island which has since borne the name of the "Batavia Graveyard". On another small island, named "Traitors Island", they also put ashore some casks containing sea-biscuit and other provisions. After searching in vain for fresh water on one or two of the neighbouring islets, the commandeur and his council decided to attempt to reach Batavia with the longboat, taking about forty men with them. In this they eventually succeeded. They left the other ship's boat at Traitors Island, in order that we might proceed with the search for water, either on the nearby islands, or by obtaining some from the wreck. Franz Gillis, the second helmsman, together with some other sailors, took this our only boat and went in search of water, leaving us where we sat, discouraged and despondent, without a drop of water or wine between us. Having had nought to drink for four or five days, we were finally reduced to drinking our own urine, and several of us perished of thirst. At last, God in His mercy sent us some rain and, having built rafts from the wreckage, we managed to obtain some sea-biscuit, water and wine. The men who had been left on board the ship attempted to swim ashore, some drowning along the way while others succeeded in reaching the place where we were.

Among them was a certain Jeronymus Cornelisz, the under-merchant who had shipped with the "Batavia", and they took him for their leader. In the beginning he behaved decently, but after some time among us he began to commit some most reprehensible actions and acts of cruelty. For a start, he had bound himself by a secret pledge to those of the men he trusted and had informed them of his plans. He had told them that he considered the number of people on our island - amounting to some two hundred souls - to be too great, and that this number ought to be reduced considerably. He had led them to believe that the commandeur, before his departure in the longboat, had suggested as such. He then ordered some of the men to take our boat and go to an island some two or three miles distant to look for water; he argued that we were too many to survive for long on the limited amount of fresh water we had managed to salvage. The members of this party soon discovered that the island they were exploring offered no comfort for men in distress. When they returned, however, the merchant ordered them to say that they had found an abundance of food and water, following which he ordered several others to go there, and some decided to go of their own initiative, in order to verify the discovery, and they left promising to light fires on the shore if they were to find water. Not finding any on this particular island, they then proceeded toward another high island where they eventually discovered water and lit their signal fires. Seeing the fires, and noting that they went on burning, the people with us cried that there must surely be water there, or the men that had gone would have perished by now. This is how luck decreed that some of our most stalwart soldiers found themselves together in a place where water could be had.

This is when Cornelisz, with the help of his lieutenants and of the soldiers whom he trusted, began to put his plan into action. They had prepared rafts, and aboard each one he put eight or ten of his own men along with two or three of the soldiers who were not in the plot. As soon as the rafts reached deep water, these brave men were quickly seized and bound with ropes by the ruffians, and thrown overboard. They then returned and made us believe that the good soldiers had been put ashore on the high island where the water was. They also took some men, women and children to a nearby islet, called Seals Island, telling us that they would look after them. But the most wicked among them went along, and murdered most of the innocents by forcing them into the water. Some of these unfortunates were able to save themselves by hanging on to floating wreckage, and thus managed to reach the high island where they joined the others and told them what had happened, warning them of the situation. With these new arrivals there were by then about fifty people on that island, separated from us. As we had lost our bravest soldiers, the ruffians started to massacre us, starting with the pregnant women, strangling men and children, acting openly and showing themselves at last for the common criminals that they were. The whole day long, their favourite saying became: "Who wants a box on the ear, then?" We expected to be massacred at any moment, and could only pray to God to deliver us from our misery. But these murderers decided to spare me and my daughter Judick, as one of their grisly assembly desired to take her for his wife. So they invited us one night to share a meal with them under their tent. I went with my daughter, not yet knowing what they wanted, and during our absence they butchered my wife and all my children together! When my daughter and I finally returned, I had every reason to weep profusely. The following day, as I wallowed in my grief and lamented aloud, some of them came to see me and told me roughly to spare them my tears, that what had happened didn't matter at all, and that if I didn't keep quiet I would soon be meeting a similar fate. O cruelty! O horror of horrors! Highwaymen strip their victims of all they possess, but often spare their lives; these brutes had robbed me of everything: goods and precious life! So, for a time, we obeyed their orders, as beasts to the slaughterhouse. Every night I told my daughter: "Come in the morning, to see whether I have been murdered!"

I will not bother to relate the many things that happened after this, except to say that my wretched flock had little to eat or drink, and many came near to dying of hunger or thirst. I myself had to feed on seal skin and to mix my ration of fresh water with salt to make it last a little longer. They forbade me to preach or pray and I spent most of my time reading on the beach, plucking grasses and leaves to assuage my hunger, making thus a dismal salad though I had neither oil nor vinegar to season it. For two months I saw neither rice nor bread. I became so weak that I could hardly stand. I had been given the task of helping launch their little boats and pull them up on the beach. Every day I would hear them say: "What are we going to do with this one?" Some wanted to cut my head off, others thought it better to poison me - it would have been a more merciful end - while some said: "Let him live a little longer; he might be useful to us persuading the ones on the other island to join us", meaning the fifty-odd people who were together on the high island where they had found water. They feared them and thought that if a ship ever came to rescue us they would get in the way, which is exactly what happened as you shall see. Meanwhile, I had started to tell you about my daughter Judick, and this is what transpired:

A certain Coenraedt van Huyssen, a native of Gelderlandt and a rather handsome young aristocrat, a member of the Assembly of these rogues, wished to take my daughter in Holy Matrimony. He claimed that he wanted to announce their betrothal formally, and to marry her forthwith in the proper manner and according to the laws of the land[3]. This project of his was the subject of much discussion between my daughter and I, the gist of which I will spare you, except to say that both Judick and I came to agree that, considering the position we were in, it was better that she should become the lawful wife of one man rather than be subjected to the foul treatment that was the lot of the other women. Thus he made, and she accepted, his formal proposal. I begged Judick to put off going to live with him until the next day - van Huyssen had agreed to this - but the rest of these murderers gathered in front of our tent and insisted that she move in with him immediately, threatening to cut the pair of us to pieces if she didn't comply. This went on for the rest of evening. She had already been forced to submit to his attentions - indeed what could have been done to prevent it? - but had assured me that she had not been mistreated. The rogues claimed that she was lucky that van Huyssen was so fond of her, and that during the five weeks that she had spent in his company, he had protected her from harm and spared her the worst - apart of course from having to submit to his lust. The other women were very jealous of my daughter, as they considered that she was enjoying too much favour. During this whole period, I tasted the worst fears. I could only communicate with my daughter under the greatest difficulties, and van Huyssen would hardly speak to me. On the rare occasions when I managed to spend a few minutes privately with her, I would repeat to her, as I had done so often in the past, what she must do if she were to find me murdered one morning, and to exhort her to keep herself ready to meet the Almighty.

Such was the situation, and the slaughter went on until barely thirty of us were left alive. Yet the murderers didn't know what to do about those who had taken refuge on the island where the water was. These numbered about fifty, as I have said before. In any case, they decided to go there in their little boats, intending to lure them into their net by sweet talk and lying promises, or at sword point if need be. They put this plan into action, and I went with them after explaining to my daughter that I hoped by this to be able to make some sort of contact with these people. As we approached the island, the people there gathered on the beach to face us, and taunted us saying: "Have things come to such a pass that you had need to bring this good man, our predikant?" We came nearer and Jeronymus falsely offered them to make peace. To this they answered that they had no use for our peace, for they knew full well that we only meant to deceive them. Two of the murderers were armed with muskets and they attempted to fire on the people, but their weapons turned out to have been spoiled and the people mocked them. Then the rogues offered to enter into a pact of friendship with them, the terms of which they had prepared in writing. They ordered me to take it to the people, which I accepted readily as this fitted well with my own plans, and I was thus able to carry out my intentions without risking any unpleasantness. I went back and forth several times and the good people wanted me to stay with them until the following day, but the ruffians wouldn't allow it and would only let me play

[3] According to Dutch law at the time, no marriage could be legal without the consent of the parents of both parties.

the shuttle between them. I had begged the good people to insist on my staying with them a month or two, as I was their predikant also, and this they did. It was finally decided that on the morrow the merchant would bring them pieces of cloth and attire, and that the peace negotiations would resume. A specific time was set for this. The following day Jeronymus, accompanied by van Huyssen, Zeevanck and three others, went back to the island, taking with them woollen cloth, wine and other provisions. The rest of the rogues, together with some of the good people and the women remained on the island opposite. Once the provisions brought by the merchant had been shared, and the wine had been poured, the murderers began to stroll with the people of the island and to engage the soldiers among them in conversation. They urged them to trust them, tempting them with large profits and with money. The good people, who understood the situation and where it was likely to lead, had sworn among themselves to try to catch the murderers and, if possible, to kill them, for they realised that these were the leaders of the ghoulish gang. They were able to achieve their goal: four were killed, one managed to escape, and the merchant was taken prisoner. Thus I was able to remain with these good people, who fed me and nursed me back to health. There was on their island a well of water that was as sweet as milk. They made me a pair of clogs, so that I might walk, and I shall treasure them as long as the Lord will grant me life. During my stay with them, the murderers had taken everything from me and had threatened to despatch me at any moment, and now that my son-in-law van Huyssen was dead I lived in the greatest dread for my daughter who might face rape or even beheading at their hands, all the more so as the people, after they had killed the four rogues, began to shout to those who were still prisoners of the mutineers: "Come and join us, who are not murderers!", and I even heard one of the rogues say to my daughter Judick: "If you try to go over to your father, we will cut you to pieces; it is through the doings of your father that four of us have been killed!" But the Lord protected my daughter, and she came to no harm. Yet the death and the capture of their fellows had considerably weakened the party of the ruffians, and they went back to the "Batavia Graveyard". It would take too long to relate the whole story, how the Lord miraculously provided for the good people, giving them water, fowls, fish and other edible beasts, even eggs by the basketful; some of these beasts, which we called "cats" (wallabies), had a flavour that could rival some of the best viands I have ever tasted. What could I say of the muskets and pikes that they contrived to make, how is it possible that men could be so ingenious? They also showed me the greatest possible kindness, they would embrace me and would gladly have carried me in their arms. Meanwhile, the murderers had formed a new government for themselves, and they came back to us on the 17th of September 1629. I had set down the terms of a peace agreement between us, which stated that they would undertake not to harm us, but when I took it to them they just tore it in pieces and, rushing upon us, wounded four of our number with their muskets, one of whom later perished of his hurt. They had just retreated from our island when we sighted a ship coming from Batavia to our rescue. At this sight, the more pious among us jumped with joy and gave thanks to the Lord, and some went in their little boat to meet the ship and warn its crew of their danger. The ship's company was thus forewarned, which was just as well, as we have since come to know that the rogues had made a plan to seize the ship and to use it to make their escape with the jewels and the gold to some place of their choice. Later enquiries have also shown that Adriaen Jacobsz, the skipper of the "Batavia" who was later imprisoned with the murderers, had plotted together with some of them and in particular with Jeronymus to seize the "Batavia" and make away, and had only been prevented from doing so by the ship running aground. I understand that closer enquiries are being made into this matter. In any case, we know with certainty that they had planned to take over the ship that had come to rescue us, and in this they would have succeeded if it had not been for the good people of the island who foiled the plot. I would write of this at greater length, but time is running out. Some of the rogues went aboard the ship, trusting to their luck, and I also went, taking with me the captive merchant. The ruffians were immediately arrested, bound with chains and put in irons. The following day, those of the murderers who were still on the "Batavia Graveyard" were captured by commandeur Pelsaert and his men. After they had been tried, the commandeur decided to hang some, and to cut off the right hand of Jeronymus Cornelisz[4], which was done. If ever there was a man who was Godless in his extremity, he was that man. To listen to him, you might have thought he was blameless. Even as he ascended the scaffold, he was yelling "Revenge! Revenge!" So that he remained an evil and Godless man to the end. The divine Justice and Vengeance were visited upon him, for he was a most evil murderer. On board the ship he had often shown his evil nature by his actions and speech, but I had never realised just how Godless he really was. Some of the other rogues were given their punishment on board the ship, others were placed in irons and taken to Batavia.

Here you have the general outline of the story. It would have taken too much time to give you all the details, indeed a large volume could be written on this sorry subject. If the tale seems to lack order and clarity, it is first because time is running short and the ships are getting ready to sail for home, and second because of the great distress that we have just experienced and which has left our minds in much confusion. I had not intended to write at such length. My purpose here is to sound a warning to the Honourable High and Mighty Lords, that they must on all occasions take into their service good, God-fearing and trustworthy men, particularly as captains of their ships and merchants, for the success of their entire enterprise depends on it. I consider this to be of the utmost importance.

The disastrous events that I have just related took place between June the 4th and September the 17th 1629, at which time the ship arrived to save us.

The End

---

[4] This contradicts the story as told by Francisco Pelsaert. In the minutes of the trial, he relates that Jeronymus Cornelisz was sentenced to have both hands cut off before being hung, and goes on to state a little later that the sentence was duly carried out.

# *Acknowledgements*

*The author wishes to thank the following people and organizations, who have contributed in different ways to this book, and especially Mrs Chantal Attali, without whose painstaking and efficient assistance it would not have seen the light of day and Mrs Phillida Stephens for her patience and care in translating the text as faithfully as possible from the original French:*

- Association pour l'étude et la documentation des textiles d'Asie — *Paris (France)*

- Mr Paul Albert (Graphic Design) — *Perth (Australia)*

- Professor Gabriel Arvis — *Paris (France)*

- Axi Press — *Lelystad (Netherlands)*

- Mr François-Gilles Bachelier — *Noumea (New Caledonia)*

- Battye Library (State Library of W.A.) — *Perth (Australia)*

- Master mariner Jean-Louis Boglio — *Brisbane (Australia)*

- Mr Max Cramer — *Geraldton (Australia)*

- Mr Robbert Das — *Marina Baie des Anges (France)*

- Mrs Silvia David — *Noumea (New Caledonia)*

- Mr Pieter Dorst, First Secretary of the Royal Dutch Embassy — *Paris (France)*

- Miss Pat Gallaher, Senior Librarian — Geraldton Public Library *(Australia)*

- Mr John Gliddon — *Dongara (Australia)*

- Mr Emmanuel and Mr Jean-Philippe Godard — *Paris (France)*

- Mr Stéphane Goiran — *Noumea (New Caledonia)*

- Mr Jean Guillou — *Noumea (New Caledonia)*

- Miss Frédérique Jacquot — *Strasbourg (France)*

- Mr Dave Johnson and Son — *Geraldton (Australia)*

- Mrs Maria La Lima — *Walters Arts Gallery — Baltimore (U.S.A.)*

- Mrs Eliane Labussière-Van Duren — *Noumea (New Caledonia)*

- Mr Wilhelm Lanting — *Miami (Australia)*

- Miss Frédérique Lazarini — *Paris (France)*

- Mitchell Library — *Sydney (Australia)*

- Mrs Glenys Mc Donald — *Northampton (Australia)*

- National Library of Australia — *Canberra (Australia)*

- Het Koninklijk Penningkabinet — *Leiden (Netherlands)*

- Professor Philippe Morat — Museum National d'Histoire Naturelle — *Paris (France)*

- Mr Didier Murcia, Barrister-Sollicitor — *Perth (Australia)*

- Mr Marcel Petron — *Carcès (France)*

- Mr Saaltink, Conservator of the Westfries Museum — *Hoorn (Netherlands)*

- Mr Hans Smit — P.R. en Promotie "Stichting Nederland Bouwt V.O.C. Retourship" — *Lelystad (Netherlands)*

- Miss Myra Stanbury — Curator of the Museum's Maritime Archaeology Department — *Fremantle (Australia)*

- Mr Stiller, Mrs Wolff and Mrs Lichtenwagner — Rijksmuseum — *Amsterdam (Netherlands)*

- State Department of Fisheries — *Perth (Australia)*

- Textielmuseum Nederlands — *Tilburg (Netherlands)*

- Mr Johannès Wahono — *Noumea (New Caledonia)*

- Mr Greg Wallace, Branch Curator — Geraldton Region Museum — *Geraldton (Australia)*

- Mr Jan van Zijverden and Mr Wildeman, Scheepvaartmuseum — *Amsterdam (Netherlands)*

- Western Australian Herbarium — *Kensington (Western Australia)*

---

- Translation of the "Ongeluckige Voyagie Van't Schip Batavia" provided courtesy of "The West Australian" — *Perth (Australia)*

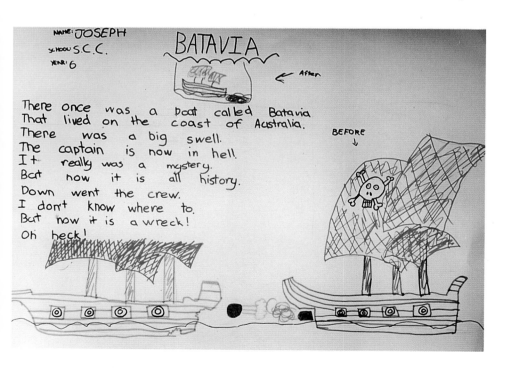

*Above and next pages :*
*The* Batavia *tragedy as pictured by children of our time, as we near the end of the century.*
*A competition open to the primary schools of Geraldton (June 1993)*

# Picture credits

# Index

# *Bibliography*

| | |
|---|---|
| **Anonymous** | Ongeluckige Voyagie Van't Schip Batavia Nae de Oost-Indien Gebleven op de Abrolhos van Frederick Houtman, op de hooghte van 28 1/3 graet, ly-Zuyden de Linie Aequinoctiael, Uytgevaren onder den E. Francoys Pelsert *(Jan Jansz, Amsterdam 1647)* |
| **BACH John** | A Maritime History of Australia *(Book Club Associates, Sydney 1976)* |
| **BASS George F.** | A History of Seafaring Based on Underwater Archaeology *(Walker and Company, N.Y. 1972)* |
| **BATESON Charles** | Australian Shipwrecks - Vol. I (1622-1850) (A.H. and A.W. Reed, *Sydney 1972)* |
| **BEYLEN J. (van)** | Schepen van de Nederlanden *(Amsterdam 1970)* |
| **BEVACQUA Robert** | Archaelogical survey of sites relating to the Batavia shipwreck - P. 60-78 in Early Days Journal Vol VII, Part VI *(Royal Western Australia Historical Society 1974 )* |
| **BLAINEY Geoffrey** | The Tiranny of Distance *(St Martim's Press, N.Y. 1968)* |
| **BOECK Eerste & Van LODEWYCKZ Willem** | Werken Uitgegeven Door De Linschoten-Vereeniging VII - De Eerste Schipvaart der Nederlanders Naar Oost-Indië Onder Cornelis de Houtman - 1595-1597 |
| **BOXER C.R.** | The Dutch Seaborne Empire *(London 1965)* |
| **BROEZE F.J.A. & BRUIJN J.R.** | Nederlandse Scheepsrestern in West Australië (Medelingen van de Ned. Ver. voor Zeegeschiedenis N°24, 1972) |
| **BROEZE Frank & HENDERSON G.** | Western Australians and the Sea - Our Maritime Heritage (Western Australian Museum, *Perth 1986)* |

| | |
|---|---|
| **BRUIJN J.R., GASTRA F.S. & SCHEFFER I.** | Dutch-Asiatic Shipping (Vol.2, Outward-Bound Voyages from Netherlans to Asia and the Cape (1595-1794) *(Den Haag 1979)* |
| **CARDON Dominique** | Les "Vers" du Rouge (Cahiers d'Histoire et de Philosophie des Sciences n°28, *Paris 1990*)<br><br>Guide des Teintures Naturelles (Delachaux et Niestlé) |
| **DEACON C. and K.** | Australia Down Under - Exploring Australia's Underwater World (Double Bay - *Sydney 1987*) |
| **DIESSEN (van) J.R.** | Het Centrum van het Nederlandse koloniale rijk in Azië en zijn cultuurhistorische nalatenschap (Jakarta/Batavia - De Bilt 1989) |
| **DRAKE-BROCKMAN Henrietta** | The Wicked and the Fair (1957)<br><br>Voyage to Disaster (Angus and Robertson, *Sydney 1964*) |
| **EDWARDS Hugh** | Islands of Angry Ghosts (*London 1966*)<br><br>Australian and New Zealand Shipwrecks and Sea Tragedies (Mathews/Hutchinson, *Sydney 1978*) |
| **GRETLER Priska & PARTHESIUS Robert** | "BATAVIA 1987" (Stichting Nederland Bouwt V.O.C.-Retourship)<br><br>Batavia De terugkeer van een Retourschip (Stichting Nederland Bouwt V.O.C.-Retourship 1991) |
| **GOLDSMITH F.H.** | Treasure Lies Buried Here (C.H. Pitman, *Perth 1946*) |
| **GREEN Andrew** | The Batavia Wreck (P. 34-35 in Scuba Diver -August/September 1992) |
| **GREEN Jeremy N.** | The Lost Gateway (P. 46-50 in Hemisphere Annual III, 1981-1982)<br><br>"Maritime Archaeology and the Indian Ocean" (The Great Circle Vol.2 n°1)<br><br>The Loss of the Verenigde Oost-Indische Compagnie Retourship BATAVIA, Western Australia 1629 - An excavation report and catalogue of artifacts (BAR International Series 489 -1989) |
| **GREEN J., HENDERSON G. & SLEDGE S** | Papers from the First Southern Hemisphere Conference on Maritime Archaeology (Oceans Society of Australia, *Melbourne 1977*) |
| **HENDERSON Graeme** | Unfinished Voyages : Western Australian Shipwrecks (1622-1850) (University of W.A. Press - *Nedlands 1980*)<br><br>Maritime Archaeology in Australia (University of W.A. Press - *Nedlands 1986*) |

| | |
|---|---|
| **JACOBS Els M** | In Pursuit of Pepper and Tea - The Story of the Dutch East India Company (Netherlands Maritime Museum, *Walburg Pers 1991*) |
| **VAN LINSCHOTEN Jan Huyghen** | "Voyage ou navigation de Jan Huygen Van Linschoten aux Indes orientales ou portugaises comprenant une courte description de ces pays et de leurs côtes, avec l'indication des lieux habités, ports principaux, rivières, caps et pays jusqu'à présent découverts et reconnus par les Portugais, dans lequel sont peints non seulement les coutumes et mœurs tant des Portugais résidant dans ces contrées que des Indiens natifs et de leurs temples, idoles, habitations, avec les arbres, fruits, plantes, épices les plus remarquables et productions semblables comme aussi les coutumes du même peuple tant dans la religion que dans son gouvernement et économie domestique, suivi d'une courte description des négoces, comment et à quel prix ils sont traités et conduits, avec les faits et événements les plus remarquables survenus pendant sa résidence dans ces pays. "Le tout décrit et recueilli par lui-même et très utile, avantageux et agréable pour tous les curieux et amateurs de choses rares." |
| **LONEY Jack** | An Atlas History of Australian Shipwrecks (A.H. and A.W. Reed, *Sydney 1981*) |
| | Wrecks in Australian Waters (Newport Vic. ND - Australian Sports Public) |
| **McDONALD Glenys** | The Castaways, a Fate Worse Than Death ? or A Glimmer of Hope ? (An argument in favour of Port Gregory as the landing site for the two Batavia Mutineers in November 1629) - *1991* |
| **MILLER Russell (and the editors of Time-Life books)** | The East Indiamen (Time-Life Books Inc., *N.Y. 1981*) |
| **MUCKELROY Keith** | Archaeology under Water (McGraw Hill, *N.Y. 1980*) |
| **MURDOCH Priscilla** | Duyfken and the First Discoveries of Australia (Antipodean Publishers, *Sydney 1974*) |
| **NOBLE Captain J.** | Hazards of the Sea. Three Centuries of Challenge in Southern Waters (Angus and Robertson, *Melbourne 1970*) |
| **NOURY Catherine** | La Renaissance du Batavia (Le Chasse Marée n°58 -Août 1981, *Douarnenez - France*) |
| **PELSAERT Francisco** | Remonstrantie (Rijskarchief voar de Centrale Regeringsarchieven *Tot 1795 - 1626*) |
| **PRAUSE Otto** | A Tale of Bloodshed from Old Western Australia (P. 64-67 in "1993 Boat Directory") |

| **RHODES Captain F.** | Pageant of the Pacific, Being the Maritime History of Australia (F.J. Thwaites, *Sydney 1934*) |
|---|---|
| **ROSS Marvin** | The Rubens Vase, its History and Date (Journal of the Walters Art Gallery, *Baltimore 1943*) |
| **SAUERACKER Gerhard** | The Abrolhos Islands "Keep your eyes open" (P.18-25, Australasia's Geographical Magazine n°4) |
| **SCHILDER Günter** | De Ontdekkingsreis van Willem Hesselsz. De Vlamingh in der Jaren 1696-1697 (Martinus Nijhoff, *The Hague 1976*)<br><br>Voyage to the Great South Land - Willem de Vlamingh - (1696-1697) (Royal Australian Historical Society, *Sydney 1985*) |
| **SIGMOND J.P. & ZUIDERBARN L.H.** | Dutch Discoveries of Australia - Shipwrecks, Treasures and Early Voyages off the West Coast (Rigby Limited, *Adelaïde 1979*)<br><br>Nederlanders Ontdekken Australië - Scheepsarcheologische Vondsten op Het Zuidland (Unieboek BV - *Bussum 1976*) |
| **STORR G.M., JOHNSTON E R.E. & GRIFFIN P.** | Birds of the Houtman Abrolhos - Western Australia (Western Australian Museum *1986*) |
| **THEVENOT Melchisedech** | Histoire des Naufrages - Chapter 7, entitled "Relation du naufrage du vaisseau hollandois, le Batavia, commandé par François Pelsart, sur les rochers de Frederic Outhman, près les côtes de la Concorde, dans la Nouvelle-Hollande, en 1630" (*Paris 1663*) |
| **THROCKMORTON P.** | The Sea Remembers (Artists House, *London 1987*) |
| **UREN Malcolm** | Sailormen's Ghosts : The Abrolhos Islands in Three Hundred Years of Romance, History and Adventure (Robertson and Mullen, *Melbourne 1940*) |
| **VIATTE Françoise et PINAULT Madeleine** | Sublime Indigo (Office du Livre S.A. Fribourg-Suisse et Musées de Marseille) |
| **(Van der) VIN Dr. J.P.A.** | De Stenen Kracht - 5000 Jaar intagli en Cameeën - 22 Juni 1990 - 2 Juni 1991 (Het Koninlijk Penningkabinet, *Leiden 1990*) |
| **WARWICK Mark** | The East Indiamen, Dutch merchant ships pioneering a new, faster route to the East. Made early contact with the west coast of Australia (P. 38-51, Australasia's Geographical Magazine n°2)<br><br>Merchant Voyages (P.20-29, Sportdiver in Australia and the South Pacific n°25) |

| **WILSON S.J.** | Doits to Ducatons - The Coins of the Dutch East India - Company Ship "Batavia" Lost on the Western Australian Coast 1629 (Western Australian Historical Society, *Perth 1989*) |
|---|---|
| **(Van der) ZEE Ad & PARTHESIUS Robert** | Batavia Guide (Stichting Nederland Bouwt V.O.C.-Retourship, *Lelystad 1992*) |

*Design :*
DEMAIN
Noumea - New Caledonia

*Typesetting :*
Pascal LE MOAL
Noumea - New Caledonia

*Printing :*
KALEIDOSCOPE PRINT &
DESIGN
Perth - Western Australia

*Printed in october 1993*